SPANISH THEATRE

STUDIES IN HONOUR OF VICTOR F. DIXON

Edited by

Kenneth Adams, Ciaran Cosgrove and James Whiston

TAMESIS

First published 2001 by Tamesis, London

ISBN 1 85566 072 5

Tamesis is an imprint of Boydell & Brewer Ltd
PO Box 9, Woodbridge, Suffolk IP12 3DF, UK
and of Boydell & Brewer Inc.
PO Box 41026, Rochester, NY 14604–4126, USA
website: http://www.boydell.co.uk

A catalogue record for this book is available
from the British Library

Library of Congress Cataloging-in-Publication Data
applied for

This publication is printed on acid-free paper

Printed in Great Britain by
St Edmundsbury Press Limited, Bury St Edmunds, Suffolk

CONTENTS

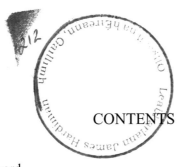

EDITORS' FOREWORD

Our first duty of thanks is to the contributors to this volume, all of whom responded with enthusiasm to our invitation to write an article celebrating Victor Dixon's long and fecund harvesting of the fruits of Golden Age and Modern Spanish Drama. The initial wise counsel of Ann MacKenzie, who, as well as helping us with the contributors' list, advised us to seek John Varey's views on the publication of the Festschrift, was the beginning of the happy outcome that has seen this book of essays brought to the light and life of the published word. A sad omission from the volume is the article from John Varey himself, which he promised to us in the very letter in which he endorsed the project for publication in Tamesis Books, but which he was unable to write, because of his untimely death. We note also with sadness the passing away of the distinguished Spanish playwright Antonio Buero Vallejo who, as with John Varey only months before his death, had taken the trouble to record his own endorsement, and which we are privileged to publish at the beginning of this volume.

Publications such as this Festschrift inevitably need the financial support of enlightened patrons. We are pleased to express our most grateful thanks and to acknowledge the assistance received from the Provost of Trinity College, Dublin, Dr Thomas N. Mitchell, who gave the project a very generous grant from the Provost's Academic Development Fund. Other generous donations were received from The Trinity College Trust, from the Instituto Cervantes in Dublin, and from the College's Dean of the Faculty of Arts (Letters). We also wish to thank those colleagues and former students of Victor Dixon who contributed, through the *tabula gratulatoria*, towards ensuring the financial viability of the venture.

The editors wish also to acknowledge the invaluable collaboration of Eithne Healy: her patient and good-humoured acceptance of the tentative starts and the many drafts from our multiple editorial hands deserves more than just a ritual mention. She worked tirelessly throughout. Last, but not least, our grateful thanks to Mary Costello who did the final corrections to the typescript, and spent long hours in the closing stages ensuring a happy termination to the work.

VICTOR DIXON

No estoy seguro de si los hispanistas son conscientes de lo importante que su labor ha sido y es para los escritores de nuestro país. Sobre todo en una época en que todo lo que se hacía dentro de España era, por una insuficiente comprensión de las posibilidades reales que existían para escribir una literatura crítica y de calidad, sistemáticamente negado o relegado, los hispanistas fueron casi nuestra única opción de contacto y reconocimiento exterior. Gracias al talante inquieto y abierto que su profesión de estudiosos e investigadores les daba, mostraron una percepción y una amplitud de miras de la que resultaron aportaciones decisivas en la construcción de la historia de nuestra literatura de los últimos años. Y, si me lo permiten, destacaría también algo más personal, pero no menos importante: el enorme amor por su profesión y por aquellos escritores a los que dedicaban sus trabajos, que constituyó una fuente de impagable calor humano y amistad.

Victor Dixon es uno de esos estupendos profesionales enamorados de la literatura española que me ha honrado con su afecto y su trabajo. El inicio de nuestra relación se remonta a los años sesenta. Son casi cuatro décadas de amistad en las que siempre he recibido de Dixon amabilidad, entendimiento, apoyo y una consideración de mi obra que ha llegado a conmoverme en más de una ocasión. He disfrutado, asimismo, de la impagable sensación de tratar con alguien que adora el teatro, que lo comprende en su más íntima profundidad, que habla no sólo desde un extraordinario acervo de conocimientos, sino también desde el corazón. Cuando la afición teatral de este especialista en Lope y el teatro del Siglo de Oro se dirigió hacia el teatro español contemporáneo, tuvo la gentileza de fijarse en mi producción y así, *El concierto de San Ovidio, Historia de una escalera* y *En la ardiente oscuridad* fueron montadas por él en el teatro universitario de la Universidad de Manchester. Además, le debo varios penetrantes estudios críticos, entre los que cabe destacar su aportación fundamental al análisis de los *efectos de inmersión,* la acertada valoración de *La Fundación* a la luz de *La vida es sueño* y un original y brillante escrito sobre *El Concierto de San Ovidio* a partir de la significación de su epílogo. Este último trabajo se recoge en un volumen monográfico dedicado a mi obra que con el título: *El teatro de Buero Vallejo: homenaje del hispanismo británico e irlandés* fue editado por Dixon junto con David Johnston.

Ahora, la Universidad de Dublín publica este libro dedicado a Victor

Dixon y me ofrece la posibilidad de homenajearle yo a él, siquiera modestamente, con este breve escrito. El motivo de la publicación es conmemorar sus veinticinco años como catedrático de español en Dublín. Una vez, en la correspondencia de más de treinta años que hemos mantenido, me envió un modelo de examen para que viese cómo orientaba la enseñanza de mi teatro. Allí estaba yo, junto a Lorca, los escritores modernistas, la novela del XIX...... Siendo mucha su dedicación por mí en lo ya señalado, convertir la obra de un autor en objeto de enseñanza es una forma especial de difundirla que la graba indeleblemente en las abiertas mentes de los estudiantes. Y es por eso que, aunque por motivos distintos a los de sus alumnos, también he de estarle agradecido por su magisterio.

Antonio Buero Vallejo

Who is Victor? What is he? –
Victor Frederick Dixon

KENNETH ADAMS

Victor Dixon, officially emeritus since 1999, continues to light the blue touch paper, with the desired pyrotechnic effect, but refuses to obey the other instruction, i.e. to 'retire', since he still beavers away at his research and chips in some specialist teaching. Holder of the Chair of Spanish in Trinity College, University of Dublin, for precisely a quarter of a century (1974–99), he became the longest-serving incumbent in that post 'in diesen heil'gen Hallen' so far, eclipsing Camilo José Cela's *Don Gualterio*, i.e. Professor Walter Starkie, he of the fiddle-raggle, or was it taggle-faddle? Not that Victor, in his harlequincarnation – 'Vesti la giubba' – would be at all averse to such a walk-about part. I first met him over thirty years ago: 'Ah, fors' è lui'?, I thought. It was at a conference in UUT (University of Ultima Thule), some-where up in a bonny, since devolved land. We were at a conference postpran-dial party, and Victor looked dashing in a trademark yellow jumper. Indeed, he is quite notorious for his assiduous, avid attendance, wherever it might be, as a conference-goer, often a *conferenciante*, and consistently a contributor from the floor, party-trouper to boot.

His interest in all things brightly and beautifully histrionic and thespian covers the whole gamut of textual criticism, editing, translating, directing and actual acting. His enthusiasm for live performance knows no bounds. One year he was putting on the *Sibila Casandra* in an ice-cold, draughty College Chapel, on a dank December evening – 'Che gelida manina' for each and every one; another time he came on as a bigamist, with or without his wife's permission, in the leading male role in *Salad Days*. Oh, and I mustn't forget to mention Victor's fine operatic voice, which if not quite up to perturbing a quiet Spanish Sunday (à la Plácido Domingo), has often been heard in formal and spontaneous performance.

Little did I suspect, however, before I had even completed my first lustrum, that Victor was already waiting in the wings: my *Pioneer* pater had been posted to Pitsea, therefore not many stones' throws away from a lurking, if smallfoot, London-born yet formatively Essex man. I soon returned to darkest Devon – 'Gott! welch Dunkel hier!' to listen to a few more all clears, while he in his turn was within range of the nasty Nazi doodlebug. Come to think of it, not a bad nickname for the real V.1's energy and single-minded thrust. This was the time of Flanagan and Allen's classic hit 'Run, rabbit, run' and their never to be forgotten 'Oo do you fink you're kiddin', Mr 'Itler', not to mention George Formby, forever 'waiting by the lamp-post at the corner of the street in case a certain little . . .' Gracie Fields with 'The biggest aspidistra in the world' came by. Ah yes, 'in them days' the ukelele was ubiquitous.

In the proximity of such curious names as Theydon Bois, Thorpe-le-Soken, Stanford-le-Hope, Ongar, Weeley, Burnham-on-Crouch and Foulness, Victor was soon to take the stage as a tyro Hispanist, as he boned up on significant words such as *celaje*, prior to making an exhibition for himself at Cambridge. His Wootton-Isaacson award launched him on his sure-footed career and after a bit of statutory squarebashing, 'Fuor del mar', and now armed with a sparkling degree – 'Lucevan le stelle' – he made his debut on the university lecturing stage, first at St. Andrew's, his doctorate shortly under his yellow jumper, and then at Manchester, spending three years in the former university and thirteen in the latter, with an interposed year in New York (1964–65), at Adelphi (where, theatrically, else, might one ask?) . . . 'Avant de quitter ces lieux'.

By 1974 he had landed the Chair in Trinity College, Dublin – 'Mir ist so wunderbar', he thought, where he immediately led the department and continued that task for the first twenty-one of his eventual twenty-five years in post. His devotion was unstinting: he immersed himself in the job and also played an active role in the work of the then incipient drama department, since to be endowed with its own Chair, thanks to the sponsorship of a universally known soft drinks company. Victor hardly ever concerned himself with extradepartmental high office. Treading those boards held little appeal for him, neither did the caffeinated chit-chat of the Common Room, nor indeed 'Viva il vino', let alone 'Show me the way to the next whisky bottle.' He was, however, sometime Proctor, where he was again able to indulge his passion for performance, by reading out whole afternoonfuls of repetitive, *Sanctae Trinitatae* [*sic*!] Latin at degree ceremonies, with enviable, if masochistic relish and a dutiful dollop of unmacaronic delivery.

Even as a long-standing – and sometimes falling-about – Hispanist myself, I cannot claim great expertise in Victor's chosen field, for him the very antithesis of 'Ecco l'orrido campo'. Faced with a choice between unctuous eulogy and *verrucae omneque*, I will simply attempt a more or less logical, systematic and arguably dispassionate statement of what I can see he has achieved over the now more than four decades of his *ejercicio*. Victor wrote his doctoral thesis for Cambridge (1959) on Lope's protegé Juan Pérez de Montalbán ('The Life and Works. . .'), though no full-length book was spawned therefrom and should, I imagine, still be written: indeed, Montalbán helped to put Victor in the limelight, but the latter rarely returned to the former afterwards.

No, Victor *es de Lope*, the two of them having 'been together now for forty years, and it don't seem a "play" too much'. He has spent much of his research career appropriately probing *la naturaleza del monstruo*, as evidenced by his many papers, plus editions and translations of Carpian theatre. Victor became a kind of 'der Vogelfänger bin ich, ja', as he pursued *el Fénix*. The ghost, of course, speaks to him constantly, as evidenced by the first lines of some of the plays (my source is María Cruz Pérez y Pérez, *Bibliografía del teatro de Lope de Vega,* Madrid, C.S.I.C., 1973): 'Nunca tuve mejor suerte' (*La ejecutada ley*), on getting his Chair; 'No sé qué tengo de hacer' (*La locura por la honra*), on being faced with new administrative headaches; 'Buena fiesta se previene' (*La Madre Teresa de Jesús*), on throwing his first annual departmental party; '¿Qué nuevas hay de mi esposa?' (*La corona merecida*), on attending yet another distant conference; '¡Salid allá fuera, bestia!' (*Los carboneros*), on clashing with a crusty colleague; 'En fin, Mustafá, han llegado' (*El valor de Malta*), on noting the arrival of departmental reviewers; '¿En qué vendrá a parar esta locura?' (*La corona mayor*), on deciding to stand down from the headship, . . . and the one nobody else knows about, 'A desnudarme comienza' (*El maestro de danzar*) . . . '¡Ya llega el aplauso!' (*Dineros son calidad*).

Victor's approach is meticulous as he trawls with his tireless toothcomb, searching out every emblem, innuendo, rhyme, syllable and trope. This is in keeping with his classic, scholarly approach. So 'Nessun dorma', while he is about. Nonetheless, as one would expect from a student of *comediantes*, he is in no way devoid of his own *vis comica*, since his writing blends the gravy of *gravitas* with a leaven of *levitas*. Moreover, though for him text is paramount, he is always aware of the writer's active presence and a play's staging potential. Neither is he merely interested in the surface, audio-visual side, but has written also on deeper implicative aspects, such as character, theme and social content.

The research output has been steady and progressive since the late 1950s. In keeping with Victor's utter professionalism, there are no hasty potboilers in his work, and only the very occasional short contribution that might be termed a 'note' or a 'query'. He gives each of his topics a thorough, solid and substantial going-over, always scouring the bibliography unstintingly, so as to support his arguments, and paying appropriate acknowledgment and attention to his peers.

I will turn to his book-length studies first: these are all editions and/or translations of Lope, with the exception of the editing, shared with David Johnston (The Queen's University, Belfast) of a volume of papers on Buero Vallejo, though I note *en passant* that it too has a xanthic cover. The first here, without translation, is *El sufrimiento premiado* (London: Tamesis, 1967), never properly edited before. Several years later he edited his sure favourite *El perro del hortelano* (London: Tamesis, 1981), which, inevitably as *The dog in the manger,* has since appeared as a blank verse translation in a separate volume (Ottawa: Dovehouse, 1990).

Victor is also a great fan of *Fuenteovejuna*, the Spanish text of which he edited in 1989 (Warminster: Aris and Philips), with a parallel English blank-verse translation. Within the glossy, yet again yellow cover characteristic of that series – and compare Juan Ruiz's 'Blanca farina yaze so negra cobertera' (*Libro de Buen Amor*, 17c) – is a very solid, scholarly piece of work. Its editor has studied all the *variantes* and sifted through the several previous translations, with his explanatory textual notes amounting to as many as one per verse of the play.

There is also a splendid *separata*, of hefty pamphlet length, this time in a paler shade of yellow, on *Characterization in the Comedia of Seventeenth-century Spain* (Manchester: Manchester University Press, 1994), being originally a public lecture. Here he lets himself range widely over plays by several dramatists within the one study. In its published form it clearly transcends the oral presentation and acquires the usual, daunting apparatus: its main thrust is that of the role of characterization and where it comes in any order of primacies, if such exist, à la A.A. Parker. Victor clearly joins the club of those who reject the virtually Thomist position of the late, learned *montevideano*. A year or so later, he synthesized the broad Golden Age drama in his weighty Chapter Five of *The Oxford Illustrated History of Drama* (ed. John Russell Brown, Oxford: Oxford University Press, 1995).

In the Golden Age sphere, Victor's articles are mainly, though not exclusively, monographic, mostly of course on Lope, occasionally on Calderón and Tirso, once on Villaizán y Garcés, and from time to time, though somewhat reluctantly – 'O wie ängstlich!' – on Montalbán. It is in the range of angles covered that Victor's work is most impressive. He is interested not only in matters of textual detail for editing purposes, making plays available in English to non-Hispanic readers but also: the huge problem of authorial attribution, given such a plethora of good, bad, indifferent, repetitive and often parasitical *comedias*, pinpointing their dates, learned sources and other parallels within and without the Spanish dramatists; characterization; the function and effect of metrics, with their varying rhyme and syllabic schemes, symbols and emblems; as well as staging and the spectacle itself; evidence of targeted, favoured actors and actresses; involvement of the playwright himself; and last but not least thematic matters from aesthetico-moralistic impact, to the development of *dénouement* and socio-political topics such as the peasant's position or the attitude towards the Americas.

I should perhaps, without producing a formal, comprehensive *bibliografía victoriana*, itemize plays that he has covered and also revisited over the years as well as themes and topics and the work of other dramatists. For example:

Plays

Antonio Roca:		*Homenaje . . . Fichter* Madrid:Castalia, 1971, 75–88.
El Arauco domado:		*Renaissance Studies*, 6 (1993), 249–69.
El Caballero del Sacramento:		*Actas del Cuarto Congreso Internacional de Hispanistas*, Salamanca, 1971 (1982), 393–403.
El castigo sin venganza:	(i)	*Modern Language Notes* 81 (1970), 957–66.
	(ii)	*Studies in Spanish Literature of the Golden Age presented to E.M. Wilson*, ed. R. O. Jones, London: Tamesis, 1973, 63–81.
	(iii)	*Actor y técnica de representación del teatro clásico español*, ed. J. M. Díez Borque (London: Tamesis, 1989), 55–74.
	(iv)	*Revista Canadiense de Estudios Hispánicos*, 21 (1994), 39–60.
	(v)	*The Knowledges of the Translator: From Literary Interpretation to Machine Classification*, eds M. Coulthard and A. Odber de Baubeta (Lewiston: Edwin Mellen, 1996), 213–42.
El perro del hortelano:	(i)	A critical edition, with introduction and notes (London: Tamesis, 1981).
	(ii)	*The Dog in the Manger*, a verse translation, with introduction and notes (Ottawa: Dovehouse, 1990).
	(iii)	*Revista Estudios*, 189–90 (1995), 73–86.
	(iv)	*Cuadernos de Teatro Clásico*, 8 (1995).
El sufrimiento premiado:	(i)	A critical edition, with introduction and notes (London: Tamesis, 1967).
	(ii)	*En torno al teatro del Siglo de Oro: Actas de las Jornadas XX y XIII* (Almería, Instituto de Estudios Almerienses, 1996), 193–202.
El villano en su rincón:	(i)	*Cuadernos de Filología*, Universidad de Valencia, núm. 3, 1981.
	(ii)	*Bulletin of the Comediantes*, 50 (1998), 5–20.
Fuenteovejuna:	(i)	*Criticón*, Université de Toulouse-Mirail, num. 42, 1988.
	(ii)	A critical edition and verse translation, with introduction and notes, Warminster: Aris and Philips, 1989.

	(iii)	*Cuadernos de Teatro Clásico*, 4 (1989).
Juan de Dios y Antón Martín:		*Hispanic Review*, 37 (1969), 303–6.
La dama boba:		*Anuario Lope de Vega*, 3 (1997), 51–65.
La ingratitud vengada:		*En torno al teatro del Siglo de Oro: Actas de las Jornadas XXX y XIII* Almería, Instituto de estudios almerienses, 1996, 193–202.
La villana de Getafe:		*What's Past is Prologue: a collection of essays in honour of L. J. Woodward* (Edinburgh: Scottish Universities Press, 1984), 34–45.
Lo fingido verdadero:	(i)	*Revista de Crítica Literaria*, núm. 4/5, 1997–98 (1999), 97–114.
	(ii)	*Cuadernos de teatro clásico*, 11 (1999), 53–71.
Peribáñez:		*Bulletin of Hispanic Studies*, 43 (1966), 11–24.

Topics

Topics he pursues in relation to some of these, further Vegan plays and a range of other dramatists are:

Chile:		*Bulletin of Hispanic Studies*, 70 (1993) 79–95.
Corrales:		*Edad de Oro* (Universidad Autónoma de Madrid), 5 (1985), 35–58.
Decameron:		*El mundo del teatro español en su Siglo de Oro: ensayos presentados a John E. Varey*, ed. J. Ruano de la Haza (Ottawa: Dovehouse, 1989), 185–196.
Emblems:		*Emblemática*, 9 (1992), 83–101.
Metrics:	(i)	*Editing the Comedia*, eds Frank P. Casa and M. D. McGaha *Michigan Romance Studies*, vol. 5 (1985), 104–25.
	(ii)	*The Golden Age Comedia: Text, Theory and Performance*, eds Charles Ganelin and Howard Mancing (West Lafayette: Purdue University Press, 1994), 384–402.
New World:		*Renaissance Studies*, 6 (1993), 249–69.
St Patrick of Ireland:		*Hermathena*, 121(1976), 142–58.
Translation:		*Prologue to Performance: Spanish Classical Theater To-day*, eds Louise and Peter

Fothergill-Payne (Lewisburg: Bucknell
University Press, 1991), 93–112.

'Traducciones de Calderón al inglés en el
siglo XX', *Calderón en escena: siglo XX*,
[exhibition catalogue] Madrid: Comunidad
de Madrid, 2000, pp. 249–53.

Other playwrights

Calderón:
Los cabellos de Absalón: (i)   *Hacia Calderón* 3 (1976), 84–96;
    (ii)   *Bulletin of Hispanic Studies*, 62 (1984),
       304–316

Pérez de Montalbán:
Ph.D. Thesis: 'The Life & Works . . .', Cambridge
    University, 1959.

Segundo Tomo: *Hispanic Review*, 28 (1961), 91–109.
Para todos: *Hispanic Review*, 32(1964), 36–59.
Vida . . . San Patricio: *Bulletin of Hispanic Studies*, 52 (1975),
    227–34.

Tirso de Molina:
El vergonzoso en palacio: *Revista Estudios*, nos. 189–90, (1995),
    73–86.

Villaizán y Garcés: *Hispanófila*, no. 13 (1961), 5–22.

Thus far I have scarcely mentioned Victor's further intense interest in modern Spanish drama, notably in the plays of the late Buero Vallejo. Dixonian publications on Buero include, as I mentioned above, the joint editing of a volume of studies with David Johnston, *El teatro de Buero Vallejo: homenaje del hispanismo británico e irlandés* (Liverpool: Liverpool University Press, 1996), to which Victor also contributes an article on *El concierto de San Ovidio*. The piece is quite typical of this scholar who always 'does his homework' very thoroughly, conducting a tireless search, far beyond the confines of any average or middling-to-good library, for whatever may be germane to the topic, involving even newspaper notices and inaccessible, to me at least, journals.

In qualitative terms, too, Victor consults works which pertain to the profundities of philosophy, psychology etc., such as Borel's 'Quelques aspects du songe', Diderot's *Oeuvres* or García Lorenzo's 'Elementos paraverbales. This 'article', no *articulito* indeed, shows an area of intellectual

---

exploration, with which the *comedia* writings are often less concerned. Victor's own words here indicate an awareness of more uncertain, if more profound, issues:

> Pero si el más hondo motivo de nuestra intranquilidad es haber sentido . . . una problemática trágica inherente a la naturaleza y existencia humanas y más allá de soluciones utópicas, filosóficas o religiosas, se nos está pidiendo . . . una respuesta a la angustia del hombre ante su propia aniquilación.
>
> (op. cit. p. 52).

He also writes on the so-called 'Immersion Effect' in *Themes in Drama 2: Drama and Mimesis*, ed. James Redmond (Cambridge: Cambridge University Press, 1980) pp. 113–37, and again in *Anthropos*, 79 (1987), 31–6. Also of fascinating interest is the influence of H. G. Wells on Buero (in *Antonio Buero Vallejo: Literatura y Filosofía*, ed. Ana María Leyra (Madrid: Editorial Complutense, 1998), pp. 145–64. Yet another article examines an aspect of Buero's link with the Golden-Age drama, namely with *La vida es sueño* (*ESTRENO*, Studies in Contemporary Spanish Theater, 2, Pennsylvania State University (1999), pp. 195–204), which ties in neatly with Buero's oneiric exploration in *El concierto*.

Given Victor's vigorous pursuit of research, even after his emeritification, it comes as no surprise that his output is now describing a virtually exponential upward curve. The above research record can be seen as the major part of an inverted iceberg. The submerged tip is still substantial, in that it comprises all of the 'routine' activities that teaching academics perform. Apart from all of Victor's teaching down the years and the administrative chores, he has also participated in those usually unsung activities, such as external examining at undergraduate and graduate level, notably in France and Spain as well as on English-speaking territory. He has been active throughout, behind the scenes as it were, in membership of journal editorial boards, and the refereeing of articles, as well as writing numerous book reviews. Last but not least, he did invaluable work as Golden-Age drama 'correspondent' for the *Year's Work in Modern Language Studies* in the late 1960s and early 1970s.

I cannot finish without referring to two of Victor's other passions, one now in prolonged abeyance, the other still up and running. Yes, there was Victor the fitness fanatic, the striving sportsman, as he padded the parks and the roads in preparation for the marathon. In a field of 12,000 he was for once, sadly, not the winner, but he still merits the attachment of *ludorum* to his name, in every sense. He also used his training runs to express his abhorrence of litter louts: here, he enacted a sort of lonely, long-distance paper chase, Dublin pavements and kerbsides providing such public-spirited chaps with more than ample opportunity. The other *afición* [sic?] shows the influence of Creationism, since, yea verily, the Gospel of St John I:1 informs us that 'In the beginning was the word': close by is the cryptic crossword. Our esteemed subject can adroitly turn a carthorse into an orchestra, an Antipodean aborigine into a Saturnalia, or the scene of a matricide into a domain, while that old standard 'I ask me, has Will a peer?', would to him be mere bard's play, so I'm sure that he could figure out the following, 'in jig time', as the Irish say:

1. Phone : ' 'Ello, order later!' (2, 5, 3, 9).
2. Ramsbottom: Wet Lancashire in Extremadura? (13).
3. Age? Develop? (4, 2, 4).
4. Grip no coal, save ozone. (10, 2, 7).

One of the still performing popular-song survivors of the era with which I began is Dame Vera Lynn, who even now delivers an evocative rendition of the – for many contemporaries – indelibly poignant 'We'll meet again, don't know where, don't know when'. In Victor's case I seem to think we will, at a venue near us, for a long time to come. Being still quite a leveret, he cannot bring himself to proclaim 'e non voglio più servir' . . . unlike Leporello. No, he will never leave the stage . . . not even kindly.

Postscript

By way of acknowledgement, I must reveal my 'subtle' variation on William Shakespeare's *Ariel* song and the line from Franz Schubert's musical version in the title to my whole piece, since Victor's wife is indeed Sylvia. I also append a list, in order of appearance, of the arias that I have plundered, as follows: 'In diesen heil'gen Hallen' (Mozart's *Die Zauberflöte*) 'Vesti la giubba' (Leoncavallo's *Pagliacci*), 'Ah fors' è lui' (Verdi's *La Traviata*), 'Che gelida manina' (Puccini's *La Bohème*) 'Gott!, welch dunkel hier!' (Beethoven's *Fidelio*), 'Fuor del mar' (Mozart's *Idomeneo*), 'Lucevan le stelle' (Puccini's *Tosca*), 'Avant de quitter ces lieux' (Gounod's *Faust*), 'Viva il vino' (Mascagni's *Cavalleria Rusticana*), 'Show me the way to the next whisky bottle' (Weill's *Mahoganny*), 'Ecco l'orrido campo' (Verdi's *Un ballo in maschera*), 'Der Vogelfänger bin ich, ja' (Mozart's *Die Zauberflöte*), 'Nessun dorma' (Puccini's *Turandot*), 'O wie ängstlich' (Mozart's *Die Entführung aus dem Serail*), 'O welche Lust?' (Beethoven's *Fidelio*), 'e non voglio più servir (Mozart's *Don Giovanni*).

For those who find cryptic crosswords unfathomable, the answers to 1, 2, 3, 4 above are as follows: *El perro del hortelano, Fuenteovejuna*, Lope de Vega, *Vergonzoso en Palacio*. Further, my contribution would not be complete without a valedictory sonnet of the kind that Lope 'might' have written:

VÍTOR, VÍTOR, VÍTOR

En un rincón de Irlanda no villano,
habitando su ebúrneo palacio,
vergonzoso no, ni nunca reacio,
con perro muy fiel, lopesco hortelano.

Pliegos sueltos lee, pluma en la mano,
y emblemas tiene en flavo cartapacio;
sus ojos de lince, que él no es batracio,
para todos pesquisando no en vano.

Bien premiado sufrimiento, a tu lado
una dama imboba, Don distinguido
amiguillo de Tespis, yo te alabo.

Pues por ti como quien tanto ha acertado,
verdadero mostrando lo fingido,
doy a esta mi semblanza fin y cabo.

Alfonso VIII and Raquel De Toledo

DON W. CRUICKSHANK

The legendary love-affair between Alfonso VIII of Castile (born 1155 or 1156; reigned 1158–1214) and the young Jewish woman, Raquel of Toledo, provided the plot for several Spanish plays, notably Lope de Vega's *Las paces de los reyes* (c. 1610), and *La judía de Toledo / La desgraciada Raquel*, written by Mira de Amescua in the 1620s, although printed versions attribute it to Diamante, who was born in 1625.[1] (One explanation is that Diamante rewrote Mira's play, but followed it closely.)[2] The best-known dramatized version is García de la Huerta's *Raquel*, which dates from the 1770s.[3] Like the story of the lovers of Teruel, the story reached a wider audience: Grillparzer wrote a version (*Die Jüdin von Toledo*, c. 1850). It gave rise to historical novels, etc., in various languages. When we try to trace the story's pedigree, however, we run into difficulties.

Alfonso's most important contemporary historians, Lucas de Túy (c. 1160–1249), in his *Chronicon mundi*, and Rodrigo Ximénez de Rada (c. 1170–1247), in *De rebus Hispaniae*, mention no love-affair. Nor does the so-called *Primera crónica general*, begun under Alfonso X, great-grandson of Alfonso VIII, except that a later hand has added the following in the margin of one manuscript:

> Este monesterio [Santa María de las Huelgas, near Burgos] fizo fazer el rey don Alffonso por tres cosas: . . . la terçera por que este rey . . . ouo de fazer pesar a Dios en siete años que moro en la juderia de Toledo con una judia despendiendo y [= allí] mal so tienpo. Et deste peccado ouo Dios grant sanna contra el, et fizole ueer en uision de como gelo querie

---

[1] H. A. Rennert, in 'Mira de Amescua y *La judía de Toledo*', *Revue Hispanique*, 7 (1900), 119–40, is sure Mira was the author. So is Donald A. Murray, in his doctoral dissertation 'Mira de Amescua's *La desgraciada Raquel*': Stanford, 1951: see John J. Reynolds and Szilvia E. Szmuk, *Spanish Golden-Age Drama / El teatro del Siglo de Oro* (New York: MLA, 1998), pp. 249–50. Lope's play was printed in his *Séptima parte* (Madrid: Viuda de Alonso Martín for Miguel de Siles, 1617), the Mira-Diamante play in *Escogidas 27* (Madrid: Andrés García de la Iglesia for Francisco Serrano de Figueroa, 1667).

[2] See Edward M. Wilson and Duncan Moir, *The Golden Age: Drama 1492–1700* (London: Ernest Benn, 1971), p. 137.

[3] See the modern edition by René Andioc (Madrid: Castalia, 1971). The first performance was in Oran in 1772, but a revised version was premiered in Madrid in 1778.

calomiar, la qual uision uio el en Yliescas una mannana en amaneçiendo a
dos annos despues de la batalla de Alarcos . . . et le dixo: ". . . por el
peccado que feziste con la judia et dexauas la reyna tu muger por ella, . . .
por esso fuste uençudo en la batalla de Alarcos, . . . et [Dios] quieretelo aun
calomiar en los tus fijos uarones, ca todos morran et non fincara
generaçion de ninguno dellos . . .". Quando el rey don Alfonso ouo oydo
esto, fico muy triste en so coraçon, repentiendose mucho de sus peccados,
et de alli adelante puso de fazer el monesterio de Burgos . . .[4]

At Alarcos (19 July 1195) the *almohades* won a decisive victory over the
Christians, although Alfonso managed to hold Toledo. Several points make
us deeply suspicious of this marginal afterthought. First, Alfonso's vision is
in 1197, two years after Alarcos, but the foundation of Las Huelgas was rati-
fied by Clement III ten years earlier, in 1187; the foundation proper dates
from around 1179.[5] Second, nothing is said about the death of the king's
unnamed mistress. Third, the prediction of the death of Alfonso's sons, God's
punishment for his sin (as with King David for Bathsheba, a parallel which is
mentioned) is worthless, since it was written long after they died. Fourth, any
account which refers to a period of seven years is likely to have been inspired
or contaminated by folk elements. Finally, the handwriting of the marginal
note is up to a century later than the main text.

Ostensibly next in chronological order is the version in the *Castigos y
documentos que daba* [*el rey don Sancho IV*] *a su hijo*. This version refers to
the seven-year infatuation with an unnamed *judía*, a sin punished by defeat at
Alarcos, expiated through Las Huelgas, and forgiven in victory at Las Navas
de Tolosa (1212, perhaps the most significant battle in the Reconquest).
Sancho IV reigned from 1284 to 1295, but the *Castigos* have been dated to
1350–60, and the longer version (containing our story) to even later.[6]

The first chronicle to refer to the murder of Alfonso's mistress (unnamed)
is the *Crónica general de España de 1344*, the *Segunda crónica general*.[7]
This version does not mention Alarcos, Las Huelgas or Las Navas, and
reduces the affair to seven *months*.

Lope is not likely to have consulted these early versions. If he consulted

[4]   R. Menéndez Pidal ed., *Primera crónica general de España que mandó componer
Alfonso el Sabio y se continuaba bajo Sancho IV en 1289*, 2 vols (Madrid: Gredos, 1955),
II, 685n (editor's square brackets removed for ease of reading). One other manuscript (of
seventeen) includes the story, but in the text proper.
[5]   *Diccionario de historia eclesiástica de España*, 4 vols (Madrid: CSIC, 1972–1975),
III, 1576, s.v. *Monasterios*.
[6]   P. Groussac, 'Le Livre de *Castigos y documentos* attribué au roi D. Sanche IV',
Revue Hispanique, 15 (1906), 212–339 (p. 332).
[7]   Quoted by James A. Castañeda in his first edition of the play (Chapel Hill: Univ. of
N. Carolina, 1962), pp. 17–18; see also the Portuguese version, in Luís Filipe Lindley
Cintra ed., *Crónica geral de Espanha de 1344*, vol. IV (Lisboa: Imprensa Nacional, 1990),
pp. 281–83.

any chronicle, the most likely is Florián de Ocampo's edition of *Las quatro partes enteras de la cronica de España*, sometimes called the *Tercera crónica general*.[8] Here we need note only that the king's mistress has an attribute rather than a name: 'avie no[m]bre fermosa', that the duration was 'poco menos de siete años', and, in addition, that 'los omes buenos d[e]l reyno . . . d[e]gollaronla a ella, e a quantos estaua[n] co[n] ella'.

The Ocampo text matches the details of Lope's play, but he could also have consulted the ballads published by Lorenzo de Sepúlveda in *Romances nuevamente sacados de historias antiguas de la Crónica de España*.[9] In particular, Durán's number 928, 'Muerto era ese buen rey', tells the story of Alfonso and Raquel:

> Olvidó el Rey á la Reina,
> con aquella se ha encerrado.
> Siete años estaban juntos
> que no se habian apartado,
> y tanto la amaba el Rey
> que su reino habia olvidado.

This version goes on to mention the mistress's murder (again, naming her only Fermosa), and the king's anger, dissipated by the vision of the angel. Neither Ocampo's prose nor Sepúlveda's verse makes any link with Alarcos.

The association of great defeats with the sins (usually sexual) of monarchs (or others) is a recurring motif in Spanish literature and historiography. The first battle referred to in this way is Guadalete (711): the defeat of King Rodrigo by the Moors. The King Rodrigo cycle of ballads, deriving partly from Pedro del Corral's *Corónica sarracina* of c. 1430, attributes the defeat to God's anger at Rodrigo's rape of La Cava, daughter of Count Julian, and sees the king's anguish after the defeat as part of his personal expiation. Another example is Fernando de Herrera's attribution of the disaster of Alcázarquivir to divine disapproval of the pride of King Sebastian and his troops.[10] This view was reiterated by Juan de Mariana in his *Del rey y de la institución real*, and raised to the status of a historical principle:

> Echad una ojeada en torno vuestro y recordad la historia de todas las
> naciones que se han visto afligidas por grandes calamidades y pasadas á

---

[8] First ed. Zamora: Agustín de Paz and Juan Picardo for Juan de Espinosa, 1541: see fol. ccclxxxvii[r] (also quoted by Castañeda, ed. cit., pp. 19–20). Lope could most readily have consulted the edition of Valladolid: Sebastián de Cañas for Antonio Cuello, 1604, fol. 345[r], from which I quote.

[9] (Antwerp: Iuan Steelsio, 1551; there were several later editions.) Reprinted in Agustín Durán ed., *Romancero general*, 2 vols (Madrid: Hernando, 1926) (BAE, vols X and XVI), II, 4–11.

[10] 'Por la pérdida del rey don Sebastián', in Arthur Terry ed., *An Anthology of Spanish Poetry 1500–1700*, Part I (Oxford: Pergamon, 1965), pp. 105–8.

sangre y fuego. Encontraréis siempre indudablemente que han tenido lugar en ellas crímenes atroces antes de ser destruidas. No hace mucho se ha sufrido en Africa una tremenda derrota, que ha cubierto de infamia y sangre á los portugueses. Atribúyese generalmente á la temeridad y audacia del príncipe . . .; mas creo que puede atribuirse á la cólera de la Divinidad.[11]

Mariana adds that the defeat of the Armada of 1588

no es mas que la venganza de los graves crímenes que en nuestra nacion se cometen, y si no me engaña el corazon, la de las mal encubiertas liviandades de cierto príncipe [Philip II], que olvidándose de su dignidad y de su edad ya avanzada, era fama que por aquel mismo tiempo se entregaba desenfrenadamente á la lujuria . . . (*ibid.*)

Even the failure to follow up a victory properly could be attributed to 'los pecados de la cristiandad, y porque quiere y permite Dios que tengamos siempre verdugos que nos castiguen.'[12] Small wonder that in 1629 (the year of the birth of Don Juan de Austria II, living proof of a royal pecadillo) Philip IV suggested that 'God is angry with me and my kingdoms for our sins, and in particular for mine.'[13]

Given this tradition, it is no surprise that Mariana, in his *Historia general de España*, recounts the Alfonso–Fermosa story as a moral lesson:

Tuuose por cierto, que con aquel desastre tan grande [Alarcos] castigò Dios en particular vn pecado del Rey: y fue, que en Toledo menospreciada su muger, se enamorò de cierta Iudia: que fuera de la hermosura, ninguna otra cosa tenia de estimar. Era este trato no solo deshonesto, sino tambien afrentoso a la Christiandad. Los Grandes mouidos por tan grande indignidad, y porque no se esperaua emienda, hizieron matar aquella muger, andaua el Rey furioso por el amor, y deseo. Vn Angel que de noche le aparecio en Illescas le apartò de aquel mal proposito: . . . le amenaçaua si no boluiesse en si: y le apercebia esperasse el premio de la castidad, si la guardasse, y temiesse el castigo, si la menospreciasse.

(Book IX, chap. xviii)[14]

A modern psychoanalyst might attribute this 'vision', had it actually taken place, to the king's sense of guilt, but it was natural, in Mariana's vision of history, that Alfonso, having mended his ways, should reap the *premio de la castidad* at Las Navas. The story of a ruler who let an 'inappropriate relation-

---

[11] Juan de Mariana, *Del rey y la institución real*, Book III, chap. x: see his *Obras*, 2 vols (Madrid: Atlas, 1950) (BAE, vols XXX–XXXI), II, 557.

[12] Cervantes, *Don Quijote*, I, xxxix ('Historia del cautivo').

[13] J. H. Elliott, 'Self-Perception and Decline in Early Seventeenth-Century Spain', *Past and Present*, 74 (1977), 46–7.

[14] Quoted from the edition of Madrid: Carlos Sánchez, 1650, I, 441–2.

ship' interrupt a successful career, only to recover his senses and go on to even greater success, was also an admirable one on which to base an edifying play.

Mariana says nothing about the length of the affair; he implies that the king was involved in it at the time of Alarcos, when he was about thirty-nine. None of the early versions names his mistress: she is La Fermosa, if she has any title. On the other hand, most versions refer to the seven-year period. Almost certainly the reference to this length of time (the commonest folk-tale period) caused Lope to think of the biblical Rachel, for whom Jacob had to serve her father seven years, and then another seven: Lope's text refers to this (1484–85).[15] But providing a name for the heroine is not Lope's only contribution to the story.

In *Las paces de los reyes* Lope devotes Act I to presenting Alfonso as a promising young ruler. The boy-king frees himself from the oppressive tutelage of his uncle, King Ferdinand of León, and acquires the sobriquet *el Bueno*. In Toledo cathedral, his sword is miraculously girt on by the image of Santiago himself:[16] in return he promises that Spain's nobles will carry his sword on their chests, a reference to the establishment of the Order of Santiago during his reign. Spain's Jewish community is not mentioned. At first sight, Act I serves only to establish Alfonso's character. However, some of the events surrounding the king's capture of the fortress of Zurita are thematically linked to the Raquel plot. Zurita is held by its letter-of-the-law *alcaide* Lope de Arenas. Arenas is loyal, but he has sworn not to relinquish the castle to Alfonso until the king is fifteen. We glimpse him dallying in the castle garden with Costanza, confident that the castle is impregnable. Costanza is his wife, but his failure to guard against treachery costs him his life: he is killed by Dominguillo, whom he trusted. Lope's use of the Dominguillo character, plus other details, suggests that he used either Ocampo's *Tercera crónica general* or the Sepúlveda ballad 'En Castilla reina Alfonso'.[17] The dalliance in the garden is not mentioned in these sources, which supports the view that Lope introduced it for thematic reasons.

Act II opens years later. The king has grown up and gone on a crusade

---

[15] Some credit for this suggestion goes to Emilio Cotarelo y Mori, in 'Mira de Amescua y su teatro', *BRAE*, 17 (1930), 467–505, 611–58; 18 (1931), 7–90; see 17, p. 644; but for the link with the biblical Rachel, see Castañeda, ed. cit., pp. 24, 44. Line-references are to his edition (see n. 7 above).

[16] Lope had probably heard of the ancient wooden statue of Santiago, now in the Capilla de Santiago at Las Huelgas. Ferdinand III (1217–52) allegedly used its movable arm to knight himself. In Mauro Castellá Ferrer, *Historia del Apostol de Iesus Christo, Sanctiago Zebedeo* (Madrid: Alonso Martín de Balboa, 1610), fol. 4, there is a reference to monarchs being crowned by Santiago.

[17] Arenas is killed with 'un gran venablo' while sitting helpless in the barber's chair; Dominguillo's treachery is both punished and rewarded (his eyes are put out, but he is to be fed for the rest of his life).

with Richard the Lionheart, whose daughter Leonor he has married and brought back to Toledo (the real Leonor/Eleanor was the daughter of Henry II, not of Richard, who was her brother). In the royal garden, by the Tagus, he sees Raquel and her sister Sibila bathing, and is captivated by Raquel. Although he knows by the girls' clothes that they are Jewish, he sends his aide Garcerán Manrique to talk to them. As he waits, he is joined by a gardener, who comes on stage singing:

> Hortelano era Belardo
> en las huertas de Valencia;
> que los trabajos obligan
> a lo que el hombre no piensa.   (1356–9)

Asked by the king if he has seen Raquel and her sister, Belardo says he has, and that they are very beautiful, though with one fault:

> Sí vi, y en extremo bellas;
> pero tienen una falta,
> si no me engaña la muestra:
> que pienso que son judías.   (1387–90)

When the king suggests he use the less pejorative term 'hebreas', Belardo attacks the fashion for politically correct euphemisms, such as Frondoso was to use later in *Fuenteovejuna*.[18] More amused than angry, the king presses for information about the girls, prompting a sarcastic response:

> ¿Cuándo vistes gente destas
> que fuese pobre jamás?
> Un coche y gentil merienda
> las trujo adonde las veis.   (1437–40)

Aware of the reason for the king's interest, Belardo ends with a remark of which Mariana would have approved:

> [el cielo] os defienda
> de dar en tan gran error;
> porque si cristiana fuera,
> ya tuviérades disculpa;
> mas, en su ley, es bajeza [. . .]
> ¡un hidalgo como vos!   (1443–8)

Characters named Belardo in Lope's plays are reckoned to represent Lope

---

18 See lines 290–320 of the first act.

himself.[19] Here, as elsewhere, he goes in for plain words, even when they are unwelcome to his listener. The words jar against our modern sensibilities, but contemporaries presumably applauded the sentiments and were unaware of the prejudice. But even the more biddable Garcerán, who brings Raquel to the palace, has an appropriate answer, when Alfonso asks him what he should do:

> Pensar
> que es de tan infame ley,
> y ganar tan gran vitoria
> como el vencerse a sí mismo.   (1470–3)

Garcerán has already referred to King David's punishment for yielding to his desire for Bathsheba (1256–9). Alfonso, however, cannot overcome his feelings. He neglects to review troops brought by Count Nuño Pérez, while a conversation with Garcerán shows that he is literally deaf to his aide's advice: he can think only of Raquel.

Others can see where the affair may lead. One of these is Raquel's pessimistic father David, who, with her more optimistic brother Leví, sets off to try to talk to her. Encountering the gardener Belardo, they ask if they can talk to the 'dama':

> ¿Es una que no ha comido
> tocino en su vida?   (1759–60)

asks Belardo. 'Sí', meekly replies David. Since we never see David or Leví again, and never hear what they may have said to Raquel, we are left with the suspicion that they were used to get Belardo on stage, or even to serve only as a butt for his doubtful jokes.

The act ends with a thunderstorm. Muttering about the heavens getting angry, Belardo recalls that

> Santiago, decía mi abuela,
> cuando los truenos oía   (1789–90)

The reference to Santiago reminds us of the promising young king of Act I. Nearby, Alfonso too notices the storm, which, significantly, is confined to the royal garden, while over the city the sky is clear. At the darkest point of the storm, the king – and the audience – hears a mysterious voice, singing:

> Rey Alfonso, rey Alfonso,
> no digas que no te aviso:

---

[19] J. M. Cossío, *Lope, personaje de sus comedias* (Madrid: Real Academia Española, 1948), p. 74. See also Carmen Riera Guilera, 'Un curioso jardín de Lope: notas al romance "Hortelano era Belardo" ', *Papeles de Son Armadans*, 77 (1975), 213–26.

>   mira que pierdas la gracia
>   de aquel Rey que rey te hizo [. . .]
>   advierte que por la Cava
>   a España perdió Rodrigo.   (1833–48)

In a scene which recalls *El caballero de Olmedo* (written years later),
Alfonso attributes everything to 'hechizos de Leonor'; he identifies even the
silent Sombra as a product of his own fear, much as Don Alonso does:

>   ¡Viven los cielos, que fue
>   sombra de mi miedo mismo!   (1859–60)

We feel that the king, like Don Alonso, is determined to do what will ruin
him, despite all advice. As in *El caballero*, Lope uses the audience's familiarity with traditional songs or ballads for additional effect: as noted earlier,
the King Rodrigo cycle attributed the Moorish invasion to divine anger at the
king's rape of La Cava; while the lines adapted from the Siege of Zamora
cycle ('Rey don Sancho, rey don Sancho, / no digas que no te aviso') remind
us of internecine strife among the Christian community: the kind of strife
that Alfonso's behaviour presumably threatens.

In Act III the nobles Illán de Toledo, Blasco de Guzmán, Beltrán de Rojas
and Garcerán Manrique are summoned to speak with the queen and her son,
Prince Enrique. The queen persuades them that the king's relationship with
Raquel is not only an affront to her but a threat to the kingdom's stability,
because of its duration:

>   Siete años ha que encerrado
>   con aquella hebrea hermosa,
>   segunda Cava de España,
>   vive retirado a solas.   (1960–3)

As we have seen, this is the second reference to La Cava. The Moors have
destroyed Almodóvar, taken Ciudad Real, and now allegedly threaten Toledo.
Like the king, the nobles have a glorious past and disreputable present, especially Garcerán Manrique:

>   Y tú, Garcerán Manrique,
>   que del Asia honrado tornas,
>   ¿cómo no ves que te llaman
>   autor de tan torpe historia?
>   Tú ayudas a tu señor
>   a que como bestia corra
>   sin freno por tantos vicios.
>   Dime: ¿con qué te soborna?
>   ¿Has mezclado allá tu sangre?   (2034–42)

Further insults follow, including another, from the prince, involving 'impure' blood: the prince suggests that Don Illán must have 'some reason' for standing up for Raquel:

> ¿Tenéis vos por qué volváis
> por esa hebrea?   (2084–5)

The 'some reason' may not be immediately clear to a modern audience, but Don Illán's indignant reply shows that **he** gets the point: the prince is accusing him of being Jewish. Between them, the queen, her son and the nobles refer to Raquel (here or later) as La Cava, Circe, Medea and Helen, standard metaphors for seductresses.

Sharply contrasted with this tense and angry scene is the next, involving Alfonso and Raquel; but if the audience was hoping for as broad a series of hints at unbridled passion as the censors would tolerate, they must have been disappointed. First, sister Sibila is present as gooseberry; second, the lovers are going fishing: the scene is an innocent one, portraying two lovers who enjoy each other's company, whatever they are doing (although bad omens are introduced later). A message is brought to Alfonso: he has to leave. The reason for his departure is hardly state business (he wants to prevent a quarrel between friends), but it contradicts the claim that he was so besotted with Raquel that all business was ignored. The message is false, a ruse to facilitate Raquel's murder. The murder takes place on stage, but Garcerán has had second thoughts, and is absent.

Alfonso's first reaction to the murder is fury: the assassins will die exemplary deaths. Just as he is planning these, the *angelus ex machina* appears and tells him how angry God is. Instantly, he is chastened and full of forgiveness. The last scene shows an improbable reconciliation between king and queen, in which Alfonso, claiming to see how blind he has been, even begs Raquel's murderers not to mention the matter again. (A cynic might ask why the principle applied to Dominguillo, of reward for the treason and punishment for the traitor, is not applicable here too.) Alfonso has been presented in such a way that this change of heart could be made convincing only by attributing it to supernatural pressure – and of course Lope is only following his sources.

At first sight, then, this is a straightforward play: a young king with great potential becomes besotted with his mistress, neglecting both his wife and his role as monarch. To make matters much worse, his mistress is Jewish. After removal of the mistress, the king recovers his senses, and goes on amply to fulfil his early promise. However, there are several oddities: first, Belardo's initial blinkered attitude undergoes a change. Although he believes that only the death of Raquel will bring peace to the kingdom, the sight of armed men in the garden prompts him to run and warn her:

> Advierte, hermosa Raquel [. . .]
> que con turbado semblante,
> capas y espadas diversas,
> caballeros de Toledo
> hoy han entrado en la huerta:
> no son de amistad señales,
> sino de traición y fuerza.   (2369–76)

She calls him a 'labrador honrado y noble' for his pains. Second, Raquel
reveals as she dies that she is a Christian; third, the altruism of the nobles is
placed in doubt by their killing of Raquel's sister, simply 'por que sea / esta
venganza famosa' (2440–1), and by their intention to kill Belardo. Belardo
escapes by offering to show them where the 'treasure' is: their acceptance of
his offer portrays them in their real colours.

Lope has a history of presenting characters and situations in such a way
that we feel obliged to reflect on them, rather than jump to conclusions. Thus,
he arguably mocks the so-called code of honour by presenting its adherents as
either risible or repulsive, for example in *Los comendadores de Córdoba*.[20]
The argument for that play is plausible, although some ambiguities remain.
The portrayal of Raquel in this play is also ambiguous: she is ostensibly
Jewish up to the moment of her death, when she reveals that she is a
Christian:

> Muero en la ley de mi Alfonso;
> testigos los cielos sean.
> Creo en Cristo, a Cristo adoro.   (2435–7)

This subtle use of the possessive adjective (he is 'her' Alfonso too: see also
2366), the manner of presenting her death – both brave and Christian –
together with the dubious motives of her killers, creates sympathy for her. No
earlier version of the story makes her convert: clearly this was Lope's deliberate invention. However, one feature of the story may have given him the idea:
Raquel was supposedly housed in the Palacios de Galiana, who was
converted to Christianity:

> [. . .] a los palacios llevé
> aquella mujer sin fe,
> que así tu fe contradice.
> Ya está en ella como el dueño,
> supuesto que Galïana
> se volvió después cristiana.   (1453–8)

---

[20] Melveena McKendrick, 'Celebration or Subversion?: *Los comendadores de
Córdoba* Reconsidered', *Golden-Age Studies in Honour of A. A. Parker, Bulletin of
Hispanic Studies*, 61 (1984), 352–60.

Covarrubias tells Galiana's story:

> En Toledo huuo vna Princesa Mora, hija de Gadalfe; a la qual su padre
> edificò vnos palacios ricos y de gran recreacion en Toledo a la orilla del
> Tajo . . . en la huerta que llaman del Rey. *Dizen que se convirtio*, y fue
> primera muger del Emperador Carlo Magno . . .[21]

In addition to the obvious attempts to make Raquel sympathetic, we
should note that the 'seductress' epithets used by her enemies are unjustified:
the relationship between her and Alfonso is instigated and maintained by the
king. There is no evidence to support the queen's claim that

> Raquel reina, Raquel tiene
> de Castilla la corona;
> da banderas a las armas,
> y a las letras nobles ropas.
> Ella castiga, ella prende [. . .].   (1968–72)

The queen, the prince and the nobles are portrayed unsympathetically, but
some justification for their behaviour is provided by the claim that Alfonso's
obsession with Raquel endangered Christian Spain. While the play does not
try to situate its plot in precise relation to the historic battles of Alfonso's
reign, the implication is that but for the removal of Raquel, the victory of Las
Navas might not have been won.

It has been suggested that, *for its time*, this play did not present Jewish
characters intolerantly. In so far as Raquel is disapproved of more for her religion than for her race, this is true. But much more striking than Raquel and
her family, who do not directly endanger Christian Castile, are the constant
references to the Moorish threat, which can be overcome only by defeating
the Moors and expelling them. As the victor of Las Navas, Alfonso was an
ideal monarch to present as a crusader. Indeed, the campaign which led to the
victory was granted official crusade status. On the other hand, Alfonso did
no crusading in the Holy Land: this deliberate embroidery is an indication of
how Lope wished to present the king. Not only the king, but his queen too:
Leonor has implicitly inherited the crusading spirit of her 'father' Richard I,
and threatens to return home to him if the nobles will not do their duty
(2043–50).

Las paces de los reyes is not Lope's only treatment of the story: we also
find it in Canto XIX of his *Jerusalén conquistada*. Earlier cantos deal with
the fictitious exploits of Alfonso in the Holy Land, to which he was supposedly accompanied by Garcerán Manrique, his aide in the play. Lope's

[21] Sebastián de Covarrubias Orozco, *Tesoro de la lengua castellana o española*
(Madrid: Luis Sánchez, 1611), fol. 423ᵛ (s.v. *Galliana*, emphasis mine). The palace is
referred to in *Don Quijote*, II, 55.

Jerusalén was published in 1609, the year when the expulsion of the Moriscos was decreed, although a first draft was ready in 1605. It has been argued that he wrote Cantos XIX and XX about 1608.[22] Morley and Bruerton suggest that the play was written between 1604 and 1612, and favour 1610–12.[23] That is, it was probably written while the expulsion of the Moriscos was under way, an expulsion which it clearly advocates. The play does not ask questions about racial and religious stereotyping: if anything, it reinforces intolerance in an intolerant age. However, skilful dramatist that he is, Lope also appeals to the audience's sentimentality with the 'true' story of a tragic love-affair.

A brief look at other dramatized versions of the story, or of similar stories, casts more light on what is happening in this play. Mira's *La judía de Toledo* makes little use of Lope's plot, although it borrowed the names of Raquel and her father David. It opens with the news that Alfonso has ordered the Jewish community to leave Toledo. The chief rabbi and Raquel's father persuade her to see the king and use her charms to induce him to revoke his decree, knowing what other results her visit may have: reference is made to David and Bathsheba (3a).[24] It would have been easy to present Raquel as a tragic victim, but the author keeps reminding us of her religion ('Lástima es, por vida mía', says one character, 'que lleve el diablo esa cara' – 4b). Mira also suggests that Raquel is motivated partly by ambition for power, once she discovers her influence over Alfonso: one of her speeches includes the words 'Ambición, tú me vendiste' (17c); even so, love is dominant: 'Quitadme á Alfonso, si acaso / la vida quereis quitarme', she says later (17c). Her murder is partly sanitized by its taking place offstage, yet the play ends with Alfonso swearing vengeance on her murderers: the unconvincing reconciliation scene is absent. This play is arguably a sincere attempt to write a tragedy, which is not quite successful because the author's prejudices, or his awareness of his audience's intolerance, interfered with his presentation of Raquel.

In his play, García de la Huerta relied partly on Mira for his presentation of Raquel as enjoying her power, but he has one striking departure: Raquel has an ambitious Jewish adviser, Rubén. The disaffected nobles do not murder Raquel themselves: they make Rubén kill her, ostensibly lessening their guilt at his expense. As she dies, Raquel claims that love has caused her death, has been her only crime: an obvious attempt to arouse sympathy. She is

---

[22] Frank Pierce, *The Heroic Poem of the Spanish Golden Age: Selections* (Oxford: Dolphin, 1947), p. 66.

[23] S. Griswold Morley and Courtney Bruerton, *Cronología de la comedias de Lope de Vega* (Madrid: Gredos, 1968), p. 372.

[24] The most accessible text is in Ramón de Mesonero Romanos ed., *Dramáticos posteriores a Lope de Vega*, 2 vols (Madrid: Atlas, 1951) (BAE, vols XLVII, XLIX), II, 1–18.

no secret Christian, but the appeal for sympathy and the distancing of her from Rubén imply that García de la Huerta is capable of some sophistication in his presentation of Jewish characters. This distancing partly backfires when she describes Rubén as an 'hebreo vil'. To present one 'Hebrew' using the name as a term of abuse to another tells us something about the prejudices of the author, and his assumptions about those of his audience.[25]

This prejudice is most visible when we compare the story of Raquel with another 'true' story which has marked similarities, and which also inspired several plays. In the 1340s, Crown Prince Pedro of Portugal allegedly fell in love with Inés de Castro, a lady-in-waiting of his wife Costanza. Inés, though not Jewish, was also an outsider, at least in Portuguese terms: she was Spanish. In 1355 a group of Portuguese nobles murdered her, although by then Costanza had died. Once again, the assassins persuaded themselves that they were acting in their country's interests. In the dramatized versions, Pedro's father, the king of Portugal, disinherits him for his liaison with Inés. But Pedro becomes king after all, and has Inés's body exhumed, enthroned and crowned. Her murderers are comprehensively put to death.

The argument that the dramatists' treatment of these stories is constrained by historical fact, or by what they thought was historical fact, is untenable. Dramatists of the sixteenth and seventeenth centuries disregarded historical fact when it suited them, with Aristotle's support. In any case, their sources of information about the relationships between Pedro and Inés, or Alfonso and Raquel, are scantier than the plays imply.

What we have in the relationships of Alfonso and Raquel, and Pedro and Inés, are similar stories which receive very different treatment. The story of Pedro and Inés is a story of true love conquering death, of a young woman who, but for envy and prejudice, should have been queen – who did become queen, in a way. Pedro's impropriety in having two children by Inés while Costanza was still alive is ignored. As confirmation of the undying love of Pedro and Inés, there was the fact that they are buried side-by-side at Alcobaça, like the lovers of Teruel.

The story of Alfonso and Raquel, on the other hand, is dramatized as an aberration. When the emperor Titus gives up Bérénice in Racine's play because his people will not accept a Jewish empress, the tragedy lies in the void between the ruler's public duty and private wishes. In Lope's play, Alfonso is not required to give up Raquel: all he has to do is accept a *fait accompli*, unlike the heroic King Pedro, who refuses to do so. Lope's dramatization of the story of Alfonso and Raquel is a moral tale, not a tragedy. It does not contemplate the dilemma of Titus because, even as a royal mistress, Raquel was unsuitable, since she was Jewish, even if she had

---

[25] The passion of King Juan for the Jewish Micol, in Vélez's *Si el caballo vos han muerto*, has an obvious debt to the Raquel story, and could be examined here, if space allowed.

adopted Christianity. The Mira version is sometimes less overtly prejudiced, but it also fails to present Alfonso with a tragic dilemma. The same can be said of *Raquel*.

The dramatic character Raquel encapsulates the ambiguities felt in Golden-Age Spain towards people of Jewish origin. The range goes from Alfonso, who can cope with Raquel's origins or beliefs (apart from his latent guilt, which can be brought to the surface), to characters who believe that the only good Jew is a dead one. Raquel is not ridiculed by a loyalty divided between her ducats and her daughter; her dilemma, where she has one, involves love and power. But she too bleeds, when pricked, although she has no need to say so. Where the prejudice is most visible, is in what is done to make her sympathetic: Lope makes her a Christian, while García de la Huerta sacrifices another Jewish character.

Any final view on the authenticity of the stories about the Alfonso–Raquel love affair must take account of the following points. First, the lack of contemporary references; second, the lack of any seven-year gap in the historical Alfonso's career; third, the contradiction of one version of the story by the dates of real events; fourth, the suspicion that the 'horror' aroused by Alfonso's relationship with a 'Hebrew' is the product of a less tolerant age, e.g., the reign of Henry II (1369–79) onwards. Anti-Semitism in Spain received a huge boost from the Black Death (1348–50) and later plague outbursts, which were allegedly propagated by Jews poisoning wells; the Trastámara regime found anti-Semitism a convenient plank in the campaign to discredit Pedro I of Castile, whose relations with his Jewish subjects had been good. Anyone reluctant to believe that such a story is pure fabrication should remember our modern variation on the theme, which claims that Princess Diana was assassinated by counterparts of mediaeval Portuguese or Spanish noblemen, acting in the interests of the monarchy, though without its consent: this kind of story creates myths.

Why choose Alfonso VIII for such an invention? First, in a society which linked military success to divine favour, the climb from the nadir of Alarcos to the zenith of Las Navas was perfect material. Second, Alfonso was the king who was rebuked by Innocent III (in 1205) for philo-Semitism.[26] Third, when troops were being marshalled in Toledo for the campaign which led to Las Navas, some Aragonese soldiers attacked the ghetto, and Alfonso restrained them. Fourth, a subconscious link may be due to the fact that Las Huelgas, founded by Alfonso, became a recognized residence for cast-off royal or aristocratic mistresses, as in Calderón's *El alcalde de Zalamea:*

[26] See Edward A. Synan, *The Popes and the Jews in the Middle Ages* (Macmillan: New York and London, 1965), pp. 100–1.

> ¿Pues no hay, sin que yo me case,
> Huelgas en Burgos, adonde
> llevarla, cuando me enfade?
>
> (Calderón, *El alcalde de Zalamea*, I, 336–8)

This last point is weak, since it is uncertain when Las Huelgas began to acquire this reputation. Finally, Toledo played a prominent role in Alfonso's reign. The Palacio de Galiana (1095–1102, 1452–8, 1701–4) does not figure in the *Primera crónica general* account of the reign,[27] but the Huerta del Rey (1304) is obliquely referred to in the context of the gathering of troops in Toledo before the battle of Las Navas:

> et porque en las angosturas de la çipdad non fuesen ellos apremiados, ell noble rey don Alffonsso . . . dioles fuera de la çipdad en la ribera del rio Taio huertas et huertos et otros uergeles de deleycte en que tomassen solazes et sabores, que el fiziera criar pora si pora tomar la su real maiestad sabores et solazes quando ell en essa çipdad fuesse et quisiesse salir a andar . . .[28]

One can see how the pieces of the myth could be fitted round Alfonso. Sentimentalists may be disappointed, but the story of Raquel and Alfonso is even less likely to be true than that of La Cava and Rodrigo, although they are probably related. Castañeda (ed. cit., pp. 30–33 [see above n. 7]) is understandably reluctant to reject the story as an invention, but he does not refer to the inconsistency over the date of Las Huelgas. With the help of a simple table we can see how the *Crónica de 1344* offers the simplest (earliest?) version, with a plausible period of seven months, and how the late interpolation in the *Primera crónica general* and the revised *Castigos* between them added a name and references to Alarcos, Las Huelgas and Las Navas, as well as the implausible folk-tale period of seven years:[29]

Source	Name	Period	Alarcos	Las Huelgas	Las Navas
1344	–	7 months	–	–	–
PCgeneral	Fermosa	7 years	✓	✓	–
Castigos	–	7 years	✓	✓	✓

---

[27] It figures, though, in the account of Alfonso VI's *cortes* of Toledo: *Primera crónica general*, II, 615–17.

[28] *Primera crónica general*, II, 689a, 25–34.

[29] One historian who deserves credit for scepticism about the story, especially the seven years, is Alfonso Núñez de Castro, in his *Corónica de los señores reyes de Castilla, . . . Sancho el Deseado, Alfonso el Octauo, y Enrique el Primero* (Madrid: Pablo de Val for Antonio Riero y Tejada, 1665), Chapter XVI, which he ends with the words 'No me dilato mas en desvanecer esta calumnia' (p. 92).

On the other hand, Lope deserves more credit than he has received for
dramatic unity in this play. If his subject-matter had been only the love affair
of Alfonso and Raquel, Act I would have been out of place, as has been
suggested.[30] The unifying theme is Santiago: Santiago, y cierra, España.
Santiago Matamoros, 'que por el cielo corría / con su espada y rodela'
(1791–2), the Santiago who girt on Alfonso's sword in Act I, symbolizes the
Reconquest, but only by 'closing ranks' behind him was it achieved. 'Las
paces de los reyes' may be as much a reference to the co-operation between
the kings of Castile, Aragon and Navarre, which made the victory of Las
Navas possible, as it is to the reconciliation between Alfonso and his queen.
(By the same token, lack of understanding between the kings – or between
Alfonso and Leonor, thanks to Raquel – had led to defeat at Alarcos.)
Updated to 1610, Lope's message may be that Spain should unite to expel the
descendants of those who took part in the invasion 'caused' by the sin of Rodrigo with La Cava. Our modern feelings about racial or religious intolerance
should not prevent us from comprehending the widespread contemporary
view that the Expulsion was the final act in the Reconquest. We should
remember, too, the belief that the Expulsion was a step towards the destruction of Islam and the recovery of Jerusalem:

> Despues de destruyda la secta Mahometana, en España, y echados los
> Moros, se tratará en ella, de la recuperacion de la tierra Santa de
> Hierusalem . . .[31]

Not surprisingly, Santiago had a role to play:

> Lo mismo [the destruction of Islam] significaron los prodigios, y visiones,
> del año 1609, sucedidos en san Tiago de Galicia, a donde entre la serpiente,
> o dragon, con sus escuadrones malignos aparecidos alli en el ayre, y entre
> el Leon co[n] sus exercitos victoriosos, se percibiero[n] bien aquellas vozes
> sensibles, *Cierra España cierra* . . .[32]

Did Lope believe this? Or did he, as so often, skilfully choose a subject of
enormous topical interest for his *Jerusalén conquistada* and *Las paces de los
reyes*?

[30] E.g., 'the first act is actually independent of the last two': Castañeda, ed. cit., p. 59.
[31] Marcos de Guadalajara y Javier, *Memorable expulsión y justíssimo destierro de los
moriscos de España* (Pamplona: Nicolás de Assiayn, 1613), fol. 160[v].
[32] Pedro Aznar Cardona, *Expulsión justificada de los moriscos españoles* (Huesca:
Pedro Cabarte, 1612), II, 146[v]. I am indebted to my colleague Grace Magnier for this and
the previous reference, as well as for the information in note 16.

Lope, Lorca and Littlewood. The Reception of Spanish Theatre in the North of England

DEREK GAGEN

In March 1926, reviewing a production of Jacinto Benavente's *La malquerida*, translated as *The Passion Flower*, James Agate wrote:

> In the Continental theatre Jacinto Benavente is the name which ranks next to that of Bernard Shaw, and it is the natural order of things that the work of this great dramatist should be entirely unknown to the British Stage. The new management at the Everyman Theatre has done something to repair this neglect. *The Passion Flower* is at least a beginning.[1]

Since Benavente had received the Nobel Prize for literature in 1922 and had been the subject of an authorative book-length study by Walter Starkie in 1924, Agate's irony seems justified. His point, however, is one that was often made. We tend to feel that Spanish theatre in the twentieth century did not until very recently receive due attention outside the ranks of professional Hispanists. Indeed it has largely been the latter – and not least the dedicatee of this volume – who were responsible in Britain in the latter half of the century for establishing and sustaining awareness of modern Spanish drama.

It is precisely the recent change in the situation that is now leading scholars to investigate the position. Over the past two decades London in particular has seen several productions of Golden-Age classics, of the major plays of García Lorca – including his 'lost' or 'impossible' theatre – and more recently of other Spanish-language and Catalan-language dramatists.[2] David Johnston has considered at some length the cultural marginalisation that has heretofore rendered the reception of Spanish drama such a problematic

---

[1] James Agate, *The Contemporary Theatre. 1926* (London: Chapman and Hall, 1927), p. 73.

[2] For an illustration of this cultural invasion see John London, 'Spanish Drama in London, January to August 1987–1988', *Estreno*, 14 (1988), p. 40. This was a special number on 'Modern Spanish Drama on the Professional English-speaking Stage' and included a bibliography. It was, however, largely oriented towards reception on the American stage.

business.[3] My own more modest purpose is simply to relate this question of cultural diffusion to theatre in the north-west of England and to propose that the Spanish theatre had been less hidden earlier in the twentieth century than the lamentations of commentators have suggested. This particular interest stems from some work that led to my Swansea Inaugural Lecture, *Coming to Terms with the Civil War. Modern Productions of Lope de Vega's 'Fuenteovejuna'* (University College, Swansea, 1993). While on the staff of the University of Manchester, I had been told of a staging of *Fuenteovejuna* in the early days of the Spanish Civil War and had discovered that this production was not mentioned in any of the accounts of the reception of the play outside Spain. This spurred me to look into the background to the 1936 performance and to relate it to what other investigators, such as Teresa Kirschner and Jack Weiner, had uncovered relating to *Fuenteovejuna*'s diffusion in France, Germany, Russia and elsewhere. I was left, however, with a nagging curiosity. Was there evidence that theatre people in the north of England were less ignorant of Spain's recent drama than was generally supposed? After all, I had myself seen English translations of plays by the Martínez Sierras on the shelves of the Central Reference Library in Manchester, and they were, moreover, in some cases acting editions in multiple copies such as would be used by the many local drama societies of the twenties and thirties. Furthermore, I know that the world premier of Buero Vallejo's *La doble historia del doctor Valmy* had been given at the opening of the Gateway Theatre in Chester in 1968, and that several performances of Lorca's work had been given in the region in recent years. Was the Spanish theatre really so 'invisible', to use Ruiz Ramón's term?[4]

Before we can answer such a question, we need to look at what we mean by theatre, above all in the early twentieth century. As we shall see, the 1936 *Fuenteovejuna* was played in the Lesser Free Trade Hall, Manchester, by a radical group called Theatre Union, the predecessor to Joan Littlewood's celebrated and highly influential post-war company, Theatre Workshop. No doubt the management at the receiving houses and Music Halls, such as the Palace Theatre, the Opera House, the Ardwick Hippodrome, or any other of the professional spaces in Manchester, would not have welcomed such a group playing such a work. However, although the stage of theatrical development reached in Spain and Britain was very different, the two traditions did overlap in one respect. Spain could boast a twice-nightly commercial theatre,

---

[3] David Johnston, 'Las terribles aduanas: the Fortunes of Spanish Theatre in English', *Donaire*, 1 (September, 1993), 18–24. David Callahan, 'Harley Granville-Barker and the Response to Spanish Theatre', *Comparative Drama*, 25 (1991), 129–46, offers a suggestive consideration of why the plays of Martínez Sierra and the Quinteros appealed to pre-war audiences.

[4] R. Ruiz Ramón, 'La invisibilidad del teatro español contemporáneo', *Estudios de teatro español clásico y contemporáneo* (Madrid: Fundación Juan March/Cátedra, 1978), pp. 125–46.

based on short runs, to compare with the British Repertory movement and this was, at one stage, to lead to a number of productions of Spanish plays in the British provinces, albeit productions that attracted a very different audience from that found at Littlewood's *Fuenteovejuna*.

Apart from Madrid – and to a lesser extent Barcelona – our knowledge of the day-to-day working of twentieth-century Spanish theatre has until very recently remained relatively limited. The publication in 1990 of *La escena madrileña entre 1919 y 1926. Análisis y documentación* (Madrid: Fundamentos, 1990) by Dru Dougherty and María Francisca Vilches, the first part of a massive study of the Spanish stage between 1900 and 1936 – followed subsequently by their *La escena madrileña entre 1926 y 1931. Un lustro de transición* (Madrid: Fundamentos, 1997) – has at last allowed us some insight into the repertory, audience, box-office and ideology of the Madrid theatre of the period. The authors' view is that, despite all the talk of a crisis in the theatre, 'nunca el teatro ha ofrecido mayor índice de actividad teatral, han confluido tantos destacados autores e importantes obras, ni ha existido una nómina tan amplia de excelentes críticos'(p. 13). Nonetheless, the bulk of the audience was middle class, the bulk of the material was comedy, and the stage was dominated by the established playwrights, the *autores consagrados*. In the 1920–21 season, ten dramatists had between them two hundred plays staged in the Madrid commercial theatre. In the previous season, forty plays by the Quintero brothers were put on.[5] At the same time, a strong influence on the Madrid stage was foreign theatre. Most of this was low-quality French boulevard theatre, although some serious foreign playwrights were performed, notably Pirandello. Of the *autores consagrados*, the leading figures were clearly Benavente and the other epigones of naturalism, the purveyors of lighter traditionalist pieces, notably the Quinteros, and writers of *astracán* farces, among whom Pedro Muñoz Seca held sway.

A picture presented in these terms suggests at first sight that Spain was taking very little note of those avant-garde developments in staging and direction that were taking place throughout Europe. This was, however, far from the case. A number of small experimental groups were putting on what tended to be termed *nuevo teatro*. (We should recall the cult of *lo nuevo* observed by Ortega y Gasset in *La deshumanización del arte* in 1924.) The major initiative here was the Teatro de Arte run between 1917 and 1925 by Gregorio Martínez Sierra at the Teatro Eslava in Madrid's Calle Arenal, just

---

[5] Dru Dougherty and Maria Francisca Vilches, *Escena madrileña* (Madrid: Fundamentos, 1990), p. 38. Callahan, 'Harley Granville-Barker' notes that the repertory format of the Madrid stage, and the need to produce new plays so as to attract 'the small play-going population', accounted for the distinctive quality of these Spanish playwrights. The point is in general well made. Nonetheless the 'repertory' programme with which Martínez Sierra came to be associated at the Teatro Eslava was to be very different. Those plays of the Martínez Sierras that the Granville-Barkers translated derived from the 'Teatro poético' period.

off the Puerta del Sol. Aided by Cipriano Rivas Cherif, who had studied with
Edward Gordon Craig, Martínez Sierrra was the first practical man of theatre
in Madrid to act like a modern Director, building up a programme of established plays alongside new works.[6] These were free to flop as, most memo-
rably, was the case of García Lorca's *El maleficio de la mariposa* in March
1920.

It is an error to suppose that these developments were ignored in Great
Britain. It was undoubtedly Martínez Sierra's vision of a theatre with a clear
agenda, repertory and direction, that appealed to Harley Granville-Barker
who, with his wife Helen, translated several plays by Martínez Sierra (and *his*
wife, though her role as co-author was unacknowledged) in the 1920s.
Granville-Barker's vision of an 'exemplary theatre', his blueprint of a
National Theatre, made him see the Spanish dramatist and director as a soul
mate. The somewhat soft-centred feminism of Martínez Sierra's plays – due
in no small measure to his wife's active, even preponderant, collaboration –
would make them for a time particularly appealing to foreign audiences, and
especially to the decent theatre-goers of provincial British cities in the early
years of the century. The Spanish plays that achieved early success in Britain
tended to be the products of the *Teatro poético* movement rather than
Benaventean naturalism. Of course, the avant-garde and *modernista* reaction
against naturalism was not the only innovative development in early twentieth-century European drama. Aesthetic reformers were at the same time
often political radicals aiming at democratizing the theatre. Even before
Romain Rolland's *Le Théâtre du peuple* (1903), there had been attempts at
creating People's Theatres, and a 'World Congress on People's Theatre' was
held in 1899. Bradby and McCormick see four broad categories of People's
Theatre:

1   Theatre as a substitute for religion.
2   Political theatre.
3   Decentralized theatre.
4   Community theatre.[7]

In Spain there were some early attempts at *Teatro del Pueblo*. In the
1921–22 season, a group under this name performed in Madrid at the
socialist Casa del Pueblo 'por no encontrar teatro en esta corte'. Their repertory, like that of their British equivalents later, would be 'teatro clásico y
teatro del pueblo'. As the work of Christopher Cobb has shown, throughout

---

    [6]   Julio Enrique Checa Puerta, *Los teatros de Gregorio Martínez Sierra* (Madrid:
Fundación Universitaria Española, 1998).
    [7]   David Bradby and John McCormick, *People's Theatre* (London: Croom Helm,
1978), pp. 13–16. In *Dreams and Deconstructions. Alternative Theatre in Britain*, ed.
Sandy Craig (Ambergate: Amberlane Press, 1980), p. 30, Craig differentiates between
'political theatre' and 'political plays', which seek to mould middle-class opinion.

the 1920s and 1930s commentators noted the absence of the *pueblo* from the commercial theatre: leftist critics such as Sender and Araquistáin – and not so leftist critics such as Enrique de Mesa – called for a genuinely popular theatre.[8] In doing so they were echoing the pleas of Unamuno in his essay 'La regeneración del teatro español' of 1895. That is to say, it had become part of a politically correct tradition to believe in a 'público posible', an audience that Dougherty describes as 'tanto más creíble cuanto más abstracto'.[9] That audience became less abstract in the crisis years of the 1930s but only one of Bradby and McCormick's categories apply to Spain, namely political theatre. The picture in Britain was to be very different and this is reflected in the reception there of Spanish Theatre.

A British equivalent of *Teatro del Pueblo* first appeared in the United Kingdom in the final years of the Great War and developed strongly after the General Strike of 1926 in the form of the Workers' Theatre Movement (WTM). This evolved in the direction of agit-prop during the thirties but was more influential in London, where it gave rise to the Unity Theatre, than in the provinces.[10] The more mainstream provincial theatre was much stronger in Britain than in Spain: Bradby and McCormick's third and fourth categories (decentralized and community theatre) were greatly in evidence. Here the North of England and West Midlands were to have a significant role through the repertory movement, the pioneer of the regional reps of the post-war period.

The repertory theatres had come into being as a reaction against the second-rate fare offered by the commercial stage in the provinces. Audiences, both the enlightened middle class and 'the self-educated, self-improving, self-conscious working people',[11] as well as the actors and actresses, sought a different kind of theatrical organization. Miss Horniman in Manchester from 1908, Basil Dean in Liverpool and Sir Barry Jackson in Birmingham from 1911, invigorated the British stage in that their theatres, being local and permanent, were not touring houses but the home of established companies able to offer a varied programme. To quote Grace Wyndham Goldie, repertory theatres 'were created as a result of the rebellion of individuals or groups of individuals against the *average* quality of the commercial play and the commercial production'.[12] It was off Shaftesbury

---

[8] Christopher Cobb, *La cultura y el pueblo. España 1920–1939* (Barcelona: Laia, 1980) includes representative statements from Sender, Díaz Fernández and others.

[9] Dru Dougherty, 'Talia convulsa: la crisis teatral de los años 20' in Robert Lima and Dru Dougherty, *Dos ensayos sobre el teatro español de los 20* (Murcia: Universidad de Murcia, 1984), p. 117.

[10] For a brief account see Bradby and McCormick, *People's Theatre*, pp. 97–99.

[11] Robin Thornber, 'First Tragedy . . . Then Farce. The Regional Reps', in Craig (ed.), *Dreams and Reconstructions*, p.165.

[12] Grace Wyndham Goldie, *The Liverpool Repertory Theatre 1911–1934* (Liverpool: Liverpool University Press, 1935).

Avenue, in the repertory theatres of the provinces, or in houses away from the West End such as the Everyman, Hampstead, where Benavente's *The Passion Flower (La malquerida)* was played, that Spanish theatre was first staged in Britain in the early twentieth century.

It seems that the United States may have shown the way. Works by Benavente and Martínez Sierra were staged there from 1917, albeit with only moderate success.[13] Significantly, Norman MacDermott had chosen to open the Everyman in Hampstead on 15 September 1920 with a production of Benavente's *Los intereses creados*, attended by a legal threat over translation rights and a hilarious (in retrospect) series of mishaps as flats collapsed and the curtain was torn.[14] Yet, despite receiving only guardedly favourable notices, Benavente's farce, translated as *Bonds of Interest*, set the tone for the reception of modern theatre from Spain in the 1920s. In London, Agate reviewed Martínez Sierra's *The Kingdom of God (El reino de Dios)* at the Strand – the West End breakthrough – in October 1927, and three plays by the Quintero Brothers, two at the Court and one at the Lyric, Hammersmith, in October 1928.[15] The plays were *Fortunato (Fortunato)*, *The Lady from Alfaqueque (La consulesa)* – with the young Gielgud in a leading role – and *A Hundred Years Old (El centenario)*, all available in translations by the Granville-Barkers.[16] However, it was the provincial repertory theatre that was following close upon the heels of Broadway in those years. Barry Jackson's Birmingham Repertory Theatre produced Echegaray's *The Cleansing Stain* in 1920, though the thirteen performances proved to be a commercial failure. In the following year both *The Romantic Young Lady (Sueño de una noche de agosto)* and *The Two Shepherds (Los pastores)* of Martínez Sierra had

---

[13] Rosemary Shevlin Weiss, 'Benavente and Martínez Sierra on Broadway', *Estreno*, 14 (1988), 30–33. It is unfortunate that Isabel Martínez Moreno ignores these earlier productions in her survey 'Recepción crítica del teatro español en la prensa inglesa: 1939–1950', *Revista de Literatura*, 56 (1994), 129–44. Productions of Martínez Sierra and Benavente in wartime London were revivals of texts given their British premier some twenty years earlier. It should be added that translated texts were abundant. The *Cameo Series*, 19 vols (London: T. Fisher Unwin, 1899–1902) included works by Echegaray, and a translation of *El gran Galeoto* by H. Lynch had been published by John Lane, London, as early as 1895.

[14] Norman MacDermott, *Everymania. The History of the Everyman Theatre Hampstead 1920–1926* (London: The Society for Theatre Research, 1975).

[15] Agate's reviews are reproduced in his *Red Letter Nights. A Survey of the Post-Elizabethan Drama in Actual Performance on the London Stage, 1921–1943* (London: Jonathan Cape, 1944).

[16] Callahan, 'Harley Granville-Barker' offers a lucid and detailed consideration of these versions, which were still being used by companies well after the Second World War. For Gielgud's performance see John Gielgud, *Early Stages*, 2nd edn (London: Hodder and Stoughton, 1974), pp. 80–81. Another member of the cast, and stage designer, was James Whale, the future director of *Frankenstein:* Agate particularly praised the sets. Gielgud recalls that Granville-Barker attended, indeed took over, the rehearsals at one stage.

successful productions and were included in the repertory over several seasons, *The Romantic Young Lady* being revived as late as 1949. In the 1922–23 season at the Liverpool Repertory Theatre, *The Romantic Young Lady* was also played: Wyndham Goldie calls it a 'slight charming piece . . . about which some playgoers wrote delighted letters but which one critic and some of the public found trivial' p. 139). Agate was to see Martínez Sierra's plays as 'light' when reviewing *The Kingdom of God (El reino de Dios)*,[17] and wrote that the leading actresses in Benavente's *The Passion Flower* spoke not with the harshness required by the text but 'with all the accent of Kensington High Street shortly after six'.[18] Yet the directors of the Liverpool Repertory clearly preferred the far from harsh Martínez Sierra and Quintero Brothers.

Martínez Sierra was represented in the 1927–28, 1928–29 and 1932–33 seasons and the Quinteros in the 1928–29, 1929–30 and 1932–33 seasons. Martínez Sierra's *The Kingdom of God* was something of a triumph in Liverpool at Easter 1933, Wyndham Goldie noting that the 'lovely Spanish sets gave the play an air of sunniness and gaiety which seemed to prevent its sentiment from becoming a too tearful sentimentality' (p. 192). Hardly surprisingly, Agate had savaged the piece in 1927, while noting that the audience was moved by it. British commentators often observed that the simplistic sentimentalism of the Quinteros and the Martínez Sierras struck a chord with the new middle-class repertory audience. Characteristic was J. C. Trewin in *The English Theatre* (London: Elek, 1948) comparing Pirandello, 'a cerebral dramatist with a habit of discussing abstract themes and forever speculating about reality' with 'the much more lucid' plays of these Spanish dramatists, 'naturalistic trifles, simple and gracefully sentimental' (p. 86).

That *El reino de Dios*, a work that most certainly qualifies as 'gracefully sentimental', had triumphed in Liverpool in the Spring of 1933, in the midst of a merciless depression, may suggest that the repertory movement was losing touch with part of its original audience, or indeed was finding a new middle-class audience similar in make-up and desire for escape as those in Madrid and Barcelona. By 1933, however, Lorca was staging *Bodas de sangre* in Madrid, and in the following February *Love on the Dole* was produced at the Manchester Repertory Theatre in Rusholme, in the working-class suburbs of South Manchester. The audience, the repertory, and, above all, the organization of theatrical activity were changing in Britain, and Spanish theatre was to be represented in Theatre Union and Theatre Workshop, two theatre groups that were to be central to that change.

At the same time, with the advent of the Republic, theatrical activity was

---

[17] Agate, *Red Letter Nights*, p. 189. Again Callahan, 'Harley Granville-Barker' clarifies that, although 'light' compared with the Benavente familiar to British audiences – that is, the Benavente of *La malquerida* – these plays catered for a British repertory audience that in its social composition closely mirrored that of Madrid.

[18] Agate, *The Contemporary Theatre*, p. 76.

taking on a new character in Spain. Hispanists are, of course, familiar with
the new outreach organizations that developed with the encouragement of the
Republic. The *Patronato de Misiones Pedagógicas* undertook a variety of
official initiatives: the *Teatro del Pueblo* and *Teatro Ambulante* of Alejandro
Casona and, most famously, *La Barraca* of García Lorca. The latter appears
to provide the paradigm for the British initiatives in that, first, it was soon –
for good reasons – to be a radical or leftist undertaking[19] and, second, it
included elements of the classical *Siglo de Oro* in its repertory, played in a
modern manner. Lorca's idealism comes through in dozens of interviews,
most notably in that with Mildred Adams where he emphasized that, as well
as the classics, 'We are also going to give them plays, plays of today, done in
the modern manner, explained ahead of time very simply, and presented with
that extreme simplification which will be necessary for the success of our
plan and which makes the experimental theatre so interesting.'[20] Echoing
Luis Araquistáin's pleas in *La crisis teatral* (1930) for a people's theatre
using avant-garde or experimental techniques, Lorca parallels the project of
working-class drama in Manchester that was, like *La Barraca*, to include in
its programme a memorable *Fuenteovejuna*.

   The organizing figures here were to be Ewan MacColl, the unlikely pseudonym of Jimmy Miller, and Joan Littlewood. MacColl was the son of a pair of
fiery Communists living in Salford but hailing from Falkirk in Scotland. He
left a wonderfully vivid account of his Salford upbringing – very much the
'classic slum' relentlessly analysed by sociologists – and of how he joined the
flourishing theatre groups so much a feature of life between the wars in the
Northern industrial towns.[21] Alan Davies in his extraordinary study *Leisure,
Gender and Poverty, Working-Class Culture in Salford and Manchester
1900–1939* (Buckingham: Open University Press, 1992) barely mentions the
theatre, yet MacColl and Howard Gurney make clear that the Workers' Arts
Club, the Clarion Players, and in 1931 the agit-prop group Red Megaphones,
led an active street-life, rather as Rafael Alberti and the *Octubre* group
sought to do in Spain in 1933 and 1934 with their puppet farces such as
Bazar de la Providencia.[22] MacColl and his comrades wrote little agitational
sketches, and then more ambitious scripts; since 'it was deadly serious, we
believed we were helping to change the course of history and we'd begun to

---

[19] I touch on the animosity of right-wing elements towards *La Barraca* in *Coming to
Terms with the Civil War*, p. 8.

[20] Federico García Lorca, *Obras completas* (Madrid: Aguilar, 1963), p. 1703.

[21] MacColl, 'Theatre of Action, Manchester' in Raphael Samuel, Ewan MacColl and
Stuart Cosgrove, *Theatres of the Left 1880–1935* (London: Routledge & Kegan Paul,
1985), pp. 205–55. Considerable further detail is provided by Joan Littlewood, *Joan's
Book* (London: Methuen, 1994).

[22] Howard Gurney, *The Theatre Workship Story* (London: Eyre Methuen, 1981), p. 3.
For Alberti's political puppets see my 'Puppets and Politics: Rafael Alberti's *Dos farsas
revolucionarias*', *Quinquereme*, 7 (1984), 54–73.

believe we were changing the course of theatrical history' (Gurney, p. 3). MacColl was always to be one of the awkward comrades to deal with. In words strongly reminiscent of attacks by Lorca and Alberti on the established Spanish theatre of the period, he firmly stated his belief that 'the West End theatre, or the formal theatre of that time, was not concerned with the lives of ordinary folk'. He nonetheless became equally discontented with the methods of the Communist-dominated Workers' Theatre. He and other amateurs – again like the young dramatists in Spain – began to read avidly of the experimental developments in design and staging that are associated with Adolphe Appia, Stanislavsky, etc. It was of course a tremendously exciting time to be around in Manchester. Gurney describes the excitement vividly:

> In terms of material prosperity, the gap between North and South was a great deal wider than it is today. Culturally, Manchester was the Second City, a position she has maintained to this day. The first Repertory Theatre in Britain has been opened in 1908 by Miss Horniman in the Gaiety Theatre. Many realistic plays of provincial life were produced there including several of the 'Manchester School' of Stanley Houghton, Harold Brighouse and others. Though the Gaiety had become a cinema in 1921, its influence on the cultural life of the city was still evident in the 1930's. There were pre-West End openings at three theatres, strong progressive amateur drama groups like the Unnamed Society and Rochdale Curtain Theatre, and in 1933, Walter Greenwood had written *Love on the Dole* (dramatized in 1934), based on his experiences in various unskilled jobs and unemployment. (Gurney, p. 6)

In Spain's second city they boasted of a different language and culture from the capital: in Manchester, 'Second City' or no, they could not. Into this melting pot came Joan Littlewood, a working-class girl from London who had, nevertheless, studied at RADA. She and MacColl collaborated in a group called Theatre of Action in 1934. MacColl and his friends corresponded with groups all over the world. One friend, Alf Armitt, learned French in order to read Appia. Ernst Toller came to Manchester to direct a production of *Draw the Fires (Feuer aus den Kesseln)* at the Rusholme Rep. This was a space, like those where the Littlewood group played, that drew a more working-class and student audience than Miss Horniman's Gaiety. In his autobiography Anthony Burgess recalled Littlewood's dynamism and seriousness that put to shame the stumbling approach of the Manchester University Stage Society.[23] These radical theatrical experiences parallel those of Alberti and his wife María Teresa León in Spain, going off to Germany and the Soviet Union to study staging and direction.

It is clear, granted the benefit of hindsight, that the Lorcas, Albertis and

---

[23] Anthony Burgess, *Little Wilson and Big God* (London: Penguin, 1988), p. 180.

Casonas, the MacColls and Littlewoods, were far more attuned to theatrical developments than the West End, Broadway or Madrid commercial stages. Early in 1936 MacColl, after a year exploring further the Soviet and continental theatre, founded Theatre Union. Its manifesto shows how the Northern non-professional groups were moving towards a position identical to that of Lorca. It calls for the theatre to face up to the problems of its time but, like the programme of *La Barraca*, sees a place for the great playwrights of Antiquity and the Renaissance:

> To those who say that such affairs are not the concern of the theatre or that the theatre should confine itself to treading the paths of 'beauty' and 'dignity', we should say 'Read Shakespeare, Marlowe, Sophocles, Aeschylus, Aristophanes, Calderón, Molière, Lope de Vega, Schiller and the rest'. (Gurney, p. 24)

It comes as no surprise, then, that on the outbreak of the Civil War in Spain, Littlewood and MacColl decided to mount a production of Lope de Vega's *Fuenteovejuna* in the translation by John Garrett Underhill under the title *The Sheep Well*. Both MacColl and Gurney have vividly described the rehearsals and performances at the Lesser Free Trade Hall, which played to packed houses. (Gurney's description of the 'terrifying screams' emanating from Littlewood during a rehearsal of the so-called rape scene is particularly lively.)

The production of *Fuenteovejuna/The Sheep Well* had an immediate significance in terms of the British perception of Spain's Civil War. For MacColl,

> In every respect *Fuenteovejuna* was the ideal play for the time. Its theme, the revolt of a village community against a ruthless and bloody dictator, was a reflection in microcosm of what was actually taking place in Spain.

But, against a longer perspective, in MacColl's view the challenge of Lope's text had obliged the group to extend their 'stylistic vocabulary':

> It occupies a very important place in our calendar of events for not only was it the first time a play by Spain's most important dramatist had been performed in Britain, it was also the first time that we had dared to step outside the territory of agit-prop-cum-expressionistic theatre.[24]

Theatre Union continued in action until 1942 and then was dissolved, as actors were called up for military service. Whereas Lorca's *La Barraca* came

---

[24] Ewan MacColl 'Preface' in *Agit-Prop to Theatre Workshop. Political Playscripts 1930–1950* (Manchester: Manchester University Press, 1986), p. xl.

to offer a model for Spain's *Teatros Nacionales* that were set up in the early years of the Franco period, the Littlewood company was revived in 1945 as Theatre Workshop and *The Sheep Well* was to reappear in its repertoire in 1955 at what was to be its most celebrated home, the Theatre Royal, Stratford, in the East End of London. Their programme continued to blend the radical traditional with the radical modern. The 'popular theatre' of Aeschylus, Sophocles, Shakespeare and Ben Jonson was specifically mentioned in the 1945 Manifesto of Theatre Workshop (Gurney, pp. 41–42). Not surprisingly, they staged an adaptation of *La Celestina* in February 1958, some five years before Casona's celebrated adaptation at the Bellas Artes, Madrid.

However, Theatre Workshop's most unexpected contribution to the diffusion of Spanish theatre in Britain had come in 1945 in Kendal, in the Lake District, when the Littlewood/MacColl enterprise reappeared after the Second World War. The Director of Education for Westmoreland was a friend of Joan Littlewood and had offered her new company rehearsal space in a school. They began their programme with a ballad opera, *Johnny Noble*, by MacColl, and *The Flying Doctor*, adapted from *Le Médecin malgré lui* by Molière. After a tour in August and September 1945, they returned to Kendal and there began rehearsing García Lorca's *Don Perlimplín*.

This was a singularly unlikely choice. Basing it on the ancient commonplace of *El viejo y la niña*, Lorca had drafted the play in his early experimental period, certainly by 1926. It had been due to be given its premier by the experimental group *El Caracol* in February 1929 but the performance was suspended when the Queen Mother died. Shortly afterwards the play was banned for bizarre reasons, possibly political but officially as an outrage against public decency, an anarchist tract having identified the traditional figure of Perlimplín with King Alfonso.[25] In 1932, Pura Ucelay, intent on founding a new women's club in Madrid and having resigned from the Lyceum Club Femenino, invited Lorca to direct its theatrical activities. She learned of the fate of *Don Perlimplín* and, anxious to include it in their first evening of amateur drama – it was to accompany Lorca's *La zapatera prodigiosa* – presented herself at the *Dirección General de Seguridad* and requested a copy of the play. She was told 'lo que la señora viene buscando es verdadera pornografía: la misma portada lo dice'.[26] A determined lady, as feisty in her way as Joan Littlewood, she finally obtained the text and it was produced by the *Club Anfistora* in 1932.

It was this play that came to the notice of Theatre Workshop in 1945,

---

[25] See the introduction by Margarita Ucelay to her edition of *Amor de Don Perlimplín con Belisa en su jardín* (Madrid: Cátedra, 1990).

[26] Margarita Ucelay, 'El Club Teatral Anfistora' in *El teatro en España entre la tradición y la vanuardia*, ed. Dru Dougherty and Mª Francisca Vilches Frutos (Madrid: CSIC, 1992), p. 454.

undoubtedly through the services of Luis Meana, a lecturer in the Department of Spanish and Portuguese Studies in the University of Manchester who
had been a member of *La Barraca*, as he apparently never tired of telling his
students. Gurney describes the work as a 'beautiful, poetic, evocative play
about the love of an old man for a young woman' (p. 49). As in Spain, it
caused no end of trouble. Whether it was the idea of Belisa's night-time
lovers, or Perlimplín's suicide, it shocked the good burghers of Kendal,
notably Belisa's

> Amor, amor.
> Entre mis muslos cerrados
> Nada como un pez el sol.

Theatre Workshop's version of *Don Perlimplín* was played over the following
years all round the Lake District, touring Scotland in 1946. It was revived in
1949–50, playing the Library Theatre, Manchester, and reaching the Edinburgh Festival in August–September 1949. It brought to the provinces and to
Scotland an awareness of a very different Spanish theatre from that represented by Benavente, Martínez Sierra and the Quinteros. There are, in particular, richly comic incidents, recalled by Gurney, which occurred during the
Festival visit. The Minister of the Church in whose hall *Don Perlimplín* was
to be played 'decided that it would not be quite suitable for the building',
only changing his view when the Swedish actress Kristin Lind 'in tones of
outraged innocence, convinced him she wouldn't appear in any play that had
any suggestion of immorality' (Gurney, p. 70).

Lorca's play was to offer particularly rich potential. It will be recalled that
it uses lighting, colour, and above all music, to break loose from the bonds of
an easy naturalism. The music is what most links Lorca, who arranged all the
scores himself, with Ewan MacColl. The effects were no doubt very different
in practice: one does not immediately associate MacColl with Scarlatti. As
Luis Meana observed of the Kendal performance, 'It's marvellous, Lorca
would have loved it, but it's completely different from his production'
(Gurney, p. 49). The production by Manchester University students of
Spanish, directed in the Spring of 1964 by Victor Dixon, certainly kept much
closer to the Lorcan model, although the Arthur Worthington Hall, a seedy
and crumbling edifice, probably approximated more closely to the venues
played by Theatre Workshop.

It is somehow reassuring to know that the wonderfully shoestring
endeavours of Theatre Workshop introduced Lorca to the Edinburgh Festival
long before Víctor García and Nuria Espert took *Yerma* and *Doña Rosita la
soltera* to the much grander latter-day International Festival. The spirit of *La
Barraca* had led the way in this second stage of the reception of Spanish
theatre in the twentieth century.

Spanish theatre was to become enormously better known over the final third of the century. It was to be a Spanish play, Buero Vallejo's *La doble his-toria del Doctor Valmy*, that was chosen to open the Gateway Theatre, Chester, in 1968. (Victor Dixon took a party of Manchester undergraduates and staff to the event, but Buero would not accept an invitation to visit the University arguing that 'uno no es Lope de Vega'.) In that same year the Manchester University Stage Society, by now very different from the group evoked by Anthony Burgess in his memoir, performed Buero's *El concierto de San Ovidio*, in Victor Dixon's translation and directed by him in the new University Theatre that replaced the Arthur Worthington. Later were to come, in what we would see as the third stage in the reception process, the triumphs of Espert and Pasqual, and the crop of productions of Golden-Age classics in London, Stratford and elsewhere.

Agate's cryptic observation that it is 'the natural order of things' for worth-while Spanish drama to be ignored now seems unnecessarily carping. There was still some animus against Spanish drama in some quarters – I know of one distinguished Midlands director who was convinced of the worthlessness of Spanish culture – but Spain's twentieth-century theatre is no longer invis-ible, if it ever had been.

Women as Author Surrogates in Four Tragedies of Antonio Buero Vallejo

MARTHA HALSEY

Although brief studies have been done on female characters in Buero's theatre, none has focused on the role of women as vehicles through which he expresses his own socio-political convictions. Magda Ruggeri Marchetti describes Verónica, of *Llegada de los dioses,* as 'enésima encarnación del yo del dramaturgo' and calls Cristina, of *Jueces en la noche,* the bearer of the play's political message but does not elaborate on either statement.[1] Linda Sollich Sikka treats women's centrality to the structure of Buero's plays, showing their frequent role as catalyst.[2] John Moore[3] and William Giuliano[4] study women in Buero's earlier plays, focusing on their relationship to men. Finally, Virtudes Serrano comments briefly on Buero's 'new women', pointing out the presence, in recent plays, of independent, non-conformist and assertive female characters who are often juxtaposed to more traditional ones.[5]

In general, Buero's earlier works show women as wives, mistresses and mothers, lacking any sense of autonomy. Even such strong female protagonists as Amalia of *Madrugada* (1953) and Penélope of *La tejedora de sueños* (1952) are dependent upon men for their fulfilment. 'Por y para el amor vive la mujer, si es plenamente femenina', Buero stated early in his career.[6] Nevertheless, starting with Lucila in *La doble historia del doctor Valmy*

[1]   Magda Ruggeri Marchetti, 'La mujer en el teatro de Antonio Buero Vallejo', *Anthropos* 79 (1987), 37–41.

[2]   2 Linda Sollich Sikka, 'Buero's Women: Structural Agents and Moral Guides', *Estreno* 16 (1990), 18–22, 31.

[3]   John Moore, 'Buero Vallejo: Good Mistresses and Bad Wives', *Romance Notes* 21 (1980), 10–15.

[4]   William Giuliano, 'The Role of Men and Women in Buero Vallejo's Plays', *Hispanófila* 39 (1970), 21–28.

[5]   Virtudes Serrano, 'Introducción', Antonio Buero Vallejo, *Las trampas del azar* (Madrid: Espasa Calpe, 1995), pp. 9–43, and 'Las nuevas mujeres del teatro de Antonio Buero Vallejo', *MonteArabí* (Murcia), 23 (1996), pp. 95–104.

[6]   Antonio Buero Vallejo, 'Comentario de *Madrugada*', *Obra Completa*, II, ed. Luis Iglesias Feijoo and Mariano de Paco (Madrid: Espasa Calpe, 1994), p. 397.

(1968), Buero began to create a series of independent and liberated female characters who find meaning outside their relationship with the other sex. Some, such as Verónica of *Llegada de los dioses* (1971) and Cristina of *Jueces en la noche* (1979), are political activists. Lucila of *La doble historia*, who awakens her former student, Mary Barnes, to the realities of political torture and other atrocities, is the precursor of Cristina, who likewise awakens the conscience of a female friend. *La doble historia* and *Jueces* each contrast the traditional woman to the new, politically-aware woman just emerging in Franco's Spain.[7]

We shall see that Verónica of *Llegada de los dioses*, Cristina of *Jueces en la noche*, Amparo of *Lázaro en el laberinto* (1986), and, to a lesser extent, Patricia of *Las trampas del azar* (1994) represent the playwright, as they express his ideas on peace, justice, and other issues in an attempt to awaken the conscience of another character. At the same time, Buero seeks to move the spectator as he deals with issues that he has often treated in essays (*OC* II). Leftists and, in some cases, authentic revolutionaries, these women play roles that correspond to those of such male figures as Asel of *La Fundación* (1974), Néstor of *Caimán* (1981), Gaspar of *Diálogo secreto* (1984), René of *Música cercana* (1990), and Salustiano of *Las trampas del azar*, all obvious author surrogates.[8]

The first of Buero's female author surrogates, Verónica of *Llegada de los dioses*, has rejected her bourgeois life of privilege and the values of her class.[9] A former teacher, she instructs Julio, her younger lover, as he rebels against the corrupt world of his father, a former Nazi. The father, Felipe, has

[7]   Studies of Buero's theatre from a feminist perspective include those already cited by Ruggeri Marchetti and Serrano as well as Carolyn J. Harris, 'La mujer en el teatro de Buero Vallejo: Una lectura femenina', *Letras Peninsulares* 3 (1990), 248–57; Patricia W. O'Connor, *Antonio Buero Vallejo en sus espejos* (Madrid: Fundamentos, 1996); Eric Pennington, '*La doble historia del doctor Valmy*: A View from the Feminine', *Symposium* 40 (1986), 131–39; and Elizabeth S. Rogers, 'The Humanization of Archtypes in Buero Vallejo's *La tejedora de sueños*', *Revista de Estudios Hispánicos* 15 (1981), 340–48.

[8]   For discussions of Asel, Néstor, and Gaspar as author surrogates who express Buero's message, see Martha T. Halsey, *From Dictatorship to Democracy: The Recent Plays of Antonio Buero Vallejo* (*La Fundación* to *Música cercana*) (Ottawa: Dovehouse Editions, 1994), Ottawa Hispanic Studies, No. 17, chapters 4, 7, and 8. Interestingly enough these three characters all spent time in Franco's prisons, as did Buero himself. O'Connor discusses aspects of Buero's personality and experiences reflected in his characters, focusing on *Las Meninas, El tragaluz, La detonación, Diálogo secreto, La señal que se espera*, and *Las trampas del azar*. Her study is based on the theories of Freud, Jung, Lacan, Rank and others regarding authorial projections in literature. The women treated in the present essay are not covered, with the exception of Patricia, who, O'Connor notes, like Buero, had dreamed of becoming a painter.

[9]   Like the maid, Mami Lorenza, in *Música cercana*, Verónica's mother was seduced by her master. The latter recognized her as his daughter and sent her cheques to buy her affection and salve his conscience. Verónica has broken not only with him but also with her mother, so that at least one of the two of them can save herself. Men like Felipe,

created a new life for himself in an unnamed archipelago that suggests the Balearic islands, 'un azul remanso de paz'[10] away, he believes, from the dangers of nuclear war that obsess his son. Oblivious to planes carrying bombs that fill the brilliant blue skies, contamination of the air and water by his factories, and hunger in the islands, Felipe speaks only of the prosperity he has created with his real estate developments and other business ventures and of the peace he enjoys. As his son notes, however, this peace is fictitious; even though a beautiful park now conceals the traces of the war that once destroyed the area, land mines remain buried – mute reminders of what was.[11]

Julio escapes what he calls the 'ceguera azul' of his father only to experience another type of blindness that leaves him in physical darkness. It is the reason for this blindness – which has no organic basis –[12] that Verónica seeks to help him understand. Within the blackness, Julio, a painter, invents moving images of the members of his family and friends, ridiculous caricatures that amuse him. However, he also experiences involuntary images, sombre visions that he considers dark warnings: the nude figure of a prisoner his father once tortured and blinded, and the lifeless body of his adolescent half-sister, Nuria.[13] Julio believes that his father's torture of the man is responsible for his own loss of vision, which occurred shortly after his learning of the crime.

Verónica, since she has known Julio's world and found the courage to

---

Verónica charges, have conditioned her mother to be a slave and it is too late for her to learn the meaning of freedom.

10 Antonio Buero Vallejo, *Obra Completa* [*OC*], I, ed. cit., p. 1348.

11 Buero's strong anti-war sentiment is obvious, beginning with his earliest plays. *Aventura en lo gris*, written in 1949, has as protagonist the idealistic Silvano who, in the greyness of a country overrun by enemy soldiers with machine guns, dreams of green fields with tranquil water inhabited by beings resembling angels without wings. His message is not unlike that of *La tejedora de sueños*: 'Aprender a soñar sería aprender a vivir' (*OC*, I, p. 436). In *La tejedora* (1952), when Ulises protests that men cannot prevent wars, Penélope responds: '¿Ah, no podéis? Vosotros las hacéis para que nosotras suframos las consecuencias. Nosotras queremos paz, esposo, hijos . . ., y vosotros nos dais guerras [. . .] convertís a nuestros hijos en nuestros asesinos' (*OC*, I, p. 78). Nowhere, however, is anti-war sentiment stronger than in *Mito* (unperformed), whose dreamer-protagonist, Eloy, inspired – or deranged – by novels of science fiction, proclaims the imminent arrival of Martians to save humans from the folly of a nuclear war, ushering in a new era of peace. Reflecting the horrors of Hiroshima and Nagasaki, as well as Vietnam, the work is Buero's strongest denunciation of modern warfare and the radiation than can destroy our planet.

12 Julio suffers from scintillating scotoma, a partial loss of vision with vibrating flashes of light and what seem to be drawings characterized by the zig-zag, wall-like outlines – which the audience sees whenever Julio invents his caricatures.

13 Torture is the subject of one of the psychiatrist's case histories in *La doble historia del Doctor Valmy*: a National Security policeman who becomes impotent after castrating a political prisoner. The play deals with the destruction not only of the victim of torture but also of the torturer. Even more important, it treats society's crass indifference.

make a clear break with it, has the authority to act as his guide. She explains the errors of his vision of his world, of the caricatures that rich youths like him create to prove to themselves that they are revolutionaries. Julio's error is to disdain his enemy and to misunderstand his motives for doing so: 'Reírse de ellos es una facilidad, un escape. Es desdeñar al enemigo para amortiguar el miedo que nos inspira su poder. Tenemos que aprender a combatirlos como a lobos, no como a bichejos. De otro modo, cuando más nos riamos de sus debilidades, nos cortarán la risa y los ánimos con sus dentalladas feroces' (*OC*, I, p. 1356).[14] The images that Verónica prefers for Julio are the dark ones that disturb him rather than those that amuse him, for it is the former that will save him.

Verónica struggles to bring Julio to face the fact that his physical blindness may have a less noble than horror at discovering his father's past, suggesting that he envies the latter's skill as a popular amateur painter of insipid island landscapes even though he says he scorns it. The father's recent exhibition has succeeded whereas Julio's own failed. She hints that the youth may now doubt himself and may have become blind as an excuse not to paint. Verónica urges Julio to break the ties that bind him to the father he both admires and hates and to the latter's opulent life style: 'Creemos haber roto con este mundo y aquí estamos, disfrutando de sus comodidades . . . Cuando trazamos sus mordaces caricaturas, proyectamos en ellos nuestra propia caricatura. La explicación que te ofrezco podrá ser burguesa, pero no falsa. Es ingenuo pensar que somos diferentes y no advertir que todavía nos tienen contaminados' (*OC*, I, p. 1389). Only by understanding these ties will Julio regain his sight: 'No volverás a ver si no ves primero en tu interior' (*OC*, I, p. 1357).

The playwright himself comments on the qualities that give Verónica the moral authority to judge Julio, describing her as 'más limpia, más sana, más evolucionada [. . .] que su compañero. Esta muchacha tiene sobre Julio la ventaja de una experiencia más completa, que la ha llevado a una ruptura más auténtica con la sociedad que en la obra los rodea'.[15] These qualities also lend her the authority to rebut the father's arguments – the authority that Julio cannot possess. This confrontation, in which Verónica destroys her opponent's defences, represents the core of Buero's message; it stands as a clear indictment not only of the violence and torture in Felipe's past but of the

---

[14] Buero emphasizes elsewhere the ideas that Verónica expresses: '[U]na estimación erróneamente empequeñecedora del adversario socio-político originará errores en el modo de combatirlo. La sobreestimación acrítica de nuestra personalidad frente a las ajenas [. . .] quizá suscribe fugaces ardores beligerantes, mas no aquella firme eficacia que sólo el conocimiento y vigilancia de los defectos propios consolida' (*Obra Completa*, II, p. 276). Asel's words in *La Fundación* constitute Buero's most complete statement, in any of his plays, on revolutionary action. See Halsey, op. cit., chapter 4.

[15] Antonio Buero Vallejo, '*Sobre Llegada de los dioses*' (Interview with Ángel Fernández-Santos), *Primer Acto* 138 (1971), 31.

crimes of which the prosperous businessman is guilty in the present. The debate concludes with Verónica's explanation of the need for Julio to leave and of the revolution that she defends:

VERÓNICA   Hay muchos otros peligros aquí, y nos urge vivir. [. . .]
FELIPE   [. . .] ¿Para la revolución? [. . .] Te he entendido . . . No me
             vas a negar que eres toda una revolucionaria . . . Quizá una
             activista . . .
VERÓNICA   ¿Qué te importa?
FELIPE   Me importa porque esas revoluciones vuestras acaban
             siempre en bailes psicodélicos, en drogas . . . y hasta en el
             crimen gratuito.
VERÓNICA   (*Con sorna.*) ¡En el repugnante crimen gratuito! ¡El tuyo,
             como no era gratuito hasta te valió un ascenso! ¡Siento
             defraudarte! No me drogo y no voy a matar a nadie.
             Todavía te llevo ventaja.
FELIPE   (*Se incorpora, rojo.*) ¡También tu revolución tortura cuando
             guerrea o toma el poder!
VERÓNICA   (*Lo considera con frialdad.*) Esa no es mi revolución. Mi
             revolución despertará toda la grandeza de los hombres, o no
             será. Tendría que hacerlo, si quiere evitar que vosotros
             aniquiléis el planeta.   (*OC*, I, p. 1382)[16]

The play ends as Verónica convinces Julio to find a new life, despite his attempts to find in her a refuge and escape, 'un sueño profundo, como el de la cuna' (*OC*, I, p. 1387), to return to a childhood free of responsibilities. Although she accepts the role as mother, she refuses to shelter him: 'Yo soy tu cuna. Tu madre. Y te daré vida, aunque sea dolorosa. Vida y no muerte' (*OC*, I, p. 1387).

Before leaving, however, Julio recovers his sight for a brief moment and declares that, if it is necessary to forget the horrors of the world in order to see the marvellous skies of his island paradise, he will do so because to lose it again would be too terrible. In his weakness, Julio prefers to see physically at all costs, even if what he sees is a lie, however, Verónica, speaking as the voice of his conscience, has admonished him: 'Se puede ver sin olvidar' (*OC*, I, p. 1402). Julio falls victim to the same 'ceguera azul' as his father. However, the accidental death of his half-sister Nuria, killed by a grenade buried since the war, reminds him that the effects of the past conflict are real and cannot be erased. Unable to forget the horrors he sought to escape, Julio once again becomes blind and experiences the sombre images that, according to Verónica, can be his strength: 'Serán tu fuerza y tu misterio cuando las

---

[16] Buero distinguishes between historical violence (which he believes may sometimes be necessary) and gratuitous cruelty. Asel of *La Fundación* speaks of 'Combatientes juramentados a ejercer una violencia sin crueldad . . . e incapaces de separarlas, porque el enemigo tampoco las separa' (*OC*, I, p. 1472).

miras con los ojos abiertos' (*OC*, II, p. 1408). If he succeeds, it will be Verónica who has enabled him to do so.

Just as Verónica informs Julio's social conscience in *Llegada*, so Cristina guides Julia of *Jueces* to confront the reality of her comfortable life of privilege as a middle-class woman in Franco's Spain and of her marriage to a man she has never loved: a cabinet member during the dictatorship and now an opportunistic congressman of the transition period, for whom politics is only a way to financial gain and political power.[17] This congressman, Juan Luis, tricked his wife into marrying him by lying about her fiancé, as she will discover with the help of her friend, Cristina.

Cristina, who worked in the anti-Franco resistance some twenty-two years earlier with the youth that Julia then loved, a student who died in prison, represents the leftist activist who has remained faithful to her ideals. She carries on her face the scar received when attacked by fanatical youths with chains and knives while she was putting up posters for elections in the late 1970s. In a key dialogue she points out to Julia, whom she knew when both women were medical students, the reality of the latter's life of ritualized, conventional boredom, as she enjoys privileges that result from her husband's politics – the very politics she says she scorns. Julia represents the traditional middle-class Spanish woman of her time who closed her eyes to what was happening in the country. Cristina attempts to bring her out of the profound depression she has begun to experience after twenty years of an empty marriage: to interest her in the medical career she abandoned – or in politics. However, Julia condemns all politics as 'una engañifa' or 'mentira': whether Juan Luis's or Cristina's. The latter's response evinces Buero's own convictions, including his views on the Spanish Left and of the dangers facing the country in the late 1970s:

> CRISTINA   ¿A la lucha por un futuro más justo la llamas mentira? No vale dar la espalda a los problemas que nos acosan, Julia. Y los del país también son tuyas. (*Grave.*) ¿No te preocupa nada, por ejemplo, que siga habiendo terrorismo?
> JULIA   De izquierdas y de derechas. No tenemos remedio.
> CRISTINA   Otro día hablaremos de los remedios, pues tiene que haberlos. ¡Y no me creas una ilusa! [. . .] sé, por desgracia, lo torpes que aún son muchos de los míos. Impaciencia, oportunismo, sectarismo . . . Inmadurez, en suma, que ya se cuidó muy bien el antiguo régimen de fomentar. [. . .]
> JULIA   (*Se siente junto al teléfono.*) Juan Luis dice que la situación actual es irreversible.

---

[17] The UCD (Unión de Centro Democrático) that won the elections of 1977 was the object of ridicule due to the opportunism of many of its members. A coalition with no clear ideology, it seemed held together mainly by the personal ambition of its members.

CRISTINA   Si quiere decir incambiable se equivoca, porque todo
             cambia y siempre es posible un golpe de estado que nos
             volviese a traer unos cuantos años trágicos. [. . .] Lo sepan
             o lo ignoren, eso es lo que buscan los terroristas. Padecen
             la mística de la sangre: una terrible enfermedad . . .
             contrarrevolucionaria. (*OC*, I, pp. 1637–38)[18]

The advice that Cristina will give Julia later is that, if she wishes to live again, she must leave Juan Luis – just as Verónica's advice to Julio is that he must break totally with his father. Cristina reminds Julia that Juan Luis's actions, including his sending their money to Swiss bank accounts, affect her also. 'Si quieres enderezar tu vida y recobrar la alegría', Cristina warns Julia, 'sepárate de Juan Luis' (*OC*, I, p. 1662).

The subject of the terrorism that Cristina condemns is significant for, as the play begins, Juan Luis is being blackmailed by the ex-policeman friend who helped him trick Julia some twenty-one years earlier into leaving her fiancé, the young student Fermín. The ex-policeman, who is now master-minding a terrorist plot to assassinate an important general, can thus destroy Juan Luis's marriage if the latter denounces the plot. The deception of Julia is re-enacted in the first of a series of nightmares in which Fermín and his father appear to judge Juan Luis. We see the ex-policeman pretend to have come to arrest Julia and state that Fermín has broken under torture and impli-cated her in his illegal activities – although, as we learn later, the latter always took care to not let her get involved in them. Juan Luis then pretends to use his political influence to save Julia from arrest. This deception was followed by Julia's loss of faith in Fermín – leaving a void never filled – and her marriage to Juan Luis. The action of the play deals precisely with Cristina's attempts to help Julia find the truth about her marriage.

Julia, who has not seen Cristina since Fermín's arrest some twenty-two years previously, states that she has called her old friend for help with her depression. However, Cristina learns that Julia is unaware that Fermín died in prison and that she has always believed that he betrayed their entire group, giving their names to the police when he was arrested and tortured. Cristina then intuits that her friend has summoned her to learn about the man she once loved. Since what Julia believes was Fermín's betrayal, she has ceased to believe in anything or anyone. Now, it is as if, increasingly aware of the emptiness of her marriage, she subconsciously seeks to resurrect a more authentic past. Cristina – whose role as a physician parallels Verónica's of *Llegada* as teacher – gives the same advice as the latter gives Julio. 'Creo que

---

[18] A military plot to overthrow the Spanish government ('Operación Galaxia') had been discovered, in 1978, only the night before it was to have been attempted. 23 February, 1981, of course, saw a coup attempt that could easily have succeeded. Cristina's remarks here about terrorist violence echo Asel's warnings in *La Fundación* of the dangers of revolutionary excesses that are counterproductive.

no saldrás a flote', she warns Julia, 'si no te atreves a ver claro en ti misma' (*OC*, I, p. 1656). Cristina attempts to 'cure' Julia by bringing her to face the truth, by taking her to visit a man who was Fermín's companion in prison so that she can learn how the young student endured the beatings that resulted in his death without revealing the names of those responsible for a prison uprising. It is illogical to suppose that Fermín would have denounced Julia, whom he never involved in his illegal activities, when he did not betray others. 'Aquel polizonte os engañó', concludes Cristina. 'Y en ese engaño has vivido media vida' (*OC*, I, p. 1661).

Julia's search for the truth concludes when she learns that her husband – whom she has assumed was deceived just as she was – and the policeman were friends prior to the latter's arrival to arrest her and that the deception was planned by both men so that she would believe the worst of Fermín. It is Cristina who obtains for Julia the proof of Juan Luis's deception: a letter from a friend whom she asked to investigate the policeman's past.

Cristina helps Julia achieve the clear vision, the self-understanding, that the latter needs. Julia is now able to admit that she believed Juan Luis's lies because she wanted to, because she feared the risks of a life with him: 'Lo veo todo tan claro. [. . .] Es insoportable. ¡Dichosa Cristina, dichoso Fermín, hasta que murió! Con navajazos, cárceles y palizas, han tenido una existencia bella y noble. A mí me faltó el valor de incorporarme a esa hermosura. Yo no valgo más que tú', she admits to Juan Luis (*OC*, I, p. 1707). Ruggeri Marchetti comments: 'Es implícita la simpatía del autor por el hecho de que Julia al final rechaza ser sólo un objeto ornamental del marido para lucimiento en sociedad, así como la vida vacía que siempre ha vivido'.[19]

Julia's insight into herself, however, comes too late. Her suicide may be interpreted as a liberation from the emptiness of her life with Juan Luis, as an expiation for the guilt she feels, or simply as the result of the feeling that she herself expresses, that she is unable to go on, to change her life. However, to Juan Luis, Julia's suicide signifies, as we see in his final nightmare, the definitive victory of Fermín, the rival he destroyed. In his dream, we see a radiant Julia join the man she really loves, as she takes her place among her husband's judges – in a conclusion that strongly resembles that of Buero's earlier *La tejedora de sueños* (1952).

If Cristina of *Jueces* leads Julia to face the truth about a husband who, with calculated deception, coerced her into marrying him, Amparo of *Lázaro en el laberinto* seeks to help the latter accept his own responsibility in the fatal beating, after a protest demonstration some twenty-two years earlier, of Silvia, the student he loved. Indeed, Lázaro sees in Amparo a new Ariadne who can lead him out of the labyrinth of his doubts and fears. The truth seemingly eludes Lázaro as he remembers the incident in two different ways. In

---

[19] Ruggeri Marchetti, p. 37.

one version he intervened to protect Silvia and, in the second, he abandoned her to save himself. Since her family concealed the girl's death from him, Lázaro expects her to contact him and awaits the voice that can 'resurrect' him like his biblical namesake.

When the awaited call does not come, Lázaro transfers his hopes to Amparo, the young writer whom he hires as his secretary and with whom he falls in love because she reminds him of Silvia. It was the latter who led Lázaro to participate in the struggle for a more humane society. He tells Amparo that Silvia was 'tan inteligente y bonita como tú. [. . .] Activa, luchadora, abnegada' (*OC*, I, p. 1913). Amparo urges Lázaro to search within himself for the truth. Like Verónica of *Llegada*, who leads Julio to see the corruption of his father's world, and like Cristina, the political activist of *Jueces* who awakens Julia's conscience so that she rejects her superficial life of comfort for one of greater authenticity, Amparo is one of Buero's strongest female characters. A writer, she is ready to reject money and security, without fear for the future, for the sake of the vocation to which she is committed. When she loses her office position, it is only on the condition that her writing come first that she accepts Lázaro's offer of employment: 'A mí no me interesa prosperar. Todo ese furor por situarse, por ganar dinero [. . .] me da risa. Y asco. Nunca he escrito mejor que cuando he estado sin trabajo. Y lo que yo quiero es escribir, no convertirme en una eficiente ejecutiva. Nadie debería pensar en enriquecerse . . . Es inhumano' (*OC*, I, p. 1893).

Amparo's ideas on her writing reflect Buero's own. And Amparo's stance constitutes, at least in part, an answer to criticism or possible criticism of Buero's own works. Just before the presentation ceremony celebrating Amparo's new book, Germán, a student who considers himself more politically committed and therefore superior, calls into question what he considers Amparo's excessive concern with the intimate, subjective side of her characters and charges that literature can contribute little to positive social change if it gets bogged down in insignificant personal dilemmas instead of focusing on the important problems of the world. Amparo defends the importance of the dialectical tension between subjectivity and objective testimony always advocated by Buero, of 'la interioridad personal al lado de la exterioridad social' ('De mi teatro', *OC*, II, p. 511).[20] Germán underestimates the importance of the interior life and motivation of the individual as they relate to

[20] Amparo is reminiscent of Dama, the narrator of *Caimán*. Both women reflect Buero's views on writing. Dama introduces the action of the latter play by explaining that she is dictating a chapter of her book. A successful writer, she suspects that she may have chosen her career precisely so that she might relate the story of difficult, uncertain years of her past, to show how an ignorant, silly adolescent girl (who, we learn at the end, is the lady herself) has become a mature woman committed to social change. Her goal is to impart a sense of hope to her readers, just as Buero's own aim has been in the case of his spectators.

social and political responsibility, considering Amparo lost in the labyrinths of conscience of which she writes. In a recent interview, Buero explains: 'En Amparo estoy defendiendo mi propia creación literaria ante una crítica desnortada, con prejuicios sobre la escritura y el cambio social. Eran los postulados de la izquierda que se atenía a modelos prosoviéticos'.[21]

It is significant that ideas in opposition to Amparo's are put into the mouth of one of Buero's most despicable characters, whose inability to understand the labyrinths of conscience that he condemns comes, as we shall see, from his own opportunism and lack of scruples. Just as Verónica condemns Felipe in *Llegada* and Cristina condemns Juan Luis in *Jueces*, so Amparo assumes the role of judge of Germán. It is her own moral authority that allows her to do so. Ruggeri Marchetti speaks of the importance of the female character in Buero's theatre 'como sede de consciente coraje revolucionario o de abnegación sublime'.[22] As will become clear, Amparo belongs to not only the first, but also the second, of these categories.[23]

Amparo judges Germán for two things. First, for making inquiries, obtaining a copy of Silvia's death certificate, and, without the family's consent, presenting it to Lázaro, who is not prepared to accept this revelation. Germán insists that the truth is always best, but the truth he insists must be faced is not his own (that truth is what Amparo will next force him to confront) but Lázaro's. Secondly, she judges Germán for his opportunism and hypocrisy. A recent law school graduate, Germán has applied for a position at the same law firm as has Lázaro's nephew. When Germán states his intention to become a member of the Centro de Juristas Liberales – an association whose members he attacks in remarks to others as reactionary – in order to

---

[21] Antonio Buero Vallejo, *Buero por Buero. Conversaciones con Francisco Torres Monreal* (Madrid: Asociación de Autores de Teatro, 1993), p. 45. Buero adds: 'Culturalmente, el socialismo real ha dado lugar a una serie de injusticias lamentables. En mi opinión, la revolución habría sido mucho más auténtica y mucho más sostenible si una bien orientada libertad expresiva la hubiera revitalizado' (p. 14).

[22] Ruggeri Marchetti, p. 41.

[23] Harris, in her study of Penélope of *La tejedora de sueños* (1952), Amalia of *Madrugada* (1953), and Amparo of *Lázaro*, states that the latter, in her emancipation, representa 'una reevaloración, por parte de Buero del papel femenino [. . .], una "revisión" [. . .] del papel de la mujer en la sociedad' (pp. 255–56). However, as stated earlier, this 'revisión' really began some twenty-two years earlier with Lucila of *La doble historia del doctor Valmy*, who struggles to make others aware of the use of torture against political prisoners. Just as Cristina of *Jueces* tries to awaken the social conscience of Julia, so Lucila seeks to awaken that of her former student. Serrano omits Lucila from her list of 'new women' in Buero's theatre and downplays the independence of Verónica of *Llegada de los dioses* because of her maternal feelings for Julio. She includes Verónica with certain characters in earlier plays: 'Las actuaciones de estas mujeres se producen dentro del trazado de unos personajes construidos con rasgos tradicionalmente femeninos, como la ternura, la comprensión, la adaptación al hombre al que pretenden salvar o su desaliento ante la imposibilidad de conseguirlo' (p. 101).

help change the system from within, Amparo reveals that he really joined the association prior to applying for the position. He did so because the head of the firm to which they applied is a director of the centre.

Amparo explains that Germán's fear of unemployment, of being left behind, engenders egoism and aggressiveness, which in turn engender more fear. Through Amparo, Buero presents his critique of Spain of the mid 1980s – that of the Socialists in power since 1982 – as he condemns the deficiencies of a society that has seemingly accepted the acquisition of wealth as its major goal. Amparo passes judgement on Germán for his deception. Rejecting his contention that he entered the centre to facilitate his efforts on behalf of his social ideals, she unmasks him:

> GERMÁN   [. . .] Pero ya veo que tú tampoco entenderías . . . Creí que pertenecías al ejército de los luchadores insobornables. Me había equivocado.
>
> AMPARO   ¿De qué libro habrás sacado tú esa frase? . . . Ese al que tú llamas ejército existe. Pero no te atreves a hablar de él. Hay gente suya en algunos partidos y sindicatos, en alguna universidad . . . Entre las personas sencillas que vemos pasar por la calle. Pero guárdate de ostentar tú su representación. Tal vez hace unos años . . . No sé. Hoy ya no puedes. (*OC*, I, p. 1941)

The only persons who have the right to represent this 'ejército de luchadores insobornables', Amparo explains, are those like Silvia. When Germán defends his deception on the grounds of poverty, stating that he has every right to get ahead in any way he can, Amparo replies: 'Pero no como luchador insobornable. A ti ya te han sobornado. Ya eres normal' (*OC*, I, 1942). Through Amparo, Buero suggests that the youth is no different from others of his generation. In an interview, Buero says of Germán, who betrays his principles and his friend to further his ambitions: 'El personaje responde a una realidad que desgraciadamente es harto frecuente, una consecuencia de la fiebre de arribismo e hipocresía social en que nos desenvolvemos. El ánimo de trepar de un modo descarado afecta incluso a quienes en un tiempo tuvieron sinceramente unas ideas de compromiso con la renovación de nuestra sociedad, y hasta unas ideas revolucionarias'.[24]

Amparo's judgement of Lázaro, himself, comes when he is alone, for the last time, with Amparo, who has rejected his marriage proposal because she believes that he still loves Silvia and that it is to the latter woman that he is really proposing. When Lázaro insisted earlier that Amparo answer, in Silvia's place, his question as to his conduct twenty-two years earlier, the former responded that, if he abandoned Silvia, he would be forgiven for his

---

[24] Quoted in F[élix] P[oblación], 'Un laberinto de Buero entre pasado y presente', *El Público* 40 (January 1987), 36–37.

moment of weakness. At their last meeting, however, Amparo reveals that she is convinced that fear did prevent him from defending Silvia. And even though she can forgive him in Silvia's name for his cowardliness, Amparo is unwilling to share the burden he carries because she realizes that Silvia's ghost will always accompany him and, even more importantly, because she doubts his real love for either woman. Fear prevented Lázaro from loving Silvia to the extent that he was willing to sacrifice himself for her, and fear prevents him from remembering the past in front of Amparo:

> AMPARO   [. . .] El miedo. O sea, el egoísmo. Se engendran mutuamente. No el miedo pasajero; no el pánico de un momento de peligro. Esos sí se superan. Pero el que se lleva en los huesos, no. Entre que apaleasen a Silvia o te apaleasen a ti, creo que elegiste lo primero. Entre el yo y el tú, elegiste el yo. Porque no amabas.
> . . . .
> ¡No te lo reprocho! Es una fatalidad del tiempo en que vivimos y hasta Germán la sufre. Pero el que, en este mundo terrible, no puede retorcerle el cuello a su miedo, ese . . . no puede amar. (*OC*, I, p. 1949)

If Lázaro had succeeded in overcoming his fear, he would not have forgotten the fact. So great was – and is – this fear that his mind ingeniously invented a reassuring lapse of memory.

Amparo's love for Lázaro is as great as Verónica's for Julio. Nevertheless, Amparo reaches a different decision: to leave Lázaro so that he may be reborn, that he may learn the truth about himself. When Lázaro entreats her to marry him and lead him as she would a blind man, her reply evinces the extent of the sacrifice that her decision represents: 'No puedes imaginar . . . cuánto lo desearía. [. . .] A tu lado, como la más fiel compañera, disfrutando cada día de tu presencia, de tus palabras [. . .] Sabiendo que puedo embeberme a todas horas en tu rostro, en tu sonrisa . . . Y gozar de tus manos, y de tus besos' (*OC*, I, p. 1950). However, Amparo understands that her presence would only constitute a refuge ('amparo') and keep him from resolving his doubts.[25] It is thus out of love that she leaves him.

Just as Verónica of *Llegada* attempts to help Julio to break with the corrupt world of his father, so Patricia of *Las trampas del azar* tries to prevent Gabi from repeating the errors of the latter's father, Gabriel, owner in the mid 1960s of a laboratory and factories that produce arms for export. Gabriel, like Juan Luis of *Jueces*, deceived his wife before their marriage, never revealing that a childhood prank of his caused the terrible scars on her

---

[25] Ruggeri Marchetti says that Amparo leaves because she has no respect for a man unable to face the truth about himself (p. 40). However, the major reason suggested in the play is a genuine concern for Lázaro's future.

back. These resulted from shattered glass when a roof tile he threw broke a street lamp as she happened, by a strange coincidence, to pass by. It is not clear if Gabriel really loved his wife-to-be, whose scars repulsed him, and why he has never been sincere with her. However, the result has been an advantageous marriage. Behind the mask, the youthful rebel was, most likely, a shrewd schemer, as his transformation into the powerful head of a firm connected to one of the most sinister of businesses suggests.

The young Gabi attacks his father for his laboratories and factories that contaminate the air with their black smoke and pollute the waters to make arms for whose use he disclaims responsibility – just as Julio attacks Felipe in *Llegada*. Gabi's attacks also recall those of his father as a youth. Some thirty years earlier, Gabriel had criticized his own father, a Francoist veteran of the Civil War who worked in Matilde's father's laboratory, for profiting from arms sales. Nevertheless, to win Matilde's hand Gabriel consented to working in this same laboratory which she would some day inherit. The young, rebellious Gabi thus resembles his father who, as a youth participated in anti-Francoist activities but who finally betrayed his ideals for wealth and power. As Serrano notes in regard to Gabriel: 'Las ideas revolucionarias han dejado paso al egoísmo conservador. El tiempo y la herencia [. . .] recibida han tendido su trampa.'[26]

It is Gabi's friend, Patricia, who forces the youth to see that he can be just as aggressive and ruthless as was his father. When Gabi discovers his father's deception of Matilde thirty years earlier, he confronts him with his suspicions that the tile that shattered the street lamp was not blown by the wind but thrown deliberately by him, not realizing that anyone was in the street. The son's attempt to force a confession from his father fails, as the latter repeats his old story of the wind and speaks of 'un maldito azar'. More importantly, Gabi destroys his mother's last illusion: that her husband loved her. As Patricia charges, Gabi has once again made his mother a victim: 'Tú has lanzado ahora tu teja. Pero no contra tu padre, sino contra los dos. Y los cristales han vuelto a herir a tu madre, acaso para siempre' (p. 135). Matilde, made by her father to feel insecure and unworthy of love because of her scars, cynically seduced by Gabriel and then tricked into marrying him, and finally destroyed by her son, takes her place as one in a long list of victimized women in Buero's theatre.

Patricia also reminds Gabi that his father once considered himself a rebel but became in Gabi's own words, 'un trepador sin escrúpulos' (p. 137). Gabi, likewise, considers himself a rebel; however, one day he will inherit the laboratory and Patricia reminds him that it will not suffice to sell it. He must

---

[26] *Las trampas del azar* (Madrid: Espasa Calpe, 1995), p. 22.

dismantle it or convert it to produce materials that sustain, rather than destroy, life:

> PATRICIA [. . .] pero mañana heredarás el laboratorio. ¿No podrá el
> laboratorio contigo como pudo con él?
> GABI   Ya veremos qué se hace con el laboratorio. Pero no seguirá
> siendo el productor de muertes que ha llegado a ser.
> PATRICIA Difícil tarea . . . No se cumpliría vendiendo el laboratorio.
> Habría que desmantelar . . . o cambiar sus programas . . .
> Aunque te atrevieses a hacerlo, ¿no crees que te lo
> impedirían? Pero ¿te atrevieses siquiera? (p. 137)

Patricia's words underscore the major idea of the play when she remarks that it is as if fate, with all its nasty tricks, were laughing at them: when they think they can reason clearly, it shows them how blind they really are. They repeat their parent's errors, although they presume to judge them.

In the end, Patricia, who has considered leaving Gabi, decides to remain with him because he is finally sincere with her, acknowledging his own weakness. 'Tú vales mucho más que yo', he states, recognizing Patricia's moral superiority, '¡A ti no te han atrapado!' (p. 137). Like Buero's other liberated women, she admits her own failings: a highly successful designer of fashions, jewelry and furniture, she has betrayed her dream of becoming a serious painter and is therefore trapped to some extent, also. However, it is through Patricia, as through Verónica, Cristina, and Amparo, that Buero expresses, not only his own ideas on peace, justice, and other issues, but also a conviction that is central to his entire tragic theatre, as the former admonishes Gabi 'que de poco sirve intentar el arreglo de este mundo atroz si a la vez no aprendemos a ver claro en nosotros mismos' (p. 136).[27]

We have seen that, in *Jueces en la noche* and *Lázaro en el laberinto*, Buero uses female characters to express his ideas on the need for authenticity and commitment in politics (Cristina) and literature (Amparo) – two areas of paramount concern in his own life. It is hardly surprising that, in *Llegada de los dioses* and *Las trampas del azar*, he chooses two other women (Verónica and Patricia, respectively) to express his continuing commitment to, and hope for, peace – including peace with, and respect for, the earth. Since the 1970s, 'Green' issues have been paramount for many feminist activists.[28]

[27] Buero stresses his belief that, in the struggle for a more just and humane society, no attempt to transform the external structures of society that neglects attention to the conduct of the individual will succeed ('Muñiz', *OC*, II, pp. 940–56). This conviction explains the constant juxtaposition of the social and the moral in his plays, which usually deal with the conduct of individuals faced with difficult moral choices.

[28] According to Bonnie S. Anderson and Judith P. Zinsser: 'The word *green* now carries the political meaning of being in favor of "Ecopacifism" and is especially associated with women'. See *A History of Their Own*, II (New York: Harper & Row, 1989), p. 430.

'Ecofeminism', a theory created during those years, 'connects male dominance and the destruction of the environment, and hopes that women can
intervene to prevent destruction of the ecosystem, whether caused by pollution or nuclear war'.[29] A song of the women's peace movement quoted by
British historian Rosalind Miles expresses the spirit of feminist activists
working on ecological and anti-nuclear issues: 'Oh sisters, come you, sing for
all you're worth, / Arms are made for linking,/ Sisters, we're asking for the
earth'.[30]

Through Verónica and Patricia, Buero suggests that belief in peace
includes love for our earth, awareness of our profound dependence upon one
another and our surroundings, and reverence for all sentient beings and our
environment. The plays studied here reflect Buero's vision of a radically
interconnected and interdependent world, of our fundamental unity with each
other and the universe. The playwright urges us to heed the voices of
Verónica, Cristina, Amparo, and Patricia just as he asked us to heed that of
their distant precursor, Penélope of *La tejedora de sueños*, who cried out for a
day when men would no longer make war, a day when there would exist a
bond of love, 'una palabra universal de amor que sólo las mujeres soñamos
. . . a veces' (*OC*, I, p. 183).

[29] *Ibid.*, p. 429.
[30] Rosalind Miles, *The Women's History of the World* (New York: Harper & Row,
1990), p. 237.

Gender Struggle and Power Relations
in *La dama duende*

MICHAELA HEIGL

In the Early Modern period, when the terms of gender were a matter of intense social debate, the theatre was one of the domains in which gender struggle was played out.[1] This focus on gender as the social organization of the relationship between the sexes reveals a general preoccupation with social and sexual relations. Indeed, the hierarchy of gender has often been employed to express or justify political subjugation, as Scott has pointed out: 'Gender is a primary field within which, or by means of which power is articulated.'[2] This nexus of gender and power have also been analyzed by critics such as Davis and McKendrick.[3] Davis, for example, suggests for the Early Modern period that the use of the male/female binary is an expression of the social relationship between master and servant, sovereign and subject. The legal subjection of wives to their husbands within the family was a guarantee for the obedience of both men and women to the slowly centralizing state.[4] The binary opposition between man and woman, the legitimization of domination and ruling power as masculine, and the control of woman, are therefore part of the meaning of power itself. To question or alter any aspect threatens the entire system.

In a society that regarded silence, chastity and invisibility as appropriate to womanhood, the theatre was a locus of subversion, disrupting ideological categories of meaning and representing transgressive alternatives to estab-

[1] See Valerie Traub, M. Lindsay Kaplan and Dympna Callaghan, eds, *Feminist Readings of Early Modern Culture* (Cambridge: Cambridge University Press, 1996), p. 4.

[2] Joan Wallach Scott, 'Gender: A Useful Category of Historical Analysis', *Gender and the Politics of History* ed. Joan Wallach Scott (New York: Columbia University Press, 1988), p. 45.

[3] See Melveena McKendrick, 'Calderón and the Politics of Honour', *Bulletin of Hispanic Studies*, 80 (1993), 135–46, especially p. 140 where she refers to the family as a microcosm of society, both family and society being based on the monarchic model. See also Natalie Zemon Davis, 'Women on Top', *Society and Culture in Early Modern France* (London: Duckworth, 1975), pp. 124–51.

[4] Davis, p. 128.

58				MICHAELA HEIGL

lished cultural relationships and the exercise of power.[5] Both the theatre and 'woman' displaced boundaries indispensable to the social order and destroyed literal and symbolic enclosures, as Ania Loomba explains:

> In both cases transience, mobility, alteration, disguise and changeability are seen as subverting a dominant need for stability . . . In both cases the fears are that social and sexual boundaries will be erased . . . Both women and theatre are seen to stray from their allotted spaces in various ways . . . Ideologically, women threaten the demarcation of the 'private' sphere and popular theatre resists the confinement of dramatic performance.[6]

In Early Modern Europe, both the stage and woman constituted a threat to the stability of social hierarchy, and the *comedia* presented a challenge to established norms at the levels of both performance and literary form. As a medium for the representation and exploration of gender roles, the *comedia* was able to use theatrical and physical space symbolically in order to discuss and/or renegotiate the social roles of either gender.

Calderón's *La dama duende* represents a struggle over the policing of multiple boundaries, portraying the cultural efforts to maintain clear-cut differences and hierarchical distinctions, constantly troubled by the mobile and potentially disruptive nature of desire. Ángela, the phantom lady of the play, has been characterized as 'a volatile packet of erotic energy, chameleon-like in her *duende*-like nature . . . unstable, volatile, multiform'.[7] Her (sexual) curiosity clearly constitutes a transgression of the constructed norm – the 'angel of the house' thus becomes Psyche or Eve, who is responsible for the fall of man and the birth of original sin.[8] Ángela's rebellion against social oppression transforms her into a *duende*, a malevolent spirit that creates confusion. The beautiful widow's thirst for knowledge, her mobility, volatility and erotic desire undermine the accepted moral order and evoke fears of instability, epitomized by the both comic and threatening figure of the disorderly woman. Ángela is, indeed, a version of the Renaissance *topos* that described women as 'a treasure which, however locked up, always escapes. She is the gaping mouth, the open window, the body that "transgresses its own limits" and negates all those boundaries without which property could not be constituted.'[9]

5   See Teresa Scott Soufas, *Dramas of Distinction: A Study of Plays by Golden Age Women* (Lexington: University of Kentucky, 1997), p. 30.
6   Ania Loomba, *Gender, Race, Renaissance Drama* (Manchester: Manchester University Press, 1989), p. 131.
7   Anthony J. Cascardi, *The Limits of Illusion: A Critical Study of Calderón* (Cambridge: Cambridge University Press, 1984), p. 25.
8   See Frederick de Armas, *The Invisible Mistress: Aspects of Feminism and Fantasy in the Golden Age* (Charlottesville: Biblioteca Siglo de Oro, 1976).
9   Peter Stallybrass 'Patriarchal Territories: The Body Enclosed', *Rewriting the Re-

The notorious woman-on-top, a popular figure in the literature, art and festivity of Early Modern Europe, challenged the opposition of 'man' and 'woman' through role reversal, highlighting the arbitrariness and violence of the gender hierarchy. Despite her popular appeal, she was often depicted as the embodiment of violence and chaos. Brueghel's *Dulle Griet*, for example, portrays a huge, armed, unseeing woman, Mad Meg, the emblem of destruction. In society, the leading head had to be a man, for woman's rule created a monster; indeed woman unhinges the social order through an interrogation of dominant ideology which depends on sexual difference, and thereby questions the validity of all hierarchical power structures. Breaking down cultural distinctions, the disorderly woman opens up possibilities for a re-signification of the social order. In Calderón's *comedias* many of the female protagonists challenge in some way the authority of the male, represented by fathers, husbands, sons, brothers or suitors.[10]

La dama duende interrogates the ways in which intelligible and coherent gender is constructed at the cost of identifications which reject woman's subservient status in the household economy and portray her as other than submissive and obedient. In seventeenth-century Spain, chastity is exalted as the most important attribute of the virtuous woman, who has to deny certain social and sexual possibilities in order to approximate the position marked out for her in the symbolic order.[11] The enclosure of female sexuality secures male subjectivity and ensures social stability; therefore, female chastity is sometimes a matter of life and death. *La dama duende* illustrates male anxieties generated by female erotic mobility and enacts a process of female objectification. On the other hand, it resists the notion of woman as an object of desire and exchange, and questions the tacit cruelties through which the final enclosure of woman's sexuality is enforced.

In *La dama duende* woman is 'kept in her place', enclosed and silenced through gender regulations. This enclosure of female sexuality and the body within the symbolic order is conveyed in spatial terms. The play focuses on the symbolic scenographic distribution of assigned spaces, granting the male protagonists a much greater freedom of movement, while confining the female character to a set of rooms.[12] Ángela's transgressions are represented

---

naissance: The Discourse of Sexual Difference in Early Modern Europe, ed. Margaret W. Ferguson et al. (Chicago: Chicago University Press, 1986), p. 128.

[10] Other examples include Cristerna in *Afectos de odio y amor* and Beatriz in *No hay burlas con el amor.*

[11] According to Lacan, the symbolic, not the imaginary, is the determining order of the subject, and Lacan draws a distinction between what belongs in experience to the order of the symbolic and what pertains to the imaginary. The 'real' as a third term, linked to the symbolic and the imaginary, stands for that which is neither symbolic nor imaginary, and remains foreclosed from the symbolic order. See his *Écrits. A Selection* (New York, London: W. W. Norton & Company, 1977).

[12] For a detailed discussion of theatrical space and its relation to gender roles see

symbolically by the movement of the cupboard to enter Don Manuel's room. Ángela tries to create space for herself and break out of her prison where she is both contained and kept under surveillance, but she cannot ultimately escape enclosure.

Doña Ángela is a young widow who has to settle some legal affairs after her husband's death, and therefore comes to Madrid.[13] Widowhood in Early Modern Europe is a position that defines woman according to her sexuality, locating her within the economy of patriarchal heterosexuality.[14] By traditional definition, a widow is lustful, and a widow at Court is therefore synonymous with a loose, scheming woman. Isabel, Ángela's maid explains to her:

> Señora, no tiene duda
> el que mirándote viuda,
> tan moza, bizarra y bella,
> tus hermanos cuidadosos
> te celen, porque este estado
> es el más ocasionado
> a delitos amorosos.
>   Y más en la Corte hoy,
> donde se han dado en usar
> unas viuditas de azahar [. . .].   (Act I, 402–11)[15]

Doña Ángela is anxiously guarded in the house of her two brothers, Don Luis and Don Juan, who are concerned with their sister's propriety. As a young widow in a rather precarious financial situation, Doña Ángela is unlikely to marry again, and any attention paid to her by men may damage her honourable reputation. Therefore, Don Manuel, who is invited to stay as a guest, is kept in ignorance about Ángela's existence. He is put up in a suite with access to the rest of the house, including her quarters, which has been hidden by a cupboard with shelves and glassware. Ángela, having been told that the cupboard can be moved like a door, gains access to Don Manuel's apartment, leaves letters and gifts, and even invites him to see her. The communication between Manuel and Ángela, however, is based on the condition that her identity be withheld. The comedy ends with a fight between Don Luis and Don Manuel, after Ángela's caprices have been detected, prompting a

Melveena McKendrick, 'Gender and Symbolic Space in the Theatre of Calderón', *Journal of the Institute of Romance Studies*, 1 (1992), 225–38.

[13] It can be assumed that Doña Ángela has come home to protect her dowry from her husband's creditors. See Margaret Rich Greer, 'The (Self) Representation of Control in *La dama duende*', *The Golden Age Comedia: Text, Theory, and Performance*, eds Charles Ganelin and Howard Mancing (Indiana: Purdue University Press, 1994), p. 97.

[14] See Valerie Traub, *Desire and Anxiety: Circulations of Sexuality in Shakespearean Drama* (London and New York: Routledge, 1992), pp. 25 ff.

[15] References are to the critical edition of *La dama duende* by Fausta Antonucci (Barcelona: Crítica, 1999).

situation in which Manuel is urged into a union with Ángela, who has sought his protection from her two brothers.[16]

Ángela's enclosure and domestication mirrors the plight of many of her contemporaries. Renaissance demarcation of domestic space restricted women's freedom to move, and sixteenth-century humanist treatises and social practices, unwilling to regard women as full-fledged human beings, relegated the feminine Other to the private sphere, converting her into a creature in need of domestication. Sumptuary, vagrancy and enclosure laws attempted to enforce social stability and prevent the subject's deviation from his/her God-given, fixed place in society.[17] The surveillance and control of women were concentrated upon the mouth, chastity and the threshold of the house, and the close link between speaking and wantonness, silence and chastity, connected with spatial enclosure, reveals a common preoccupation. Conduct books, for example, tried to 'tame' women through various techniques of controlling the body. In Vives's *Instruction of a Christian Woman*, for example, overwhelming importance was given to chastity. It has been underscored by Wayne that 'all of Vives's restrictions on the lives of women are given in the name of chastity, and the virtue was lauded and praised so much . . . that it obscured the other virtues a woman might exhibit or strive for'.[18] Women's lives had to be controlled in order to ensure chastity, and, consequently, the enclosure of the body was regarded as an emblem for social stability.

In *La dama duende*, Ángela's body becomes a site of resistance to socially prescribed gender identifications, a site marked by struggle and final reintegration. Throughout the play it changes its contours, is materialized differently according to the different role models it adopts or fails to assimilate. By exceeding socially sanctioned boundaries, Ángela's body, for example, outgrows itself, becomes grotesque, powerful, even demonic. At the end of the play, however, it recedes within the sanctioned limits of prescribed gender models. In Calderón's *La dama duende* subjectivity is not independent of history, society, political forces: 'woman' is a political category, not a natural given.

The female protagonist in Calderón's play has a multiple identity: she shifts alignments, trying to escape enclosure and the fate of being 'buried

16 For a detailed summary of the play see Alexander A. Parker, *The Mind and Art of Calderón: Essays on the Comedias*, ed. Deborah Kong (Cambridge: Cambridge University Press, 1988), pp. 144 ff.

17 Juliana Schiesari, 'The Face of Domestication: Physiognomy, Gender Politics, and Humanism's Others', *Women, 'Race', and Writing in the Early Modern Period*, eds Margo Hendricks and Patricia Parker (London: Routledge, 1994), pp. 55–70.

18 Valerie Wayne, ' "Some Sad Sentence": Vives's *Instruction of a Christian Woman*', in *'Silent but for the Word': Tudor Women as Patrons, Translators, and Writers of Religious Works*, ed. Margaret Patterson Hannay (Kent: The Kent State University Press, 1985), p. 24.

alive'. She manages to make a choice of marriage partner, and thus trespasses on the male privilege to exchange women. Ángela has given herself away, she has chosen Don Manuel as her husband, and has thus partly written herself out of the discourse which defines women as valuables or signs which need to be exchanged. This is even more remarkable if we keep in mind that Ángela lacked financial means and was therefore not very likely to remarry at all. Marriage might, however, be regarded as just another form of enclosure under the tutelage of a male family head, as Larson suggests: 'Her independence and ingenuity do lead to her goal of marriage, but marriage will in turn force her back into a more subservient role'.[19]

If Ángela's transgression is contained at the end of the play through symbolic enclosure, however this is clearly achieved at a considerable cost. As in many other Calderonian plays, coherence is accomplished through violence, here the violence of confinement, and the body, the corporeal image, has a central and irreducible place, and is clearly visible, as Francis Barker suggests:

> Whether judicially tortured as the visible sign of vengeance . . . on the transgressor, or disassembled lovingly on stage in the cause of poetry, it [the body] is the crucial fulcrum and crossing point of the lines of force, discursive and physical, which form this world as the place of danger and aspiration.[20]

Marriage provides the ideal ending of the play and the ideal type of patriarchal enclosure. Ángela's containment through the forces of power, however, is portrayed as being desperate, sadistic and violent.

Ángela's transgressions certainly endanger her life: at the beginning of the play she flees from her brother, Don Luis, who tries to ascertain the identity of an unknown *tapada* who talks to the men at court, unaware that it is his own widowed sister he pursues. This pursuit and other incidents in the play have induced Honig to assume a (possibly unconscious) incest drive on the part of the two brothers, Don Luis and Don Juan, under the disguise of a punctilious adherence to the exigencies of the honour code.[21] Fleeing from her brother, Ángela thus asks Don Manuel for protection:

> Si, como lo muestra
> el traje, sois caballero

[19] Catherine Larson, '*La dama duende* and the Shifting Characterization of Calderón's Diabolical Angel', *The Perception of Women in Spanish Theater of the Golden Age*, eds. Anita K. Stoll and Dawn L. Smith (London: Associated University Press, 1991), p. 45.

[20] Francis Barker, *The Tremulous Private Body: Essays on Subjection* (London and New York: Methuen, 1984), p. 23.

[21] See Edwin Honig, *Calderón and the Seizures of Honor* (Cambridge, Massachusetts: Harvard University Press, 1972).

> de obligaciones y prendas,
> amparad a una mujer
> que a valerse de vos llega.
> Honor y vida me importa
> que aquel hidalgo no sepa
> quién soy, y que no me siga.
> Estorbad, por vida vuestra,
> a una mujer principal
> una desdicha, una afrenta;
> que podrá ser que algún día . . .
> ¡Adiós, adiós, que voy muerta!   (Act I, 100–12)

Already at the beginning of the play the outcome of the inversion which is going to follow is foreshadowed: Ángela's transgressions are channelled into final enclosure when Don Manuel is practically forced to marry her in order to safeguard his (and her) honourable reputation. Both Don Manuel and Doña Ángela have to fulfil their roles in the service of normative heterosexuality and exogamy, because Ángela's transgression has put her life at risk, or, according to Foucault: 'Law cannot help but be armed, and its arm, *par excellence*, is death; to those who transgress it, it replies, at least as a last resort, with that absolute menace.'[22] The presence of death and violence in what is fundamentally a *comedia de capa y espada*, reminds us that Calderón's dramaturgy strikes a 'nearly perfect but paradoxical balance between the festive and the funereal'.[23] As Wardropper contends, in Calderón's comedies, although there is no death on stage, the presence of death is always in the minds of the characters and the spectators, and he concludes: 'Amusing as the comedy is, it is for ever teetering on the brink of tragedy.'[24]

Don Luis, Ángela's brother, who threatens her with a sword at the end of the play, symbolizes the power of the symbolic, enforcing the reiteration of its norms and principles. Wittig, discussing the social contract, points out that language, which is, to her mind, simultaneously abstract and concrete, determines our perception of reality: 'Language casts sheaves of reality upon the social body, stamping it and violently shaping it. For there is a plasticity of the real to language.'[25] The spectacularity of symbols of power such as the

---

[22] Michel Foucault, *The History of Sexuality. Volume I: An Introduction* (New York: Vintage, 1990), p. 144.

[23] Robert Ter Horst, 'The Origin and Meaning of Comedy in Calderón', *Studies in Honor of Everett W. Hesse*, eds William C. McCrary and José A. Madrigal (Lincoln: University of Nebraska, 1981), p. 147.

[24] Bruce W. Wardropper, 'Calderón's Comedy and His Serious Sense of Life', *Hispanic Studies in Honor of Nicholson B. Adams* (Chapel Hill: University of North Carolina Press, 1966), p. 181.

[25] Monique Wittig, *The Straight Mind and Other Essays* (Hertfordshire: Harvester Wheatsheaf, 1992) pp. 43 ff.

sword conveys the materiality of language, the rigidity of categorical thinking
and the intrinsic cruelty of the symbolic order.

Violence is done to the body that is incarcerated and circumscribed:
Ángela's territory within the house and also within the dominant social order
is carefully mapped out, as she reveals in the following apostrophe:

> ¡Válgame el Cielo! Que yo
> entre dos paredes muera,
> donde apenas el sol sabe
> quién soy . . .!   (Act I, 379–82)

Ángela, unlikely to remarry, will probably attract dishonourable attention,
and thus constitutes a constant threat to the identity of her two brothers. This
situation and its numerous variants in other Calderonian plays[26] illustrate the
nexus between woman's chastity or honourable behaviour and the coherence
of the male subject. As Crocetti puts it: 'Feminine honour hinges on . . .
vulnerable elements such as the glass(ware) placed in the false cupboard.'[27] It
might be argued that men's identity hinges on the same vulnerable element,
and only to the extent that woman erases her own desire is she able to guarantee that 'man' signifies within the symbolic. Through a licentious act on
the part of his sister, wife or daughter, a man in seventeenth-century Spain is
liable to social death through the loss of his name. To have a name is to be
positioned within the symbolic, as Sidonie Smith writes: 'To the degree that
woman contests such roles and postures by pursuing her own desire and independence from men, she becomes a cultural grotesque.'[28] When Don Luis
finds out that his brother has placed a cupboard in front of Ángela's room he
exclaims

> ¿Ves con lo que me aseguras?
> Pues con eso mismo intentas
> darme muerte, pues ya dices
> que no ha puesto, por defensa
> de su honor, más que unos vidrios
> que al primer golpe se quiebran.   (Act I, 363–68)

---

26   In the wife-murder plays, for example, women threaten their husband's good name;
other plays focus on the father–daughter, or, as here, the brother–sister relationship.

27   María Martino Crocetti, 'La dama duende: Spatial and Hymeneal Dialectics', The
Perception of Women in Spanish Theater of the Golden Age, eds Anita K. Stoll and Dawn
L. Smith (London: Associated University Press, 1991), p. 52.

28   Sidonie Smith, 'The Universal Subject, Female Embodiment, and the Consolidation
of Autobiography', Subjectivity, Identity, and the Body: Women's Autobiographical Practices in the Twentieth Century, ed. Sidonie Smith (Bloomington: Indiana University Press,
1993), p. 16.

When Ángela 'transgresses' the 'proper' space assigned to her by her brothers, moves the cupboard and visits Don Manuel's room, she tries to make room for her self-determination. She goes 'beyond the limits of her own body in an act of giving birth to her own self', as Crocetti puts it.[29] Ángela tries to re-signify her own body in an attempt to draw differently the boundaries that separate her from the world and other bodies. This displacement or shifting between different domains, this renewal of space, can also be read as a symbolic renewal: a redistribution of spatial domains implies re-signification in the symbolic. Ángela and Isabel scatter Don Manuel's clothes on the floor and this dimensional reorganization[30] might be read as a dis-placement, a re-signification of the symbolic order. At the end of the first act Don Manuel's Cosme introduces us to the realm of the supernatural, because he suspects that a *duende* caused a great deal of disorder in the room: '¡Vive Cristo, que parece/ plazuela de la Cebada/ la sala con nuestros bienes!' (Act I, 898–900).

While the *gracioso* sustains a traditional link between woman and the devil, Don Manuel sees in Ángela a beautiful angel. The two images of woman as angel and monster, bride of Christ and devil's gateway, are apparently opposed, but in reality intrinsically connected, as Auerbach notes:

> It may not be surprising that female demons bear an eerie resemblance to their angelic counterparts, though characteristics that are suggestively implicit in the angel come to the fore in the demon.[31]

The text links both angelic and diabolical attributes, and Ángela becomes a hybrid creature; she is *ángel*, *demonio* and *mujer*.

Grotesques have no consistent properties; they both require and defy definition. The anomalous, the ambiguous always belong to more than one domain at a time and thus defy conventional language categories.[32] When we perceive the grotesque we always search for clear and constant forms within an amalgam of shapes, but the grotesque is more than just a summation of its parts. Ángela as a hybrid and grotesque creature exceeds any stereotypical characterization and resists any clear-cut definition, as Larson contends:

> All of the linguistic signifiers used to characterize her (*fiera, torbellino, duende, mujer, ángel, diablo*) . . . join with the varying concepts that the male characters have of this woman, creating signs that can never

---

29 Crocetti, p. 55.

30 Crocetti, p. 58.

31 Auerbach, quoted in Larson p. 49.

32 Geoffrey Galt Harpham, *On the Grotesque: Strategies of Contradiction in Art and Literature* (Princeton, New Jersey: Princeton University Press, 1982), pp. 4 ff.

completely and concretely define the referent, precisely because they indi-cate that she is – and is not – a composite of essences.[33]

Ángela is thus neither angel nor devil; she is much more than she appears to be:

MANUEL	Imagen es
	de la más rara beldad
	que el soberano pincel
	ha obrado.
COSME	Así es verdad,
	porque sólo la hizo él.
MANUEL	Más que la luz resplandecen
	sus ojos.
COSME	Lo cierto es
	que son sus ojos luceros
	del cielo de Lucifer.
MANUEL	Cada cabello es un rayo
	del sol.
COSME	Hurtáronlos dél.
	[. . .]
MANUEL	Un asombro de belleza,
	un ángel hermoso es.
COSME	Es verdad, pero patudo.　(Act II, 2040–61)

Ángela's hybrid identity disrupts Aristotelian dialectics of the Same and the Other.[34] When Don Manuel insists on a clear identification and asks her if she is *demonio* or *mujer* she affirms 'soy / mucho más de lo que ves' (Act II, 2167–68). Ángela as a signifier embodies *différance*, she actively resists any simplistic categorization of herself, and thus stands for the complexity of reality which is adulterated when abstract concepts are imposed upon it.

Don Manuel's and Cosme's effort to establish clear categories of differ-ence shows us that 'direct perception' is a myth. The features of the *dama duende* are interpreted with the help of culturally available symbols, stereo-types and categories: Don Manuel 'dissects' Ángela's body in alignment with the canon of Petrarchan poetry and casts her as a submissive angel. Cosme, the *gracioso*, clings to stereotypes found in popular culture: woman as witch and demon. Ángela, however, attempts to free herself from cultural identifi-cations that either elevate and venerate her as an object of desire, or define her solely in negative terms.[35]

---

[33] Larson, p. 43.

[34] Aristotelian dialectics operate on a series of oppositions that have a metaphysical connotation. The Greek male understood himself as being essentially different from woman, animal and barbarian.

[35] Barker points out in connection with Marvell's poem 'To his Coy Mistress' that the

Devising new identifications for herself, she becomes in a double sense a 'spirited' being, a *torbellino*, transgressing the boundaries of her enclosure as an 'image,' a fixed 'stereotype'. Throughout the play she constantly negotiates identifications, incarnating angelic and devilish qualities, culturally sanctioned roles as well as spectres of abjection. She is, according to Larson, a 'beautiful woman, a widowed sister needing protection, a phantom lady . . . a giver of gifts, and the noble hostess of a fantastic banquet'.[36]

Her identity is also destabilized through role-play, which stages subjectivity as an effect of historical and social discourses, illuminating the contradictory, multiple constructions of subjectivity. Ángela creates a play within a play, in which she adopts the role of a noble hostess at a banquet to which Manuel is brought. Manuel assumes a role as well: he becomes the 'Caballero de la Dama Duende', a chivalric knight.

His efforts, however, to 'fix' her identity once and for all, now in terms of the canon of Neoplatonic imagery, have to fail, because none of the characterizations, stereotypes or roles she is cast in or adopts herself can fully determine her, as she herself explains:

> No soy alba, pues la risa
> me falta en contento tanto;
> ni aurora, pues que mi llanto
> de mi dolor no os avisa;
> no soy sol, pues no divisa
> mi luz la verdad que adoro;
> y así lo que soy ignoro,
> que sólo sé que no soy
> alba, aurora o sol [. . .]   (Act III, 2343–51)

Ángela is neither essentialized nor fully determined by any of the traditional social roles she is cast in, nor by any of the roles she is adopting:

> porque para con vos hoy
> una enigma a ser me ofrezco
> que ni soy lo que parezco
> ni parezco lo que soy.   (Act III, 2373–76)

She is in Eagleton's term 'unspeakable' because the symbolic order views the sign as a symmetrical unity between a single signifier and a single signified.[37] It cannot account for *différance*, where meaning is scattered or

---

dismemberment of woman's body in poetry is often a sign of discursive aggression. Barker interprets this aggressive fetishization of woman's body as a rage against the irrationality and delinquence of women (Barker pp. 86 ff).

36 Larson, p. 44.

37 Post-structuralism questions the view of language as a closed, stable system in which every signified has a corresponding signifier.

dispersed along a whole chain of signifiers, is never present in any one sign alone, and is always deferred or still to come.[38] Luce Irigaray suggests that within 'phallogocentric' language woman constitutes the unrepresentable, the sex that cannot be thought, a linguistic absence. Ángela is a cultural grotesque because she has moved beyond the specular economy of the symbolic order which encloses and circumscribes women's bodies.

Ángela is 'betrayed' at the end of the play by her jewellery and her clothes, a symbol for woman's status within the nuclear family of the expanding and upwardly mobile middle classes. Her jewellery and her clothes reveal her social status, and she is therefore recognized by her brother Don Juan, although he initially takes her to be the conventional object of desire, Beatriz. The social relations of the sexes 'bound the lady to chastity, to the merely procreative sex of political marriage, just as her weighty and costly costume came to conceal and constrain her body while it displayed her husband's noble rank'.[39] Ángela's subversive multiplicity, her 'play', signal an excess, transgressing the relation of the sexes as one of dependency and domination within a regime of reproductive heterosexuality. The social importance accorded to chastity renders woman's erotic power inordinate, and therefore generates male anxiety. Female erotic mobility threatens the process by which male subjectivity is secured. Through a dramatic transformation of women into jewels and corpses (in the wife-murder plays, for example) the erotic threat of the female body is psychically contained.[40] At the end of the play, Ángela's body will be enclosed, and she will be silenced. Chastity requires her to be still, cold and closed, whereas Ángela's transgressive mobility has rendered her unchaste: mobile, hot and open. Dominant ideology, however, requires woman's body to be rigidly 'finished'; woman has to embody a perfect and impermeable container or a *hortus conclusus*.[41]

Ángela's defeat is a spatial and semiotic enclosure, expressed in powerful imagery, capable of rendering Ángela's desolation as she is guided back to rule-bound discourse and intelligibility under the threat of the sword:[42]

[38] Terry Eagleton, *Literary Theory* (Oxford: Blackwell, 1983), p. 128.

[39] Joan Kelly-Gadol, 'Did Women have a Renaissance?', *Becoming Visible: Women in European History*, eds Renate, Bridenthal and Claudia Koonz (Boston: Houghton Mifflin, 1977), p. 160.

[40] Traub, p. 26.

[41] Stallybrass pp. 128 f. In Cervantes's *El curioso impertinente* Camila is compared to a diamond or a holy relic, which is to be revered, but should not be touched. Camila is a prized possession because she conforms to the normative ideal for womanhood: 'no hay joya en el mundo que tanto valga como la mujer casta y honrada, y que todo el honor de las mujeres consiste en la opinión buena que dellas se tiene'. Camila is also likened to a garden which may elicit desire, but is enclosed by a fence to ward off trespassers. See Frank Pierce, ed., *Two Cervantes Short Novels: El curioso impertinente and El celoso extremeño* (Oxford: Pergamon, 1970), pp. 36–37.

[42] See also Greer's interpretation of the passage, which highlights the 'pathetic sight of Doña Angela stumbling alone through the dark streets, panic-stricken and imprisoned

Aquí yerro, aquí caigo, aquí tropiezo,
y torpes mis sentidos
prisión hallan de seda mis vestidos;
sola, triste y turbada
llego, de mi discurso mal guiada,
al umbral de una esfera
que fue mi cárcel, cuando ser debiera
mi puerto o mi sagrado.   (Act III, 2930–37)

Ángela is unable to define her own identity, she is at a loss where clear categories of difference are required by a symbolic order based on delineations and the categorical distinction between self and other, man and woman, culture and nature, fiction and reality. Ángela's body is a site of the operations of power: the symbolic regulates its boundaries by marking off any unsanctioned positions as 'unspeakable', while enforcing the emulation of socially acceptable role models. Ángela experiences her own unintelligibility as an abject being on the margin of the symbolic domain, she is what cannot really *be* within the symbolic, and thus constitutes a cultural impossibility.

A coherent self is maintained unthreatened when separations are upheld. All contradictions are pushed underground, out of the conscious mind. Ángela as a libidinal creature, a monster, emerges as a spectre from the subterranean unconscious of subjectivity and civilization. Her existence within the realm of unintelligibility is discomfiting, even to herself. There is an all-pervasive sense of danger emanating from the dissolution of boundaries through carnivalesque techniques of inversion and misrule, and embodied transgression. Ángela as cultural grotesque must have unsettled the author, the spectator, and it continues to unsettle us, as a reminder of the groundlessness of our identity, of its violent 'constructedness', its dependence on untenable distinctions and Difference. Nevertheless, the *topos* of the woman-on-top, the play with the unruly woman, are powerful and may effect change as a positive agent of renewal. In Davis's words, it is 'partly a chance for temporary release from the traditional and stable hierarchy; but it is also part of the conflict over efforts to change the basic distribution of power within society. The woman-on-top might even facilitate innovation in historical theory and political behavior'.[43]

Civilization and its vital distinction between self and Other seem to rescue us from death and a loss of identity, but in reality the image of an impermeable, independent self is an effect of power structures; it can only be sustained through control. The subordination of the disorderly 'woman on top' effects the return of dualistic categories, differences and meanings,

by her own dress, fleeing from her own home to another house that should have offered her a safe haven. Instead, she fled from one prison to another' (Greer, p. 103).

[43] Davis, p. 131.

which reflect the hierarchical structures of the political field. The role of 'woman' as a silent, obedient and abstinent sign of exchange within the exchange economy of the symbolic is the socially sanctioned role, but it remains only one of the many identifications possible in Calderón's 'picture-book' of spectres.

The Caves of Toledo and Salamanca: Seats of Magic in Golden-Age Drama

ROBERT LIMA

In Spain's Siglo de Oro there was a broad interest in occultism and its practitioners, both among the general public and the elite of Church and State. Recognizing this fact, numerous writers of the period depicted occultists of varying stripes (alchemists, astrologers, magicians, sybils, witches), nationalities and faiths, both in positive and negative terms.[1] Among these, magicians garnered a great deal of attention for they were credited with the ability to perform such marvellous works as the translocation of people and things, feats of invisibility and transformation, as well as communicating with and commanding the supernatural world of spirits, angels and demons.

Many of the magicians portrayed in literature, with the possible exception of Celestina,[2] performed their rituals in caves or had their lessons therein.[3]

---

[1]   While there are plays on all these types of occultists, many of the *comedias* of the period concern magicians both within and outside Christianity. Zoroaster, for example, appears in Juan de la Cueva's *Comedia de la constancia de Arcelina* and Merlin has the leading role in Rey de Artieda's *Los encantos de Merlín* and appears, too, in *La casa de los celos y selvas de Ardenia* by Miguel de Cervantes. Juan Ruiz de Alarcón's *Quien mal anda en mal acaba* deals with Román Ramírez, a Moor who was arrested and punished by the Inquisition on charges of being a magician, in a typical *comedia* of intricate plot and superimposed identities manoeuvered by Satan. Ruiz de Alarcón also portrays another Moorish magician, Amet, in *La manganilla de Melilla*. Another reputed magician, Pedro Vallalarde, is the subject of Salvo y Vela's *El mágico de Salerno*, while the eighteenth-century dramatist Valladares de Sotomayor wrote numerous plays in which magicians are protagonists, among them *El mágico de Mogol*, *El mágico en Cataluña* and *El mágico de Tetuán*. There are also numerous plays on magic by anonymous authors.

[2]   Celestina performed her Plutonic magic in her house, in a place apart from the prying eyes of all, and her retiring thereto could arguably be interpreted as removal to a basement or similar underground area appropriate to contact with the pagan Lord of the Underworld. See Robert Lima, 'The Arcane Paganism of Celestina: Plutonic Magic versus Satanic Witchcraft in *Tragicomedia de Calixto y Melibea*', *Neophilologus*, 82 (1989), 221–33.

[3]   For instances in the pastoral narrative, see Frederick A. de Armas, 'Caves of Fame and Wisdom in the Spanish Pastoral Novel', *Studies in Philology* (Durham), 82 (1985), 332–58. For a study of Don Quijote's descent into the cave of Montesinos in Part II of Cervantes's novel, see Henry W. Sullivan 'The Beyond in the Here-and-Now: Passing

Such is the case in Pedro Calderón de la Barca's *El mágico prodigioso* (1663).[4] Almost at the conclusion of the Jornada Segunda, Cipriano, a pagan from Athens, heeds the offer of a stranger, first pretending to be a traveller and later a magician, to help him in his quest to possess the chaste Justina, whom he has glimpsed in a vision proffered by the disguised Devil. At his behest, Cipriano signs a contract in his own blood. The dramatists of the Siglo de Oro were so fascinated with the demonic pact, as said to have been executed by scholars à la Faust or, earlier, by clerics such as Theophilus of Adana, that it became a commonplace.[5]

Having signed the pact, Cipriano listens to the terms of the stranger, whom he fails to identify as the Devil:

> que en una cueva encerrados,
> sin estudiar otra cosa,
> hemos de vivir entrambos.   (p. 832)

As the act ends, Cipriano enters the Devil's cave, secreted in a forest, to learn the necromantic arts that will help him effect his seduction of the virtuous Christian woman, Justina.[6] Perhaps relying on folk belief to inform the public's imagination, Calderón does not describe the interior of the cave; in fact, Cipriano's lessons in Goetic or black magic are not staged at all. All that is known of it is what Cipriano declares in Jornada Tercera on emerging from the cave after a year of instruction:

> Este monte elevado
> en sí mismo al alcázar estrellado,
> y aquesta cueva oscura,
> de dos vivos funesta sepultura,
> escuela ruda ha sido
> donde la docta mágica he aprendido,
> en que tanto me muestro,
> que puedo dar lección a mi maestro.   (p. 833)

Through Purgatory in *Don Quijote, Crítica Hispánica* (Pittsburgh) 15 (1993), 63–84; special Issue: *The Occult Arts in the Golden Age*, edited by Frederick A. de Armas.

4   Calderón's play, a favourite in Germany, is held to have been a model for Goethe's *Faust*. See Pedro Calderón de la Barca, *El mágico prodigioso, Obras completas, I* (Madrid: Aguilar, 1959), pp. 807–45.

5   For a list of plays on the subject, see Robert Lima, 'Spanish Drama of the Occult through the Eighteenth Century: An Annotated Bibliography of Primary Sources', *Crítica Hispánica* (Pittsburgh), 15 (1993), 117–38; also integrated into 'Drama of the Occult: A Bibliography of Spanish and Latin-American Plays', Robert Lima, *Dark Prisms, Occultism in Hispanic Drama* (Lexington: University Press of Kentucky, 1995), Chapter IX.

6   The play tells the story of two who would become the early Christian martyrs St Cyprian and St Justina, Virgin.

The 'monte elevado' rises toward Heaven, the place of salvation, as the 'cueva oscura' is sited toward the opposite polarity, the place of death and damnation.[7] The symbolism may stem from Dante's *Inferno*, in which the Mountain in Cantos I and II is contrasted to the abyss of Hell, which the poet enters in Canto III. However, in this *comedia de magia*, the very mountain that thrusts towards the firmament contains the cave in which unholy rites have been performed and taught by the Devil. There is little irony in this union of positive and negative in the context of Cipriano's pagan world, where dualism was commonplace; however, Christianity's dictate that good proceeds from God and evil from the Devil presents a dichotomy that becomes highly ironic when the symbols of the two polarities are intertwined, as here.

The cave in *El mágico prodigioso* is nameless and has no tradition, nor, as noted earlier, is it described. This is not the case in other plays of the period. Most notable among magician's caves of the Golden Age are two notorious settings: the Cave of Toledo and the Cave of Salamanca. The renowned eighteenth-century Spanish critic and encyclopedist, Fray Benito Jerónimo Feijoo, addressed the matter in his essay 'Cuevas de Salamanca y Toledo, y mágica de España', referring to what he termed popular *fábulas*:

> entre los magos gentiles era circunstancia del rito destinar cuevas o sitios subterráneos a sus sacrílegas imprecaciones. La especie de que en un tiempo hubo escuelas de las artes mágicas en varias partes de España, señaladamente en Salamanca, Toledo y Córdoba (algunos ponen en vez de Córdoba a Sevilla), no sólo se derramó en el vulgo, sino también logró asenso en algunos graves escritores. . . . Créese que nos trajeron esta peste acá los moros, los cuales, aún hoy, se supone que son muy prácticos en toda hechicería. Es verosímil, pues, que juntando el vulgo una noticia con otra, la de ser circunstancia de las imprecaciones mágicas el celebrarse en cuevas, y la que en algunos lugares de España se enseñaban las artes mágicas, sin otro fundamento destinase para escuelas de ellas las cuevas de Toledo y Salamanca. (pp. 376–77)

What prompted Feijoo's critical discourse is that each of these caves had a long association with the magical tradition in Spain long before his time. Toledo, a seat of power and learning in the Moorish era and after its conquest by the Christians, had the legend of the Cave of Hercules upon which dramatists and others could draw. According to the legend, as promulgated in *Crónica del Moro Rasis*,[8] Hercules foresaw that Toledo would become a great city and so erected a great tower that his fame might prevail despite the

---

[7] See John E. Varey, 'Calderón y sus trogloditas', *Cosmovisión y escenografía: El Teatro español en el Siglo de Oro* (Madrid: Castalia, 1987), pp. 249–61, at pp. 255–56.

[8] This document was subsumed into the *Crónica General* of 1344. See Fernando Ruiz de la Puerta, *La cueva de Hércules y el Palacio encantado de Toledo* (Madrid:

passage of time.[9] The tower endured for centuries. Here the story takes a different turn, for by the eighth century C.E. the tower had been transformed into an enchanted palace that Hercules had kept locked; stories about great treasures buried within its keep persisted until the time of Rodrigo, king of the Visigoths, who set out to unearth them, as Feijoo recounts:

> algunos creen, que aquel palacio encantado, que dice el arzobispo don Rodrigo había en Toledo, y estaba siempre cerrado por no sé qué predicción creída, de que cuando se abriese se perdería España; pero el infeliz rey don Rodrigo le mandó abrir, entrando en él, halló un lienzo en que estaban pintados hombres armados de hábito y gesto de moros, con esta inscripción: *Por esta gente será en breve destruida España*, digo, que algunos creen que aquel palacio encantado no era otro que la cueva de que hablamos. (p. 378)

It was said after Rodrigo's defeat at the hands of the Muslim invaders that his kingdom fell as a result of his desecration of the ancient tower/palace erected by the Greek hero. Somehow over time, when the tower was no longer extant, the legend transformed it into the cave over which it had been erected, according to some accounts.[10] And so it was the Tower or Palace of Hercules first and, ultimately, the Cave of Toledo, a transformation for which Feijoo finds a classical antecedent: 'Que se diese nombre de palacio a una cueva, no se debe extrañar, pues palacio real llamó Virgilio a la cueva de Caco' (p. 378).

The influence of Virgil, considered at the time a white magician in Spain as elsewhere in Christendom, should not be underestimated, for he foreshadows much supernatural lore in the Middle Ages and the Renaissance, of which Dante's *Divina Commedia. Cantica I. L'Inferno* is but one example. When Dante encounters the shade of Virgil in Canto I he acknowledges the

---

Editora Nacional, 1977), pp. 53–54. The quotations from Feijoo are from *Obras escogidas* (Madrid: Perlado, Páez y Cía, l903).

9   Another such tradition is extant in La Coruña, in Galicia, with the so-called Tower of Hercules, a Roman lighthouse which still stands. *The Crónica del Moro Rasis* recounts that Toledo 'fue una de las quatro cibdades que Ercoles pobló en España'.

10   In *Crónica General de España de Alfonso X el Sabio* (1275), there is an account of a King Rocas, said to be a descendant of Hercules, who during his travels came upon a cave in the area that would become Toledo: 'fallo y una cueva en ques metio o yazie un dragon muy grand . . . e fizo una torre sobraquella cueva', Later documents added to or liberally changed the account: in the 1440 re-writing of the *Crónica General* 1344, the legend has it that it was Hercules himself who made the structure, but it was changed from a tower to 'una casa tan maravillosa, e por tal harte, que nunca en el mundo fue ome que verdaderamente sopiere dezir como era fecha'; while in an Arabic chronicle written by Al-Makkari, it is the Greeks who build the tower as a talisman to protect the city of Toledo, which it is said they founded, from the enemies predicted by their astrological readings. For these and other versions of the legend of the tower, palace and cave, see Ruiz de la Puerta, pp. 45–63.

author of the Aeneid as his master and inspiration and asks his help in over-coming the travails that lie before him in his journey through the nether world. And Virgil leads him into the pit, in a sense making Dante a disciple as he teaches him the lore of Hell and exposes him to its secrets. As the work progresses, the abilities that made Virgil a magician in Dante's time manifest themselves through the 'Words of Power' that he employs to open paths and keep his charge from being harmed by demons and souls alike as they delve ever deeper into the abyss.[11] In another context, Virgil conjures the Greek hero Ulysses with an economy of language that demonstrates his self-assur-ance as a mage (Canto XXVI, lines 78–84). Through his empowerment from 'where power / And will are one (87), Virgil is the facilitator through the cavern of the damned. It is easy to see how he came to be viewed as a great purveyor of Theurgic magic.

It is perhaps due to this positive image of Virgil that many practitioners of the art of magic in subsequent times were seen in a favorable light. One such magician was Don Illán de Toledo, whose story can be traced to Don Juan Manuel's medieval collection of didactic texts in which Patronio instructs his master Count Lucanor on affairs of state and on human nature.[12] In the be-st-known, *Exemplo XI. De lo que conteçió a un deán de Sanctiago con don Illán, el grand maestro de Toledo*, Don Illán tells his clerical visitor from Santiago de Compostela that the occult arts he wishes to learn 'non se podía aprender sinon en lugar mucho apartado e que luego esa noche le quería amostrar dó habían de estar fasta que hobiese aprendido aquello que él

---

[11] See Dante Alighieri, *The Divine Comedy. I. Hell*. Translated by Dorothy L. Sayers, (Baltimore: Penguin Books, 1964). Virgil's first use of this device occurs in Canto III, lines 94–96, when Charon refuses passage to Dante across Acheron, the first river of Hell: 'Charon, why wilt thou roar / And chafe in vain? Thus it is willed where power / And will are one; enough, ask thou no more' (p. 87). A second and similar use of the formula occurs in Canto V, lines 22–24 (p. 97), when Minos, the judge who assigns souls their appropriate sector of Hell, refuses to let Dante pass. The Word of Power is used on other occasions as well, as at the opening of Canto VII (lines 8–12) when Pluto bars the way. However, Virgil is impotent before the gates to the City of Dis (Canto VIII) and must await the arrival of a heavenly messenger, who rebukes the demons and lets Virgil and Dante enter Nether Hell (Canto IX). Only in Canto XXI, lines 79–84, does he again employ the magical formula, this time in an extended text: ' "Dost thou think, Belzecue, that I had bent/ My footsteps thus far hither", the master said,/ "Safe against all your harms, were I not sent/ By will divine, by fates propitious led?/ Let me pass on; 'tis willed in Heaven that I / Should guide another by this pathway dread" ' (p. 203).

[12] As is true of much of medieval European literature, this collection has been influ-enced by previous didactic tales. Likewise, it has influenced subsequent writers. Lope de Vega used the tale, 'Ejemplo XXV', 'De lo que conteció al conde de Provençia, cómmo fue librado de prisión por el consejo quel dió Saladín', in his *La pobreza estimada*, as did Calderón de la Barca in *El Conde Lucanor*. Quotations from don Juan Manuel are taken from the edition of *El Conde Lucanor* by José Manuel Fradejas Rueda. (Barcelona: Plaza & Janes, 1984, Biblioteca Crítica de Autores Españoles).

quería saber' (p. 83) The appropriate place is the magician's cavern, the infamous Cave of Toledo, into which they descend shortly thereafter:

> por una escalera de piedra muy bien labrada e fueron descendiendo por ella muy grand pieça, en guisa que paresçia que estaban tan baxos que passaba el río de Tajo por çima dellos. E desque fueron en cabo del escalera, fallaron una posada muy buena, e una cámara mucho apuesta que y había, ó estaban los libros el estudio en que había[n] de leer. (p. 84)

The descent into the cave here is not fraught with dire implications, as in classical accounts. Neither is Don Illán's cave presented as a hellish setting. It is impressive in its unsuspected location beneath his house, in its great depth, in its comfortable appointments. But is it only an enchantment, a magical illusion? At the end of the tale, having shown the dean his future in the Church and the ingratitude that he would show his host and teacher, Don Illán has everything return to the same setting as before the descent into the cave. He sends his would-be apprentice back to Santiago de Compostela, without satisfying his desire to advance in the knowledge of magic, but having taught him a lesson nonetheless, one that leaves him shamefaced and without response.[13] In the tale, Don Illán, the master of occult arts, emerges as a principled man and the setting in which he performs his magic as a nether intellectual haven away from the mendacity and hypocrisy of the overworld.[14] The reason behind this sympathetic portrayal is that natural magic was considered a science and its practitioners were generally thought of positively in the European Middle Ages, as in the case of Virgil.

Such a view was reflected in the *comedias* of the Siglo de Oro, in which magicians were not infrequently portrayed as wise men who brought benefits to society by the application of their esoteric knowledge to practical situations, in the resolution of political, religious or personal dilemmas. One such example is *La prueba de las promesas* (c. 1618), a *comedia de magia* with moral overtones by Juan Ruiz de Alarcón, which uses 'Exemplo XI' of Don Juan Manuel's book as its foundation, giving the classic tale an effective

---

[13] Where here the dean leaves without commenting on what he may have experienced – the panorama of his entire career in the Church – the narrator in Luis Gálvez de Montalvo's *El pastor de Fílida* (1582), where a similar situation develops in the cave of the magician Erión, declares: 'No se yo si esto fuere por fuerza de encantamiento o verdadero edificio' (p. 474). For the uses of the cave in the Spanish pastoral novel, see F. de Armas, art. cit., note 3.

[14] In Cervantes's *Los trabajos de Persiles y Segismunda* (see *Obras completas*, Madrid: Aguilar, 1962, pp. 1525–1714), the astrologer-magician Soldino inhabits a cave through which 'se descubrió el cielo luciente y claro y se vieron unos amenos y tendidos prados que entretenían la vista y alegraban las almas' (p. 1678) and within which he practices his art through intuitive knowledge: 'Aquí estoy, donde sin libros, con sola la esperiencia que he adquirido con el tiempo de mi soledad' (p. 1679).

adaptation for the stage.[15] The playwright keeps as his protagonist the self-same Don Illán who taught his apprentice a lesson through magic, but the Dean of Santiago de Compostela does not appear herein, his role having been assigned to Don Juan de Ribera, a gentleman in love with Doña Blanca, the daughter of the magus in this version. Similarly, none of the other characters proceed from Don Juan Manuel's tale. Also missing from the *comedia* is the setting of the Cave of Toledo in which 'Exemplo XI' is set. For reasons that the playwright did not divulge in the play, the magical illusion performed by Don Illán to test Don Juan de Ribera's character and love occurs in the study of the magician's house in Toledo; there is no descent into the depths of a cavern as in the medieval tale. The omission may be a reflection of the dramatist's fear that hearkening back to that topos might bring upon him the wrath of the Holy Office of the Inquisition, either in his native Mexico or in Spain. Nonetheless, the enchantment that makes Don Juan believe in his good fortune and that demonstrates how success can make an individual forgo his avowed love and solemn promises is as effective as that cast in the Cave of Toledo in the medieval version of the plot.

However, Toledo, once the most important gem captured in the early stages of the Reconquest, lost its privileged position and, as Feijoo notes, Toledo's cave passed from public lore and was replaced by Salamanca's seat of magical operations:

> La especie de la cueva de Toledo ya casi enteramente se ha desaparecido de el vulgo; mas la de la cueva de Salamanca echó hondas raíces en él, y aún se halla apoyada por algunos escritores demonógrafos . . . Lo que tiene aprehendido el vulgo es que en la cueva de Salamanca el demonio por sí mismo enseñaba las artes mágicas, admitiendo no más que siete discipulos por cada vez, con el pacto de quedarse con uno, aquel a quien tocase la suerte, destinado luego en cuerpo y alma a las penas infernales, y aquí entra la historia del Marqués de Villena, aquel mismo de quien creyó toda España ser un insigne mágico . . . De éste dicen que, habiéndose hecho consumado mágico en aquella escuela, entre los siete le tocó la suerte infeliz, pero él engañó al demonio, dejándole su sombra con la aprehensión de que era su cuerpo. (p. 377)

The Cave of Salamanca, then, provides the second major setting for magic in the Siglo de Oro theatre. One of the more fascinating historical figures associated with that site who became prominent in the works of the Golden Age was the Marqués Enrique de Villena, the Aragonese nobleman born about 1384. He published a study on astrology (*Tratado de Astrología*) and an

---

15 See José Fadrejas Lebrero, 'Un cuento de Don Juan Manuel y dos comedias del Siglo de Oro', *Revista de Literatura*, 8 (1955), 66–80. Don Juan Manuel's tale also provided the central character for José de Cañizares's *Don Juan de Espina en Milán* and the Duque de Rivas's *El desengaño en un sueño*.

influential treatise on the 'Evil Eye' (*Libro de aojamiento*, 1425), which
caused him to be branded a sorcerer and moved the Church to burn his library
upon his death in 1434. The confrontation between the Devil and a member
of the Spanish nobility could not help but be dramatic, and its appeal to the
major playwrights of this period is evident in the works they created on this
theme: Ruiz de Alarcón wrote the full-length *comedia de magia, La cueva de
Salamanca*, Calderón *Los encantos del Marqués de Villena* (presumed lost),
and Rojas Zorrilla *Lo que quería ver el Marqués de Villena*.[16] For his part,
Cervantes used the motif in a satirical manner in the *entremés* of feigned
magic *La cueva de Salamanca*, excluding the Marqués de Villena from the
cast of characters. Instead, a university student, claiming to have been robbed
on the road, takes the occasion of Pancracio's entrance to inveigh against the
poor shelter given him by his wife Leonarda in his absence and regrets not
being able to use the *ciencia* he learned in the Cave of Salamanca to better his
situation for fear of the Holy Inquisition. Then, as if suddenly inspired, he
changes his resolve and hoodwinks Pancracio into believing that the
Sacristan and the Barber who had secretly come to woo Leonarda and her
maid are in fact demons. The Student orders them to bring in a hamper of
food destined for the bacchanale which Pancracio's unexpected return had
squelched. Elated by the encounter with the pleasant 'demons', Pancracio
leads all into the dining room, there to feast and hear of the wonders of the
Cave of Salamanca.

While Cervantes eschews the cave and magicians as topics worthy of high
consideration in this *entremés*, Ruiz de Alarcón gives each his serious attention in *La cueva de Salamanca*, often demonstrating a philosophical knowledge of occult traditions as well as a sound grounding in Catholic doctrine,
which is generally blended into the dialogue without pedantry. The *comedia
de magia* features two magicians, the Marqués Enrique de Villena as a young
man (*galán*) and one Enrico, an old Frenchman who has devoted his life to
studying wherever he is, on this occasion at the University of Salamanca.[17]
The latter is the first magician encountered (Scene VI) when some gallants
fleeing the law after vengefully killing some of its officers are helped to 'dis-
appear' by the elderly magician, who later reveals to them his background as

[16] Lope de Vega's *Porfiar hasta morir* does not, as some critics would have it, deal
with the subject; Enrique de Villena is alluded to only as the master of the poet Macías,
protagonist of Lope's *comedia*, but he never appears.

[17] A large number of Ruiz de Alarcón's *comedias* are concerned with magic, astrology
(or other forms of divination), and various superstitions of an occult nature. Besides the
play under consideration, these include most notably *Quien mal anda en mal acaba, El
anticristo, La prueba de las promesas, El dueño de las estrellas*, and *La manganilla de
Melilla*. See A. Espantoso Foley, *Occult Arts and Doctrine in the Theater of Juan Ruiz de
Alarcón* (Geneva: Librairie Droz, 1972). The references to Ruiz de Alarcón's plays are
taken from the *Obras completas* (México, D.F. – Buenos Aires: Fondo de Cultura
Económica, 1957, pp. 383–470 and 742–845).

a pupil of Merlin in Italy, who taught him chiromancy, astrology and necro-
mancy. The young men decide to enlist among Enrico's apprentices. When
the Marqués de Villena makes his entrance (Scene XIII), he too divulges his
credentials as a magician, curiously coinciding with Enrico in that he studied
with Merlin as well, and in Italy. What will bring the two magicians together
is the Cave of Salamanca, as Villena reveals to Don Diego, one of the gallants
rescued by the old magician:

> La parlera fama allí
> ha dicho que hay una cueva
> encantada en Salamanca,
> que mil prodigios encierra;
> que una cabeza de bronce,
> sobre una cátedra puesta,
> la mágica sobrehumana
> en humana voz enseña
> que entran algunos a oírla,
> pero que de siete que entran
> los seis vuelven a salir,
> y el uno dentro se queda.   (pp. 410–411)

He has come to Salamanca in search of the cave and his investigation has
led him to Enrico's minute house:

> La cueva está en esta casa,
> si no mintieron las señas;
> pero que verdad dijeron
> muestra el hallaros en ella,
> porque, si no es por encanto,
> imposible es que cupieran
> dos hombres que son tan grandes
> en casa que es tan pequeña.   (p. 411)

Don Diego, now versed in the history of the cave as a result of his training,
interprets what the Marqués has heard as allegorical imagery and proceeds to
explicate that the bronze oracular head symbolizes Enrico:

> y porque excede a la naturaleza
> frágil del hombre su saber inmenso,
> se dice que es de bronce su cabeza.   (p. 412)

This is the sage who freely teaches his magical arts in his one-room
windowless house, wherein the sun can only enter through the door. This
setting is a metaphor for the famed cave. To Don Diego, what had seemed the
humblest of abodes has become glorious, as he explains to his beloved, Doña
Clara, in Scene XIV:

No ya humilde la llames, pues ha sido
oriente celestial de luz tan nueva.   (p. 415)

His description juxtaposes first the preconception of the image of the dark
cave and the revelation that it is a place that provides light – in other words,
enlightens with new knowledge; next, the nether locale of the cave and its
celestial dimension, both as orientation and as a reference to the East, from
whence esoteric knowledge comes; lastly, the old lore and the new wisdom.
Both Enrico's teachings and the place in which they are imparted are
presented in a positive manner. Yet, when in Act II, Scenes V and VI the
magicians are in Enrico's cave, there is no description given nor any indication in the dialogue of its aspects; the playwright, who had given detailed
stage directions in the previous scene for the magical tricks played on Don
Diego's servant, Zamudio, has nothing to say concerning the cave. As is the
case in Calderón's *El mágico prodigioso*, the omission leaves the reader (and
the director) to his or her own imaginings. But these are subvented by popular
belief, which is impacted upon by a long oral tradition concerning the aspect
of magical caves since antiquity, as well as by written descriptions.

Don Diego is the bridge between the supernatural inner realm of the cave
and the external world of reality. His interest in entering the grotto to learn
magic stems from practical needs in the world he inhabits: to secure his and
his fellow conspirators' freedom on the one hand, and to sexually possess
Doña Clara since he lacks the financial means to be an acceptable suitor for
her hand. When, in the last scene of Act II, Don Diego's passion for Doña
Clara drives him to attempt to take her illicitly, his action vitiates magic's
positive aspect, as William Blake has it: 'When thought is closed in caves,
then love shall show its root in deepest Hell.' Having forgone love for lust,
courtliness for dishonor, Don Diego has also perverted the esoteric knowledge provided by his study of natural magic when entering Doña Clara's
bedroom through the ruse of assuming the shape of the bronze statue he has
had delivered in a large wooden box. When Clara first opens the box, the
statue is indeed inside; but when she returns after an interruption and again
goes to it, Don Diego has taken the place of the statue through his magical
prowess. To her fear that he is an apparition and to her protestations about his
presence in her bedroom, he proclaims:

> Yo soy la verdad, señora;
> que el bronce fue la ilusión.
>   Por estar aquí Lucía
> aquella forma tomé . . .
> te escriví que si quisieras
> saber nuevas verdaderas
> de amor y misterios raros,
>   en pasando la mitad

de la noche, sola hablaras
con la estatua.   (pp. 442–43)

When he attempts to impose his nefarious will upon her, she fights him, exclaiming that his hellish magic cannot overcome her free will. But the act concludes ambiguously, without indication of whose will triumphs.[18]

The last act commences with Don Diego's declaration to Villena of his resolve to use the aid of Enrico's magic to free Don García, imprisoned as a result of the murderous conduct of the gallants early in the play. But the Marqués offers instead to intervene with the king. Yet, no doubt by magic, Don García's prison is open and unguarded when Don Diego arrives to rescue his friend. Having freed other prisoners as well, Don Diego magically sets fire to the prison records and orders the warden, who has been forced to provide them, to tell the Corregidor that he will burn as well if he does not pardon him and his cronies. Instead, the Corregidor imprisons Enrico.

The confrontation of the power of magic and the power of the state has come to a head. The king orders a convening of all concerned before a tribunal of theologians at the University of Salamanca, during which Enrico will present his arguments in favour of magic as a natural science. In Scene XV, the last in the play, the magician proceeds with great eloquence to delineate the positive aspects of his art, his long disquisition founded on a syllogistic statement:

> Propongo desta manera:
> toda ciencia natural
> es lícita, y usar della
> es permitido; la magia
> es natural: luego es buena.   (p. 461)

While his arguments ring true for many, the rebuttal by the learned Doctor is longer and more convincing; its efficacy relies on Church doctrines concerning the role of the Devil in human affairs. He posits that Satan uses those types of magic deemed licit, those founded on natural laws or on artifice, to his own ends:

> mas con capa de las dos
> disimulada y cubierta,
> el demonio entre los hombres
> introdujo la tercera.

---

[18] In Act II, Scene II Don Diego tells Zamudio what occurred thereafter, revealing that her resolve was so great and her laughter so mocking that he withdrew at light of dawn, ashamed of his actions. He does not employ the ways of magic again to obtain his desire. And yet, despite his behaviour, Doña Clara still loves him and when Don Diego inherits a title that guarantees his income, their marriage is assured.

He goes on to define this illicit form of magic:

> La diabólica se funda
> en el pacto y convenencia
> que con el demonio hizo
> el primer inventor della.   (p. 464)

Following the rhetorical practices of argumentation at the time, he proceeds to a series of proofs of his position, with the intent of influencing the thought and future conduct of his listeners:

> Pruébolo así: por virtud
> de palabras esta ciencia
> obra prodigios, que admira
> la misma naturaleza;
> luego los obra en virtud
> del pacto implícito en ellas,
> contraído del demonio.   (pp. 464–65)

At the end of the Spaniard's lengthy presentation on magic as diabolically inspired and implemented, the French magician Enrico admits that the arguments have convinced him of his error; he will abandon the practice of magic, acknowledging that it is evil and perverse.[19] Through the confrontations of these two philosophies – one pagan, the other Catholic – Ruiz de Alarcón brings to bear his knowledge of both and resolves the matter of magic's place in the scheme of Christian society. In a time and place in which the Church holds the dominant position, the debate is won by the learned Doctor, a member of the Order of Saint Dominic, which was in charge of the Holy Office of the Inquisition. Whatever the playwright's personal inclination, the *comedia*, as a public vehicle of entertainment and instruction, had to adhere to the tenets of the Church.

Curiously, in light of the importance of the cave, there is no mention of it in the Doctor's oration, nor does Enrico say anything in regard to the place where he conducted his magical operations. Is the expectation that, since Enrico will no longer function as a magician, the cave will simply be abandoned? Or will it cease to exist, as if it had been an illusion sustained by the magician? Or will it simply cease to be effective without its tenant, returning to its natural state? Or is it valid to assume that the cave will continue to be a

---

[19] Enrico's admission has another dimension, which is both religious and political: it represents the triumph of a learned churchman from Spain over a misguided magician from France; it is also the triumph of the Christian ethos under the aegis of Spain over the obscurantist practices of France that Enrico represents. Spain emerges as 'Defender of the Faith', a title the nation and its rulers cherished from Ferdinand and Isabel through the Counter-Reformation.

magical setting awaiting another who will enter its recesses to seek personal empowerment?

What of the famed Marqués de Villena? Will he be the next occupant of the nether premises? It is ironic that while Enrico is imprisoned and then made to defend his cause, the Marqués remains untouched by the authorities, no doubt untainted by his association with magic because of his social and political stature. Ruiz de Alarcón felt it necessary, at least, to address the issues of the cave and the Marqués for he has the actor who played that role step out of character to address the public:

> Y porque es justo
> que el noble auditorio sepa
> por qué dicen que engañó
> el gran Marqués de Villena
> al demonio con su sombra,
> oíd: la razón es ésta.
> Como el Marqués estudió
> esta diabólica ciencia,
> tuvo el infierno esperanza
> de su perdición eterna;
> mas murió tan santamente
> que engañó al demonio; y ésa
> es la causa porque dicen
> que con la sombra le deja.   (pp. 469–70)

It is strange that while the Marqués de Villena plays a secondary role, both as a character and as magician, and that he has been presented more as a man of reason than as a necromancer, Ruiz de Alarcón felt it necessary to address the lore regarding his involvement with the Devil in the practice of Goetic (i.e., diabolic) magic and his ultimate mockery of his master, although the latter is a mere accommodation to Christianity rather than a valid interpretation of the magical operation behind the popular belief. Having dealt with that matter, however inadequately, there is left only that of the cave and he does so with the *comedia's* final speech:

> Y con esto demos fin
> a la historia verdadera
> del principio, y fin que tuvo
> en Salamanca la cueva,
> conforme a las tradiciones
> más comunes y más ciertas.   (p. 470)

It should be noted that the lines 'principio, y fin que tuvo / en Salamanca la cueva' imply either that the *comedia* finalizes the 'historia verdadera' of the cave (meaning it will thereafter cease to be other than a natural setting), or that the play has delineated the purpose ('fin') or reason for the existence of the cave. Whether or not the cave will remain as a venue for magic is moot. In a sense, then, the dramatist has left an open ending while seeming to bring the play to closure.

Ruiz de Alarcón's *comedia de magia* is one of the two most representative plays on the Cave of Salamanca motif for it deals directly with the magical setting; it is also the most moral, since it presents the Marqués de Villena as one who has learned magic but not succumbed to the Devil's wiles, rather tricking the Old One as payment for his services.

The other play in which both the Cave of Salamanca and the Marqués de Villena are manifest is Francisco de Rojas Zorrilla's *Lo que quería ver el Marqués de Villena*. Well into the Jornada Primera the Marqués de Villena enters as the wooer of Serafina, who immediately defines him as:

> Unico sois en las ciencias,
> Dueño de las experiencias
> Sin la costa de los años.
> Sois en la escuela el mayor
> Sugeto della, esto sé.   (p. 323)

The term 'ciencias' covers not only the traditional academic areas but, as the conversation that follows indicates, also astrology. The Marqués has attained the superior status at the University of Salamanca because of his broad knowledge, having accomplished this 'sin la costa de los años', which implies both that he gained knowledge very quickly and that the years have not taken their toll, i.e., his aspect is that of a young man rather than of a man worn out by having toiled over a long time to gain intellectual distinction.

However, as in *La cueva de Salamanca*, the Marqués gives way to another figure associated with supernatural pursuits, the masterly magician Fileno. As with Villena's appreciation of Enrico in Ruiz de Alarcón's play, Rojas Zorrilla's Marqués is delighted by the encounter with the older magician at the *tertulia* in Serafina's house, a gathering of minds that she calls her *academia*. In the engaging discourse that ensues, Fileno posits as follows:

> Digo que la magia es
> La ciencia más necesaria,
> Más útil y más perfecta.
> [. . .]
> Digo que la magia es una
> Filosofía perfecta,
> Y es una ciencia evidente,
> Que si el hombre la alcanzara,
> Todo cuanto deseara
> Consiguiera facilmente.   (p. 323)

His brief *apologia* troubles the Marqués, who retorts: 'La magia está 'prohibida'. In reply Fileno, like Feijoo later on, divides the field into categories:

> La natural no lo está,
> La diabólica será
> La que lo es.

Villena immediately resolves to learn this science as well, saying: 'Eso es lo que yo he de ver'. It is this curiosity that the title of the play echoes and that Fileno will satisfy. As the act draws to an end, the magician invites the Marqués to visit his abode the next day.

Jornada Segunda, then, opens with Villena and his servant Zambapalo[20] at the cave of the magician Fileno. The *gracioso* is afraid even to knock on the door:

> Porque deste hombre me cuentan
> Que tiene en una redoma
> Un demonio.   (p. 328)

The idea of a demon in the flask seems outlandish to Villena but his servant's fear is based on his experience of having been in the cave, whose configuration he gives in great detail:

> Es larga como señor
> De otros tiempos; es estrecha,
> Como mercader de ahora,
> Y oscura como conciencia
> De letrado que recibe
> Cualquiera pleito que venga.
> Está en el zaguan la sala
> Y la alcoba en una pieza,
> Y aunque no hay cocina, es
> Todo el cuarto chimenea.
> Hay en aquesta espelunca,
> Alcázar de la Noruega,
> Un lampión, que desde el techo
> De un cordel de lazo cuelga,
> Que no alumbra tanto cuanto,
> Mancha á los que salen y entran;
> Sola la puerta es un ojo

---

[20] The servant is named after an old dance and the tune that accompanies it but the first part of his name (from the adjective *zambo*, *zamba*) also implies triply one who is knock-kneed, a half-breed (American Indian and Negro), and a variety of South American monkey. In the list of characters, the role is classified as 'estudiante gorrón', which identifies him as a sponge or hanger-on, as well as a libertine.

Por donde un rayo aún no entra.
[. . .]
No tienen polvo sus libros,
Pero como es la cueva
Tan húmeda, tiene lodo,
Ya podrida la madera.   (p. 328)

How Zambapalo got to enter the cave is not explained here but the impact of
that visit left an indelible impression, as his description makes clear. For the
Marqués, the aspect of the cave and its contents elicits not fear but admiration
for the man who has chosen to live in such humble surroundings despite his
magical powers. Nonetheless, Zambapalo appears to have cause to warn his
master not to cross the threshhold of the cave, both for the dangers it may
contain and for the negative association that doing so would create in anyone
who saw him. But the Marqués de Villena will not abandon his quest for
esoteric knowledge. The mystery of the magician and the cave lures him on
and he enters its confines as the door opens without human agency. A
moment later Villena and his servant are greeted by Fileno, accompanied by
Bermúdez, one of the competitors for a *cátedra* at the university. When he
leaves, Fileno promises his distinguished guest:

Hoy no ha de salir de aquí
Sin que antes experimente
Si hay magia [. . .]
        Pues pida
Imposibles vuecelencia,
Que á imposibles se prefiere
Mi ciencia. [. . .] . . .
Pues sin salir desta cueva
Ha de ver cuanto quisiere.   (p. 331)

Villena asks to see all that occurs that night in the city and Fileno obliges by
showing him the events in a mirror – a comic scene in which hungry university students steal a turkey, next a scene with Bermúdez hiding in a lady's
bedroom, then a scene in Serafina's house, and a return to Bermúdez as he
discovers the lady's secret and is in turn discovered – through which the
Marqués sees unravelled before him all the complex interpersonal relationships and learns that he is desired by two women. Yet, despite the magical
display he has witnessed, he is loath to admit that magic exists and the act
ends when Fileno waves his wand and the vision disappears.
    In the third and final act Fileno invites Zambapalo and the student Cetina
to visit his cave in the morning, adding as an explanation:

Mis discípulos no más
Son á los que yo convido.   (p. 341)

Thus it becomes clear that Zambapalo's first visit to the cave was in his role
as sorcerer's apprentice. Now he has been asked back, as Fileno explains:
'pero en llegando el día/ Veréis [. . .]/ *Lo que quería / Ver el marqués de
Villena.*' (p. 341). Fileno has convened his four disciples of the moment:
Zambapalo, Cetina, Bermúdez, and the Marqués de Villena. When they have
come to the cave, Fileno locks the door, tells them of the past master who
taught him magic, and informs them of his intent:

> Ese, cuando me enseñaba,
> Con condición me enseñó
> Esta ciencia no adquirida,
> Que aquí venís a aprender,
> Que su esclavo había de ser
> Como en la muerte en la vida,
> Y que de cuantos mi engaño
> Engañase la magia,
> Un discípulo le había
> De dar por feudo cada año,
> Y como faltar no puede
> Este paso [. . .]
> Cada año se ha de sortear
> Uno que conmigo quede;
> Todos suertes han echado
> Para esta satisfacion;
> Trece discípulos son
> Los que en trece años le he dado;
> Y así, si hoy os conformáis
> A obedecer lo que os digo,
> Uno de los cuatro que aquí estaís.   (p. 345)

When the four disciples voice their disbelief at his diabolic plan, since
none had made a pact, the magician voices his last dictum:

> Aqui ha de quedarse uno
> O los cuatro han de quedar.   (p. 345)

Resigned to the magician's power, each of the four selects a slip of paper from
a pot proferred by Fileno. The one who selects the unmarked piece will be the
loser. And that lot falls to the Marqués de Villena. Nobly, Bermúdez wants to
revoke the decision but Villena insists on its execution. Unknown to all, he
has formed a plan. He grabs Zambapalo before he can exit with the other two
and speaks his intent:

> El sol he de escurecer,
> No me he de apartar de aquí:
> A la noche semejante,

> Vario el dia quedará;
> Ninguno conocerá
> Propio ni ajeno semblante.
> [. . .]
> Pues ahí queda mi sombra.   (p. 346)

Suddenly, all is dark. And when Fileno attempts to grab the Marqués, his arms enfold Zambapalo instead. The Marqués de Villena has disappeared. He has left behind his 'shadow,' his servant, who proclaims in recognition, as if of a great truth: 'En efeto, los criados/ Son sombra de los señores' (346). Unlike the lame explanation in Ruiz de Alarcón's *La cueva de Salamanca*, the motif of the shadow rings true here as a feasible substitution in magical terms. The self-assurance that Fileno had demonstrated throughout now abandons the magician as he comes to his own recognition of what his failure portends when, as the stage direction indicates, he sees that '(salen por debajo de la tierra diferentes animales con luces)'. He cries out in despair at the terrible fate that awaits him:

> ¡Ay, el Marqués me engañó!
> Vive mi pena inmortal,
> Con la magia natural
> La diabólica burló.
> [. . .]
> Y al espíritu también
> Que me gobierna ha burlado.   (p. 346)

Fully cognizant that he has failed to keep his diabolical vow, Fileno resigns himself to his damnation. There is no soul searching, as with Marlowe's Faust, no hedging one's bets by calling for confession, as in Celestina's case. Momentarily, as the stage direction has it '(*Húndese debajo de la tierra*)', he is swallowed by the earth, going into depths beyond those of any cave. His descent is into Hell for, in exclaiming the word 'Infierno' as he falls, the entire magical context of the *comedia* leading up to his demise takes on the aspect of the Devil's work. Except for a few exclamations of the word 'Diablo' by the *gracioso*, Satan had been excluded from the proceedings, but now, with Fileno's final utterance, the purveyor of Goetic magic is identified as the Devil and, in that context, Fileno's damnation to Hell is established.

The aftermath of this theatrical *desenlace* is the promised reappearance of the Marqués at Serafina's house, where others have gathered at his earlier behest. The event is not anticlimactic for there are still concerns and problems to be resolved. To the many questions that the company pose, the Marqués replies:

> Burlé al mágico Fileno,
> Porque tiene tanta fuerza
> La natural magia, que

La demoniaca mesma
Quedó burlada con ser
Espíritu quien la enseña.   (p. 346)

The spirit, of course, is the Devil. In mocking his servant Fileno the Marqués has mocked the master as well. But that was not the reason for his quest. Finally, the Marqués de Villena reveals to them through individual disclosures what it is that he wants to see: the truth. As each masquerader is uncovered, each sentiment expressed, each desire made manifest, it becomes clear that illusion disguised in falsehood or in courtly manners cannot be rewarded; just as the falsehood of the magician Fileno came to an end, so too the play ends with none of the principals achieving their convoluted goals. Love does not triumph in the end for, as demonstrated in this second *desenlace*, it was perverted by all kinds of subterfuge. Even the Marqués de Villena partakes of the general disillusionment for he has indeed seen the truth that he wanted to see and hereafter must sublimate both sexual and intellectual expectations.

The topos of the cave and the magician in the plays of the Siglo de Oro, foreshadowed in Spanish literature in Don Juan Manuel's *exemplum,* attained its frequency in the *comedias* because it satisfied an intellectual need in the dramatist and addressed an intuitive curiosity in his public – the former saw the motif as an entertaining, instructive way to delve into human psychology by assessing the desire for power and control through supernatural means, while the latter was awed by the chthonic setting and the magical occurrences within and without its confines. As the Church became increasingly more powerful, both in spiritual and political terms, it interpreted as heterodox and therefore sinful all attempts at empowerment or knowledge outside what Christianity promoted as acceptable. Magic and magicians became associated with the Devil, as had witchcraft and witches, and the caves which they used were seen as malevolent places, without regard to the type of magic practiced or its ends. The danger of eternal damnation heightened the appeal of cave and magician, and this was exploited by the dramatists of the period, ever within the parameters of the Church.

In a Christian context then, the crucial element in *comedias de magia* became the struggle between good and evil, whose result for human beings could be salvation (à la Cipriano) or damnation (à la Fileno).[21] In Calderón to

---

[21] The Church faced many interpretations of the struggle; chief among them in the Middle Ages was that promoted by the Manicheans, followers of the third century Persian prophet Mani (or Manes) who proclaimed himself a new incarnation of Jesus Christ. Among his doctrines was that of the cosmic battle between the God of Light and the Lord of Darkness; the former was the Gnostic Supreme Being, the latter was the Demiurge, identified with the Old Testament Yahweh. Mani and other Gnostics held that the Jewish and Christian deity was evil: 'It is the Prince of Darkness who spoke with Moses, the Jews, and their priests. Thus the Christians, the Jews and the Pagans are involved in the same

a large degree and in Rojas Zorrilla to a lesser, the religious aspect of the agon was the climactic moment: the decision of the individual to persist in his nefarious ways or to use his *albedrío* to reclaim his Christian status (to emerge from the cave as it were). In the plays by Cervantes and Ruiz de Alarcón the focus is different, a satirical view on people's gullibity in the case of the first without recourse to magic or religion, and a largely secular treatment, although with an intellectually motivated conversion to the 'right path', by the second. The plays discussed here are exemplary of these several dimensions of the theme.

error when they worship this god.' See Francis Legge, *Forerunners and Rivals of Christianity*, 2 vols (New York: University Books, 1964), vol. 2, p. 239. In an earlier context, also out of Persia, Mithraism saw the struggle as between the divine twins Ahura Mazda, the solar deity, and Ahriman, deity of darkness.

History and Opposition Drama in Franco's Spain

JOHN LYON

One of the most interesting responses of opposition dramatists to the Franco regime was the recourse to historical subject-matter. The theatrical trend towards a thoughtful and critical approach to national history began in 1958 with Buero Vallejo's *Un soñador para un pueblo* and Rodríguez Méndez's less well-known *Vagones de madera*.[1] A continuous, though somewhat uneven, flow of historical plays followed throughout the 1960s. Rodríguez Méndez was undoubtedly the most prolific source with, amongst other titles, *El vano ayer* (1963), *El círculo de tiza de Cartagena* (1964), *La mano negra* (1965) and *Bodas que fueron famosas del Pingajo y la Fandanga* (1965). Buero Vallejo produced an immediate follow-up to his first history play with *Las Meninas* in 1960, but then abandoned the genre until he wrote *El sueño de la razón* ten years later. Other names began to emerge in this decade: Ricardo López Aranda with *Yo, Martín Lutero*, a work on Luther with clear Spanish overtones, in 1963,[2] and Agustín Gómez-Arcos with *Diálogos de la herejía* in 1964. Alfonso Sastre contributed *La sangre y la ceniza* in 1965 and *Crónicas romanas* in 1968. Alberto Miralles also staged his *Cátaro Colón* (on the life of Christopher Columbus) in 1968. It was not until the 1970s, when the crumbling Francoist regime was being forced into greater liberalization, that the trickle became a stream and the succession of historical plays took on the collective character of a genre or movement. Rodríguez Méndez continued his output with *Historia de unos cuantos* (1971) and *Flor de otoño* (1972), and Sastre with *El camarada oscuro* (1972). Other established playwrights of the opposition, like José Martín Recuerda and Carlos Muñiz, turned their attention to historical material, Recuerda with *Las arrecogías del beaterio de Santa María Egipciaca* and *El engañao*, written in 1970 and 1972 respectively, and Muñiz with *Tragicomedia del serenísimo príncipe don Carlos* in 1972. Of a younger generation, Antonio Gala produced *Anillos para una dama* (1973) and *Las cítaras colgadas de los*

---

[1] *Vagones de madera*, written in 1958, was staged in Barcelona in December 1959 and published in *Primer Acto*, 45 (1963).

[2] *Yo, Martín Lutero* has never been performed and did not appear in print until 1984 (Madrid: La Avispa).

árboles (1974) and Ana Diosdado *Los comuneros* also in 1974. Even after
Franco's death in 1975 the flow of historical works showed no signs of
abating. Domingo Miras emerged as a significant new writer of historically
based theatre with *De San Pascual a San Gil* (1975), *La venta del ahorcado*
(1976), *Las brujas de Barahona* (1977) and *Las alumbradas de la
Encarnación Benita* (1979). Buero Vallejo added a further title to his cycle of
history plays, *La detonación*, in 1977. A couple of chronicle plays on the
previously taboo subject of nineteenth-century working-class politics, *Como
reses* by Luis Matilla and Jerónimo López Mozo and *Pablo Iglesias* by Lauro
Olmo, appeared in 1978 and 1984.

What were the reasons behind this resurgence of historical drama among
opposition dramatists? It would perhaps be tempting to see the phenomenon
as a response to censorship, were it not for the continued presence of historical subject-matter in plays written during the *Transición* and well into the
period of democracy. In fact a whole new generation of playwrights continued to cultivate the genre. Works by Ignacio Amestoy, Concha Romero,
Fernando Martín Iniesta, Carmen Resino and Eduardo Galán continue, well
into the 1990s, to testify to the importance of historical truth as a basis for
contemporary society. Buero Vallejo has strongly – and repeatedly – denied
that the recourse to history has anything to do with simply avoiding censorship.[3] This is not a denial of any intention to allude to the present via a historical situation. Indeed, Buero argues that historical drama can – and should –
illuminate the present, but only on the basis of a past situation explored with
intellectual honesty and rigour, not one used merely as a pretext.

The claim that the movement came mainly as a critical reaction to a traditional and more conformist school of playwriting has, I believe, been over-
stated.[4] The older generation of Eduardo Marquina and Francisco Villaespesa
would hardly have been uppermost in the minds of most oppostion dramatists
under Franco, and those of their contemporaries who practised right-wing,
imperialist or conformist drama – Pemán, Luca de Tena, Calvo Sotelo –
hardly presented a body of work worthy of such massive opposition. For the
most part, government policy was to depoliticize entertainment, and establishment dramatists were content to express their conformity by bland
assumption rather than argument. Even a work like Luca de Tena's *¿Dónde
vas, Alfonso XII?*, frequently cited as an example of Francoist historical
drama, concentrates almost entirely on the 'estampas románticas' of the love

---

[3]   See his article 'Acerca del drama histórico', *Primer Acto*, 187 (1980–81), 19, and
his introduction to Domingo Miras, *Las alumbradas de la Encarnación Benita* (Madrid:
La Avispa), pp. 6–7.
[4]   See Martha T. Halsey, 'Dramatic Patterns in Three History Plays of Contemporary
Spain', *Hispania*, 71 (1988), 20 and 'The Politics of History: Images of Spain on the Stage
of the 1970s' in M. T. Halsey and P. Zatlin, eds, *The Contemporary Spanish Theater* (New
York: University Press of America, 1988), p. 93.

affair between Alfonso and Mercedes de Orléans. Apart from caricaturing the idea of the Republic and affirming that the monarchy is the natural, God-given form of government, the play scrupulously avoids any serious moral, social or political issues. Opposition dramatists were certainly reacting to an 'official' version of national history, but it was not one which had a significant presence in the theatre. Official history as propagated by Francoism found its expression in the state-controlled press, radio and television, in political speeches and, above all, in school textbooks.

Francoist ideology was inseparable from a certain view of Spain's imperial past and its destiny as a nation. The view of Spain as a great imperial nation chosen by God to spread the truth of Catholicism throughout the world (though regrettably diverted from this destiny by corrupt foreign influences) was central to the political philosophy of Francoism because it constituted the justification for its seizure of power. It was an article of faith that the grandeur of the sixteenth and seventeenth centuries, in which Spain had carried the true religion to the New World, was destined to be restored as the country's natural birthright. Franco saw himself, and was seen by his supporters, as leading a crusade for the recovery of Spain's traditional values and political hegemony in Europe and Latin America. To this end it was regarded as justifiable to rearrange the facts of history in support of these values and principles. In his prologue to Andrés Sopeña Monsalve's *El florido pensil*,[5] Gregorio Cámara Villar quotes the words of a history professor from Valencia university:

> El maestro ha de proceder de modo apriorístico, seleccionando hechos no sólo en función de su valor histórico absoluto, sino de su valor para la formación en este sentido patriótico nacional que preconizamos. Ha de hacer resaltar de modo interesado los hechos que muestran los valores de la raza, silenciando otros que o no la ennoblecen o pueden ser interpretados torcidamente. Se trata, repito, de hacer españoles que sientan la historia y no de formar hombres que conozcan plenamente la historia. (p. 17)

El florido pensil provides a wealth of examples from school textbooks of the time, particularly from the 1940s and early 1950s, of this kind of indoctrination and social engineering.

The impetus for this imperialist ideology was initially provided by the rise of European fascism, although the driving force behind the providential view of Spanish history was always Catholic traditionalism. Spain was seen as a nation whose Christian identity had been forged in seven centuries of struggle or 'Reconquest' against Islam, and whose unity had been sealed by the Catholic Monarchs, Fernando and Isabel. According to this version, the

---

[5]   Andrés Sopeña Monsalve, *El florido pensil: memoria de la escuela nacional católica* (Barcelona: Grijalbo, 1994).

nation had fulfilled its universal destiny during the imperial period when it took Christianity and civilization to the territories of Latin America. The process of expansion was seen as the natural continuation of the unification phase. Just as the reconquest of Spain, its unification and imperial expansion were seen as Catholic-driven projects faithfully carried out, so the process of national decline was explained by a departure from Catholic principles and a reduction of Church influence. The decline of empire had begun in the late seventeenth and eighteenth centuries, principally owing to foreign ideas and influences (the Bourbon monarchy) which had corrupted the integrity of the state. A combination of secular reform and the alien cult of rationalism had undermined the authority of the Catholic Church.[6] The nineteenth century had witnessed the collapse of most of the overseas territories, culminating in the loss of the last shreds of empire in 1898. For traditionalist ideologues, the political developments at home – the rise of liberalism and republicanism – represented a series of aberrations that 'should not have existed', since they were contrary to the model of what they imagined to be the essential qualities of the Hispanic race.[7] The early twentieth century had accelerated the process of decline with the rise of socialism and anarchism. The second Republic of 1931, according to this view, had been the last straw, attacking the very foundations of religion, state and all traditional values. Franco's military rebellion was portrayed as a holy war to re-establish those values, to save Spain from the heresy of deviant philosophies, to reunite the country under the Catholic banner and to rediscover its original essence and historical destiny.[8]

The contemporary problem and its solution were seen as an exact repetition of the situation confronting the Catholic Monarchs. The same logic was applied to both. Rodríguez Puértolas in his book *Literatura fascista española* quotes numerous passages from José Antonio Primo de Rivera, Ernesto Giménez Caballero, José María de Areilza, Dionisio Ridruejo and Antonio Tovar affirming the need to reimpose strong central authority in order to

[6]   See the *Enciclopedia Álvarez: Tercer Grado* (Madrid, 1997), pp. 471–73. This reprint of a 1966 school textbook became an immediate best-seller.

[7]   See the article by Pérez Ledesma, in *El País* (núm. extraordinario), 20 Nov. 1996, who quotes from Franco's speech in Baracaldo on 21 June 1950: 'El siglo 19, que nosotros hubiéramos querido borrar de nuestra historia, es la negación del espíritu español'.

[8]   Julio Rodríguez Puértolas in his *Literatura fascista española*, vol. 1 (Madrid: Akal, 1986) quotes a passage from Antonio Tovar: 'Los españoles tenemos la fortuna de pertenecer a un pueblo hecho para mandar . . . y nuestro deber es, entonces, potenciar en lo actual toda nuestra historia, actualizarla, movilizarla agresivamente, con estilo ofensivo y de acción directa . . . Estamos como al principio del reinado de los Reyes Católicos y todo ha de ser hecho de nuevo' (p. 344). The same conviction that Spain's future lay in the past is echoed in a passage from Feliciano Cereceda quoted in *El florido pensil*: 'Nuestro pasado nos aguarda para crear el porvenir. El porvenir que habíamos perdido lo hemos vuelto a encontrar en el pasado. ¡El porvenir de España unido después de tres siglos al destino del pasado!' (p. 192).

overcome internal divisions, achieve unity and expand the nation's influence. The striking feature of this vision is its denial of the historical process. It is predicated on an essentially unchanging national identity, an unquestionable religious faith and an indisputable destiny. The social price for being the 'chosen people' and enjoying a privileged destiny was subjection to a narrow and inflexible concept of Spanishness, conformity to a single notion of racial, religious and ideological purity, the idea of unity as uniformity.[9] The educational philosophy of the Republic was totally dismantled. The central tenets of a liberal education – stimulating the critical faculties, awakening the imagination, encouraging intellectual curiosity – were put into reverse. The watchwords became respect for, and submission to authority and the 'natural' social hierarchy. As late as 1966, the *Enciclopedia Álvarez*, in its section on 'formación político-social', inculcated the idea that all forms of human co-operation depend on a hierarchical structure of authority. In the family, the workplace, the community, society and the state, order, stability and unity would be inconceivable without hierarchy and central authority (pp. 592–603).

For most opposition dramatists, their work was a bid to reclaim their history, which had been hijacked by nationalist ideology.[10] Far from being a pretext or a disguise, history was at the heart of the debate. They were making a genuine attempt to set the record straight and to rescue their national heritage from what they saw as grotesque and politically-motivated distortions. In a recent debate on the teaching of history in schools, Antonio Muñoz Molina recalls his experience during the dictatorship:

Desde 1939 se decretó no sólo la amnesia acerca de lo que habían sido la República y la guerra, sino también la falsificación de todo el pasado anterior, a fin de ajustarlo a las directrices ideológicas de la derecha más ignorante y cerril . . . No se trata de que nos contaran una historia fascista en vez de una historia progresista: era, simplemente, que nos estaban mintiendo, que nos ocultaban otra historia verdadera y plural, haciéndonos creer que la única tradición española posible era la reaccionaria. Las Comunidades de Castilla, la Ilustración, las Cortes de Cádiz, la revolución de 1868, el progreso de las ideas krausistas, del socialismo y del federalismo, la II República, todo fue borrado, abolido, negado, con la

[9]   Manuel García Morente in his *Ser y vida del caballero cristiano* (Madrid, 1943) asserts: 'España es el único país de la Tierra en donde ser cristiano y ser español es una y la misma cosa, porque España es el único país de la Historia donde no puede haber ni ha habido ni hay diferencia alguna entre la constitución moral y religiosa y la constitución histórica nacional . . . No se puede ser español y no ser católico, porque si no se es católico, no se puede ser español' (quoted by Rodríguez Puértolas, *Literatura fascista española*, vol. 2, pp. 993–94).

[10]   See Michael Thompson's introduction to his edition of Buero Vallejo's *Un soñador para un pueblo* (Warminster: Aris and Phillips, 1993), pp. 3–6 for a concise summary of the background and general issues involved.

misma crueldad radical con que se negó la condición y hasta la
nacionalidad española a una muchedumbre de vencidos.[11]

This response is implicitly echoed in the majority of historical works
written by dramatists opposed to the Franco regime. In addition to the statement of alternative views and interpretations, they generally contain an
implied defence of the basic principles of historiography: honesty, the acceptance of ambiguity and obscurity where they exist, the emphasis on history as
process and change. They also present a challenge to Francoist social values
by the implied denial of monolithic uniformity and unquestionable authority,
and the recognition of social and religious pluralism.

    In their treatment of history, opposition dramatists responded at different
levels. Some concentrated on the destruction of official mythology – generally referred to as 'desmitificación' – either in naturalistic terms or by means
of expressionist satire. Others presented alternative interpretations of
national history (without the element of 'desmitificación'), alternative viewpoints, alternative heroes. Others involved the contemporary situation in their
portrayal of the past, whether by simple analogy or by revealing the past as
the roots of the present. Although I propose to deal with these categories
separately, for the convenience of analysis, it should be stated at the outset
that they are seldom clear-cut and separate in individual cases.

    In a social atmosphere saturated with heroic rhetoric, it is hardly
surprising that one of the commonest responses of the opposition was a desire
to discredit the imperialist mythology, particularly with reference to the
sixteenth and seventeenth centuries. The gap between myth and reality in
Spain's Golden Age forms the basis of Martín Recuerda's *El engañao* and
Antonio Gala's *Las cítaras colgadas de los árboles*.[12] Both these plays
explore the contradiction between external conquest and expansion, and
internal poverty and stagnation. Martín Recuerda's declared purpose was to
show the reverse side of the coin of Spanish imperialism: 'la otra cara del
Imperio no reflejada en la historiografía oficial y sí en la tradición literaria
española. Es, en definitiva, el grito de un pueblo por encima de la política
como ejercicio del poder y de la religión como política.'[13] Set in the 1540s, *El
engañao* depicts the efforts of Juan de Dios to establish a hospital for the
victims of Philip II's imperial wars and the opposition he encounters from the
civil and religious authorities. Martín Recuerda mounts a three-pronged
attack to discredit a false concept of imperial glory, a false concept of religion and a false concept of unity. He contrasts Philip II's grandiose political

---

[11] 'La historia y el olvido', *El País*, 9 Nov. 1997.

[12] The statement also applies to *Las Meninas*, but Buero Vallejo's work will be
discussed later.

[13] José Martín Recuerda, *Génesis de 'El engañao': versión dramática de la otra cara
del Imperio* (Salamanca: Ediciones Universidad de Salamanca, 1979), p. 29.

dream of a universal Catholic empire with the disastrous impact of his holy wars on the lives of the people. Behind the imposing façade of imperial conquest lies the reality of a deluded, impoverished and defeated population. He also contrasts two concepts of religion: a political one, measured in terms of territorial gains and numbers of alleged converts, and one based on truth, love and concern for individual human beings. The Church stands accused of pacting with the ambition of kings, while neglecting the suffering of those who are used to further those ambitions. The 'engañados' of the title are those victims of the alliance between Church and State who have been deceived into fighting and suffering for a country which ignores and despises them. Finally, *El engañao* juxtaposes conflicting models of community and society. One is an idea of community based on enforced compliance with a single doctrine, represented by the policies of king and court towards Spain and its overseas territories. The other is an idea of a diverse and plural society unified on the basis of free moral choice, represented by the hospital community of Juan de Dios.

Both *El engañao* and *Las cítaras* constitute an attack on the Francoist view of empire as the achievement of historical, geographical, spiritual and theological unity.[14] Gala's play condemns it as an irresponsible pursuit of gold and glory which destroyed native cultures and left the nation destitute and divided at its centre. Gala concentrates on the aspects of religious bigotry and racial intolerance. He focuses on an individual experience of history, a story of doomed love between a converted Jewess, Olalla, and Lázaro, a political subversive and ex-*comunero* recently returned from South America, who struggle against monumental social and religious prejudice. The title of the play refers to Psalm 137, in which the captive Israelites hang their harps on the willow trees because they cannot bring themselves to play or sing in an alien land. The 'Israelites' of Gala's play are not just the remaining Jews in sixteenth-century Spain, but all those whose beliefs – religious and political – place them outside the orthodoxy of a regime that rules by fear. *Las cítaras* clearly denies the myth of unity which is no more than an imposed religious, racial and political uniformity. For Gala, real unity can only come with the acceptance of the truth of history and the tolerance of diversity.[15]

The idea of 'demythification' was not limited to historical episodes and periods, in which the reality did not match up to the heroic myth. It also applied to the principles and motivations behind historical action. This is the

---

[14] For José Antonio Primo de Rivera, the achievement of empire was synonymous with the achievement of unity: 'Pronto se realizará el Imperio español, que es la unidad histórica, física, espiritual y teológica' (*Obras*, ed. Agustín del Río Cisneros [Madrid, 1970], pp. 422–23).

[15] In his prologue the author implies a relationship between the two attitudes: 'tengo la seguridad de que el español debe convivir sinceramente con su pasado para poder después convivir con su prójimo'.

case of *Cátaro Colón* by Alberto Miralles, for instance, which exposes some of the less admirable motivations – greed, ambition, calculated self-interest and political expediency – behind the discovery of the New World and the power struggle which ensued between Columbus and the Catholic Monarchs. Perhaps more interesting are the plays which explore, not so much hidden ulterior motives, as the tragicomic consequences of adherence to 'official' religious motives. Good examples of this are provided by Muñiz's *Tragicomedia del serenísimo príncipe don Carlos* and Miras's *Las alumbradas de la Encarnación Benita*. It is true that these works reveal – as does the historical reality – a very bizarre and distorted sense of religion. Of greater significance, however, is the fact that this distortion of the religious principle is seen as the only valid criterion, unchangeable and unchallenge-able. From this perception flow all the sophistry, self-deception and, in one case, collective hysteria that ensue.

Muñiz's *Tragicomedia* hinges on the relationship between Philip II and his demented son, Prince Carlos, and, more specifically, on the question of succession to the throne. The author's depiction of the king emphasizes the latter's obsession with religious purity and anatomical relics, which he collects with the single-minded devotion of a stamp collector, and on which he bases not only his religious faith but also his political and military deci-sions.[16] In comparison with the grotesque antics of his son, Philip's supersti-tious fanaticism has a sombre consistency. His is a madness which interprets everything in the light of an all-consuming religious obsession. But it is not his alone. The text constantly emphasizes the association between religious and secular power. Religious orthodoxy and the national interest, theology and the law, heresy and treason are all identified and indistinguishable. Equally, Philip's religious obsession and his passionate persecution of heresy become identified in his own mind with the defence of his political power and the perpetuation of his own line. For this reason, his decision to imprison and finally assassinate the unfortunate Carlos is based on what he interprets as a simultaneous threat to the faith, the nation and his own survival in power. He abdicates all personal responsibility for his action, which, in his mind, becomes an inevitable consequence of the violation of a divine principle and hence the 'will of God' (p. 137).

Like the *Tragicomedia*, *Las alumbradas de la Encarnación Benita*, written some four years after Franco's death, reveals the superstition and hysteria which lie behind the august façade of Church and State in imperial Spain. Miras is not concerned with the heresy of the *alumbrados* as such,[17] but with the process of self-delusion and collective hysteria within the convent's community, which begins with the feverish imagination of a simple-minded

---

[16] *Tragicomedia del serenísimo príncipe don Carlos* (Madrid: Preyson, 1984), p. 58.
[17] A heresy which affirmed that states of such perfection could be achieved through prayer alone that even the most licentious acts could be committed without sin.

nun and later extends into the social and political sphere. The play traces a series of developments arising from the convent's need to generate wealth and prestige and the fortuitous coincidence of Sor Luisa María witnessing an act of levitation by the prioress. This produces a convoluted process of self-delusion, casuistry and rationalization (fuelled, amongst other factors, by the envy and ruthless ambition of Sor Anastasia and the complicity of the prioress, Doña Teresa), which culminates in a situation in which the nuns are said to be possessed by devils who are nevertheless acting on the command of God. Once the idea of demonic possession with God's authority has been accepted, the process acquires its own momentum. The secular authorities become involved. The Count-Duke Olivares, Philip IV's Minister, is persuaded by the demons, speaking through the nuns, to make love to his wife in front of the high altar in order to engender an heir. The government's foreign policy in Flanders is formed around certain signs and portents indicated by the alleged demons. On the king's orders, a series of convents are founded throughout the Holy Roman Empire because they have been recommended by the head demon 'Peregrino Raro'. The whole sequence of events is driven by a kind of insane logic, in which every piece of apparently conflicting evidence is rationalized away so as not to contradict the original religious premises, which no one – not even the king – dares question. Behind it all lies the fear of the Inquisition with its awesome power. It is this repressive fear of questioning, or appearing to question, the unquestionable that produces the neuroses and the absurdly contradictory situations of the action.

There was a significant number of dramatists who, instead of debunking aspects and figures of the past lionized by the regime, chose to highlight historical periods, viewpoints of marginalized groups and communities, or protagonists which official history had either denigrated or ignored.

Buero Vallejo's *Un soñador para un pueblo* is a highly unusual case of a play which to some degree vindicates the Enlightenment policies of Charles III and his Italian minister, Esquilache, branded as alien to the Spanish tradition by Francoist historians. As we shall see later, this adjustment of the historical record was not Buero's sole or even principal objective. Nor did his treatment of the material imply a defence of absolutism or the principle of reform from above ('sin el pueblo'), as several of his progressive critics maintained. Buero's central preoccupation was the problem – unresolved in 1766 and still seeking a solution in 1958 – of the *pueblo*'s involvement in the power process. It is this question of the relationship between power and the *pueblo* which underlies most of the plays written about the nineteenth century. These include more or less all the more important plays of Rodríguez Méndez during the 1960s and early 1970s, Buero Vallejo's *El sueño de la razón* and *La detonación*, the collective creation of *El Fernando*, involving eight writers, performed by the university theatre of Murcia in 1972, Martín Recuerda's *Las arrecogías del beaterio de Santa María Egipciaca*, and *De San Pascual a San Gil* by Domingo Miras. The writers focus on the the polit-

ical and social events emanating from the War of Independence: the crisis of
the monarchy, usually involving the notoriously repressive Fernando VII, the
conflict of the 'Two Spains', the clash between the supporters of absolute
monarchy and liberalism. All these developments relate, directly or indi-
rectly, to the emergence of the *pueblo* as a force in Spanish history. That
emergence is viewed with different degrees of political and social optimism.
Domingo Miras in *De San Pascual a San Gil*, despite the farcical treatment,
offers a bleakly tragic vision of the *pueblo* purely as the victims of history,
oppressed by traditionalist self-interest and deserted by the commercial
opportunism of the progressives. Others, like Matilla and López Mozo in
Como reses and Lauro Olmo in *Pablo Iglesias*, writing in the post-censorship
era, are more interested in the *pueblo* as a rising working class and a political
resistance to the status quo.

Rodríguez Méndez's plays are characterized, not so much by an intellectual reassessment of the past, as by a radical change of viewpoint. This is a
vision of history as seen by its victims, the viewpoint of the anonymous
pueblo reacting – uncomprehendingly and inarticulately – to the larger
historical events and situations which affect their lives. His characters are
generally incapable of rationalizing the forces acting upon them or even of
seeing their own status as victims with any degree of clarity. There is no
explicit debunking of official history in these works, but the unheroic viewpoint stands in calculated contrast to the heroic mythology.[18] Set in the Restoration period between the first and second Republics, Rodríguez Méndez's
plays reflect the largely unconscious – and doomed – struggle of a people to
retain its culture and identity against the political and religious forces which
exploit or manipulate it, alienate it from power, fragment or undermine its
values. A large portion of his output is the chronicle of a people's disintegra-
tion, of which the Franco dictatorship is simply a continuation. It is worth
noting that the author's adoption of the popular viewpoint by no means
implies support for a left-wing political stance. Of all opposition dramatists
Rodríguez Méndez is perhaps the least political. He is equally sceptical of all
politicians and sees the *pueblo* as the victims of both the authoritarian right
and the revolutionary left.[19]

Rodríguez Méndez is well aware of the dangers of establishing an alternative mythology by idealizing or sentimentalizing the *pueblo*. He avoids
portraying them simply as the blameless victims of circumstances. They are
also victims of their own fatalism, the inability to identify their collective

---

[18] To an interviewer who suggested that this viewpoint might be somewhat limited, he
replied: 'Todo lo limitado que quieras, pero a través de ella, se puede desmentir la historia
oficial' (Moisés Pérez Coterillo, 'Conversación impertinente con J. M. Rodríguez Méndez
en vísperas de estreno', *Blanco y Negro*, 15–21 (Nov. 1978), p. 74).

[19] *El círculo de tiza de Cartagena* provides a good example of the *pueblo* torn
between both sides of the political divide.

interests, and lack of solidarity. The conscripts in *Vagones de madera*, being transported like cattle to the war in Morocco, are their own worst enemy. Their capacity to resist the official propaganda which justifies the war and exploits them is undermined by a latent tendency to divisiveness, self-assertion and an inability to communicate. The hired labourers on an Andalusian estate in *La mano negra* (set in 1911) endure starvation wages, physical abuse and a routine of daily prayers, yet seem unaware of the structures of inherited wealth, the Church and the forces of order which keep them in subjection. Even in a play like *Bodas que fueron famosas del Pingajo y la Fandanga*, in which we see a small, albeit doomed, gesture of rebellion on the part of the marginalized and disinherited, the heroic elements are submerged under deep layers of irony. The attitudes of this marginalized community are a bizarre mixture of rejection and imitation. In part, they are a largely unconscious parody of official religious and militaristic values (admiration for skill at *rana*, thieving and dice, canonization of bullfighters, approval of self-preservation in face of the enemy, avoidance of official duty, disrespect for hierarchies). Yet whilst being a reaction against Establishment values, these attitudes reflect many of their characteristics (notions of honour, glory, status) and are expressed with appropriate ceremony and rhetoric. Hence the alternative culture of the outsiders also emerges as a comically distorted copy of official culture. It stems both from an awareness of theemptiness of those values and from a sense of dependence on their structures.

The characters in Rodríguez Méndez's plays are not totally determined by external circumstances. In certain plays, at least, they have the capacity to respond in ways which affect the quality and direction of their lives (e.g., Julián in *Historia*), yet in general his work does not communicate any faith in the individual as an effective force in determining the course of historical events. His whole approach to historical drama gives less importance to the individual's attitudes, perspectives and imagination than we see in the works of Buero Vallejo. José Monleón's comment that Rodríguez Méndez's characters are 'aprovechados', 'infelices', 'inconscientes' or 'testigos' may require some qualification, but the critic is surely right when he detects the absence of the 'personaje que se ha comprometido de buena fe y con lucidez en la transformación real de la sociedad española'.[20] His characters have the autonomy to respond to history but show little capacity to change it.

One year after the death of Franco, yet with most of the old structures – including censorship – still in place, Antonio Gala conceived a general re-examination of national history in a series of short plays for television called *Paisaje con figuras*.[21] Gala's whole approach to these scenes implies a

---

[20] José Monleón, *Cuatro autores críticos* (Granada: Universidad de Granada, 1976), p. 19.
[21] The first series of *Paisaje con figuras* ran intermittently between February and

rejection of Francoist ideology, yet he takes neither the demythifying route of his earlier work nor the antiheroic stance of Rodríguez Méndez. Instead he elevates his own selection of individuals to the rank of hero and presents them against an impressionistic backdrop of their historical time. His heroes are seldom those who wield the political power. They represent many different aspects of Spanish life: churchmen, generals, explorers, conquistadores, bullfighters, poets, philosophers, painters, lovers. They are from a variety of racial and religious backgrounds. Gala's concept of the heroic generally involves a struggle between an individual and a prevailing social or ideological context, personal morality against political expediency, love against dogma. He celebrates the lives of people whose ideas were in conflict with the dominant culture of their time, like Jovellanos, Goya and Mariana Pineda; those who were the victims of the self-interest or the polit-ical ambition of their lords and superiors, like El Gran Capitán, El Empecinado or the actress María Calderón, locked away in a convent for the rest of her life for no other reason than having been Philip IV's lover; those who resisted the fashionable trends, like El Espartero who, in a period of military coups to 'save the nation', never took up arms against the established government.

Undoubtedly, the underlying preoccupation in these scenes is the question of Spanish identity. Gala unequivocally rejects the exclusive definition of Francoist traditionalism based on an essential Catholicism and a Castilian-centred political unity. Following on from *Las cítaras*, *Paisaje con figuras* is an inclusive exploration of all the diverse elements that have gone into the making of 'Spanishness'. He affirms the value of the Moorish and Jewish inheritance in a pluralistic vision of Spanish history. It is a celebration of diversity and richness in language, cultural heritage and religion.

In his prologue to *Paisaje con figuras*, Antonio Gala defines a nation's history as its family album, in which it can recognize its own origins and identity, an attitude which clearly accepts the exploration of the past as a means of illuminating the present. This brings us to the third main category of historical drama under Franco, in which the principal point of reference is to the present rather than the past.

In one way or another, the present situation forms a part of most of the historical drama discussed so far. History plays which confine themselves entirely to the recreation of the past are likely to be of antiquarian interest only. Conversely, those in which the past is no more than a peg on which to hang a contemporary issue would constitute a denial of the historical process. The very nature of historical subject-matter invites discussion of certain universal questions – the relationship between private and public affairs, the

November 1976, with cuts, postponements and cancellations. The longer second series did not appear until 1984. The complete two-volume collection was published the following year in Colección Austral.

ethics of power, the rulers and the ruled, social justice – which almost inevitably carry contemporary resonance. In the case of Spain, a country divided by civil war, indoctrinated by the victors with a distorted version of its own past, history becomes a relevant and living issue. The discussions it aroused – and continues to arouse[22] – are about politically-charged questions of national and personal identity. Most historical dramas thus involve some dialogue between past and present, between historical action and contemporary relevance.

In some of these historical plays, however, the reference to the present is clearly dominant. Rodríguez Méndez's *El vano ayer*, for instance, is principally (and untypically) a comment on a contemporary situation by historical analogy. Ostensibly set in 'los años de La Restauración', it describes the brutal repression of an unspecified 'popular' uprising, instigated by middle-class republicans and a general in exile who finally betray the people that follow them. Making no attempt to centre the action around recorded historical events, the author constructs his play on the basis of a parallel between attitudes of government and the middle classes under the Restoration and those under Francoism. The historical material is not explored on its own terms and appears to be conceived primarily as a functional support and illustration for the contemporary comment.[23]

In *La sangre y la ceniza*, Alfonso Sastre also concentrates his audience's attention on the present, although not exclusively through a parallel historical situation. His protagonist Miguel Servet (1511–53), physiologist and theologian, falls foul of both the Spanish Inquisition and Calvin's Reformation. He is burnt in effigy by the former and in person by the latter. Sastre focuses on the protagonist's pursuit of intellectual freedom, the right to think, debate and challenge established ideas in a Europe dominated by these two institutions, which, despite their differences, share the common conviction of being in possession of the absolute truth. It is this conviction, with its concomitant demand for ideological purity and homicidal intolerance of dissent, which forms the basis of Sastre's equation between sixteenth-century religion and twentieth-century fascism. He surrounds the fanaticism of Catholics and Protestants with the iconography of Nazi uniforms, machine guns, megaphones and fascist salutes. Many of these anachronisms are drawn from Franco's Spain. The names of certain groups and organizations, for instance 'Comité de la Salvación Pública' and 'La Falange del Amor', parody the identification between religious, military and civil authorities, as do such terms as 'subversive heresy' and the police presence surrounding Church

---

[22] A passionate debate on the teaching of history, provoked by government proposals for a revised national curriculum, took place towards the end of 1997 in the press, on television and on the internet.

[23] See Michael Thompson's unpublished Ph.D. thesis, 'The Unity of the Historical Theatre of José María Rodríguez Méndez' (University of Bristol, 1989), pp. 172–87.

leaders at Calvin's sermons. Sastre's frankly stylized and, at times, caricaturesque presentation, his blatant use of anachronism in allusions, costume and language, are all designed to lift the spectators out of the sixteenth century and immerse them in the wider and more modern implications of the conflict.

Other aspects of Sastre's approach tend towards the same purpose of bringing the content into the historical time and emotional world of the audience. The spectator is constantly reminded that a story is being told (scene titles and dates are projected on a screen) through the medium of people acting a part (use of masks, stagey asides, direct addresses to the audience). The author's stage direction stipulates that the preparations for Miguel's execution have to be set up 'sobre la idea de que se va a asistir a una representación teatral' and the scene ends with the director's voice calling for the stage to be cleared. The anti-heroic comedy surrounding the protagonist serves a similar purpose to the anti-illusionist devices, that is, to take the hero off his pedestal and make him more accessible to the ordinary person. Sastre's unheroic hero induces neither a sense of passive, trance-like admiration, because of his weaknesses, nor an attitude of rejection, because of his passion for truth and intellectual integrity. Despite his physical cowardice and abject terror at the stake, it simply appears impossible for him to recant his so called 'errors', because he cannot regard them as such. Sastre tries to provoke a critical reassessment of the hero figure and make the audience reflect on the regrettable conditions which make heroes necessary. Although he avoids Brecht's anti-heroic solution of the protagonist's recantation in his *Life of Galileo*, Sastre does seem to make Galileo's words a suitable commentary on his own play: 'Unhappy is the land that is in need of heroes'.

At first glance, Antonio Gala's *Anillos para una dama* seems to present an obvious case of demythification of a sacrosanct hero. Jimena, the middle-aged wife of the recently deceased El Cid, wishes to divest herself of all the historical baggage which being the widow of a national hero obliges her to carry, and to make public her love for Minaya, one of the Cid's generals. The Cid, seen through Jimena's eyes as a man too busy making war to make love, though arguably more human, is certainly less godlike than his usual depiction in the history books. Yet Gala's intention was not to diminish the Cid or his historical significance. Although it is about history, *Anillos* makes no attempt to demythify or even reinterpret the past. Its main points of reference are almost entirely to the present. The author's own definition of his play was 'teatro actual con referencias históricas'.[24] The attitudes, dialogue, social customs and dress are all boldly contemporary. More fundamentally, *Anillos*

---

[24] See Andrés Amorós's introduction to his edition of Antonio Gala, *Los buenos días perdidos / Anillos para una dama* (Madrid: Castalia, 1988), p. 76. The page references are to this edition.

goes straight to the heart of one of the central features of the Franco dictatorship: the link between political power and the mythification of history.

To a large extent, Franco's power rested on a providential view of Spain's historical destiny and of his own role within that destiny. National heroes and role models were essential to sustain such a view. Gala's King Alfonso is a shrewd politician who recognizes the importance of the heroic myth of the Cid and his conquests to his own power base, particularly when his military fortunes are at a low ebb (p. 240). The king admits to no longer believing in the inflated rhetoric of 'Dios', 'patria' and 'pueblo', but pleads not guilty to the charge of cynical egoism which Jimena levels against him. It is simply, he claims, that power and myth have become interdependent. The king denies Jimena, not the right to love, or even to remarry (provided that there were sound political reasons for doing so), but the right to remarry openly and publicly for love (p. 245). It is Jimena's insistence on this public dimension that changes *Anillos* from a sentimental tale of impossible love to a play with a political edge. Her love for Minaya constitutes a (tragically failed) bid for truth, openness and freedom.

Buero Vallejo's historical plays, like those of most of his colleagues, certainly contain elements of demythification or reinterpretation of the past, as well as allusions to the present. Where they differ is in their seamless combination of all these elements, attributable largely to the coherent intellectual framework which underpins their construction. Perhaps Buero's most distinctive contribution to the historical genre is his ability to synthesize apparently contradictory approaches: historical documentation and creative imagination, fidelity to the past and relevance to the present, individual and collective interpretations of history.

Buero makes a serious effort to present a true – if not strictly factual – picture of the past. Iglesias Feijoo has given us ample proof of the scrupulous research and documentation that went into the preparation of these works.[25] But the purpose of historical drama is not simply to endorse established historical interpretations. Buero also defends the use of the imagination, not just to adapt the complexities of history to dramatic form, but as an instrument of investigation and interpretation. The subtitle of 'fantasía', applied to *Las Meninas*, *El sueño de la razón*, and *La detonación*, did not reflect a simple desire to pre-empt criticism of alleged historical inaccuracies, but a calculated approach to the material. The author speaks of a need for the intuition of an 'intrahistoria posible' which the facts alone cannot give.[26] This is, in part, the intuition of the inner life of his historical characters, their motiva-

[25] See Luis Iglesias Feijoo, *La trayectoria dramática de Antonio Buero Vallejo* (Santiago de Compostela: Universidad de Santiago, 1982). Each of the relevant chapters contains a full account of Buero's historical sources.

[26] A. Buero Vallejo, 'Acerca del drama histórico', *Primer Acto*, 187 (1980–81), 19. Here Buero's use of the term *intrahistoria* seems to differ from the sense generally

tions, tensions, contradictions. Perhaps more importantly, however, it refers to an intuition of a wider significance – that is, what links the historical past to the spectator's present and what links the experience of the individual to the general historical situation.

Buero Vallejo's whole approach to historical drama is based on a concept of history as an open-ended, dynamic continuum, in which nothing – not even human nature – stands still, a view which challenges at the deepest level the static, 'essentialist' assumptions of Francoist historiography. Buero's entire output tends to illustrate his view of a constantly evolving humanity. In *El tragaluz*, an essential text for understanding Buero's idea of history, he induces the spectators to see an action from their own immediate past through the eyes of some Researchers from a remote future generation which has evolved beyond individual self-interest. The positive aspect of this vision of history is the pushing back of the frontiers of possibility. What appears inevitable or irreparable in one age may be overcome in a later period.[27] Buero's historical drama makes use of ironical interplay between past and present perspectives. Values and assumptions which were regarded as fundamental and unchangeable in the seventeenth or eighteenth century are seen from a contemporary perspective as false or ephemeral. This, by implication, casts doubt on the alleged permanence of those values by which we live in the present.[28] In *Un soñador* and *Las Meninas*, Buero occasionally invites his audience to draw their own conclusions about their contemporary situation from assertions made by his historical characters on the inviolability of their own status quo.[29] This conviction about the transience of all human affairs in the flux of history is a constant theme in Buero's later work. Following the logic of his argument, he even questions the stability of truth itself. In *Las Meninas* he begins to explore a conflict between truth and power in which truth can no longer be tolerated and is compelled to hide (pp. 226–27). By the time he comes to write *La detonación*, the historical process which confronts Larra is a rapidly mutating political charade in which truth becomes not only obscured but contaminated with self-interest. Like history, truth is not a static set of principles or beliefs, but a process of discovery.

Buero's commitment to reflect the truth of the past and the historical process is matched by an equally strong commitment to illuminate the

---

associated with Unamuno, i.e. a 'true' or 'eternal' bedrock of popular tradition lying unobserved beneath the ephemeral, hence ultimately 'false', surface of official history.

[27] For instance, *El concierto de San Ovidio* is centred on the assumption that the blind can never read and therefore never play music.

[28] See L. Iglesias Feijoo, 'Circunstancia y sentido de *El concierto de San Ovidio*', *Estreno*, 14 (1988), 19.

[29] Buero Vallejo, *Un soñador para un pueblo*, ed. L. Iglesias Feijoo (Madrid: Espasa Calpe, 1995), p. 109, and *Historia de una escalera / Las Meninas*, ed. R. Doménech (Madrid: Espasa Calpe, 1994), p. 227.

present. There is no question of one aspect or the other being dominant. For Buero, the very act of trying to understand history is an attempt to explain or serve the present. The present cannot be fully understood if it is not seen in historical perspective and the past can have no meaning for us unless it speaks to the present.[30] Again, *El tragaluz* provides a useful illustration of this principle. The investigation by the Researchers, the attempt to retrieve individual lives from the past, is a learning process for their contemporaries, a simultaneous act of judgement and compassion, self-discovery through empathy. Because what we are is explained by what has gone into forming our nature, it is constantly necessary to recover and re-examine the past. In the history plays, Buero is interested, not in establishing convenient parallels, but in illuminating a relationship of interdependence between past and present:

> El teatro histórico ilumina nuestro presente cuando no se reduce a ser un truco ante las censuras y nos hace entender y sentir mejor la relación viva existente entre lo que sucedió y lo que nos sucede. Es el teatro que nos persuade de que lo sucedido es tan importante y significativo para nosotros como lo que nos acaece, *por existir entre ambas épocas férrea, aunque quizá contradictoria, dependencia mutua.* [Italics mine].[31]

Buero explores the historical subject-matter both on its own terms and as the roots of the contemporary situation. The plays generally pose problems in the past which are still seeking solutions in the present: the question of government by consent and the involvement of the people in the power process (*Un soñador*), the conflict between truth and political power, explored under conditions of absolutist repression (*Las Meninas*) and in periods of political instability (*La detonación*), the consequences of repressive power on those who exercise it and those who suffer it (*El sueño*). At both individual and collective levels, the conflict between autocracy and rebellion, traditionalism and change, is either explicit or strongly implied in all these works. Broadly speaking, the plays are structured around the interaction of the same three worlds: the world of authority and power (not always associated with traditionalism), the world of the *pueblo* (usually the victims, though not always associated with liberalism) and, finally, the inner world of what might be termed the liberal conscience, which mediates between the rulers and the ruled. These broad issues are never treated prescriptively. What tends to emerge is a sense of interdependence: the *pueblo* as the conscience of the idealistic politician or creative artist, who in turn tries to fulfil his role as the conscience of power. Those relationships, however, remain a remote –

---

[30] The distinction between speaking about the present and speaking to the present was well made by Iglesias Feijoo, *Trayectoria*, p. 234.

[31] *Primer Acto*, 187 (1980–81), 19.

though necessary and achievable – ideal. The choices which confront Velázquez, Goya and Larra continue to reflect the author's own moral dilemmas under the Franco regime.

Buero's open-ended view of history does not exclude human responsibility and some degree of human control. History is not just something that happens to people; it is also something they help to create. From the start of his dramatic career, Buero exiled all notions of pre-established fate and destiny, so close to the hearts of Francoist historians. His whole approach to historical drama is based on the idea that individually and collectively human decisions and actions shape the course of history. In particular, Buero stresses the role of the individual in the historical process. Once again it is *El tragaluz* which develops this idea to its fullest extent. The Researchers belong to a time when the importance of the individual has been restored after centuries of collectivism.[32] He was not simply trying to redress what he saw as an imbalance here, but pointing to the essential falseness of the antithesis (popularized by Brecht) between collectivist and individualist representations of human behaviour. What Buero wishes to stress is the interdependence between individual morality and collective social patterns, with the consequent historical responsibility on the individual.

In each of his history plays Buero places an evolving individual consciousness at the heart of an evolving historical process. Each protagonist struggles with his own weaknesses and the resistance or repression of his social context to hold on to his integrity. In each case there is a process of self-discovery, leading to a climactic moment of decision. Esquilache not only sacrifices his personal ambition in the general interest, but questions his right to govern without popular consent. Velázquez learns to live as a man the principles of truth which have guided him as an artist. Goya recognizes the link between fear and tyranny in himself, and Larra realizes the limitations of his own commitment to the people's cause, the gap between his character and his beliefs. Buero invites his audience to empathize with his heroes, to the point (in *El sueño* and *La detonación*) of almost total immersion in their perceptions, memories and imagination, though without loss of critical distance or perspective. The audience shares the protagonist's internal journey towards self-knowledge, but is implicitly left with its own historical problems to solve at the end of the play. By transferring the challenges and choices to the theatre audience, the author reminds them that they are the inheritors of the protagonist's situation and reaffirms his faith in the power of individual moral stances to influence collective change.[33]

---

[32] The Researchers refer to a profound cultural change which had made them realize 'la importancia infinita del caso singular'.

[33] Buero's theory of *posibilismo* is entirely consistent with this belief. *Posibilismo* in repressive times, he argued, should not be regarded merely as a technique of evasion. The writer has a duty to 'hacer un acto de presencia actual', to try and make a difference in the

Buero Vallejo's cycle of history plays reveals both a sense of development and a fundamental unity. The plays evolve in thematic explicitness, sophistication of historical vision and technical complexity. At the same time, they are unified by a coherent philosophy of the genre he was working in and a consistent vision of history as a constantly changing, anti-deterministic process. With a clear distinction in his mind between the role of the academic historian and the historical dramatist, Buero convincingly incorporates the use of the creative imagination, the dimension of the present and the role of the individual into his vision. These underlying convictions, allied to a consistent emphasis on the theme of power, raise his work above the level of protest literature and absolve him of any charge of political opportunism in his use of history. Buero's history plays, perhaps more than the work of any of his opposition colleagues, transcend the political circumstances which gave them birth.

here-and-now. It is not enough to put your work in a drawer and wait for more liberal times. The writer should be part of the political process and probe the limitations of power. In a contribution to a round-table discussion he said: '. . . lo que sucede es que los márgenes de este posibilismo son muy diferentes en cada lugar, y, por supuesto, son dinámicos, variables, y nosotros somos unos de los factores que los hacen variar; pero debemos tener muy presente que nuestra presencia como autores tiene que ser una presencia efectiva, no una esterilidad; tenemos que hacer un posibilismo dinámico, progresivo, combativo' (*Cuadernos para el diálogo*, Núm. extraordinario (junio, 1966), 45).

'A Dramatist in His Own Right':
Juan Pérez de Montalbán and the
Authorship of *Los desprecios en quien ama*

ANN L. MACKENZIE

'Juan Pérez de Montalbán, though immensely popular in his own century, is today almost forgotten.' Victor Dixon, 'the World's leading *Montalvanista*',[1] as Jack Parker rightly calls him, made this thought-provoking observation in 1972, in his review of Maria Grazia Profeti's ground-breaking monograph, *Montalbán: un commediografo dell'età di Lope* (Università di Pisa, 1970).[2] Several decades later Dixon's comment, regrettably, is still applicable. Writing as recently as 1998, Patricia Kenworthy complained: 'Twentieth-century Hispanists, with the notable exceptions of Dixon, Parker and Profeti, have largely ignored Montalbán.'[3] This neglect seems all the more surprising given the specialist assistance to researchers provided by Profeti's outstanding bibliography of Montalbán's works, published in 1976, updated in 1982, and continued by Vega García-Luengos in 1993, thanks to which, as Kenworthy points out with only slight exaggeration, 'we know the exact location (and the library call numbers!) of every edition of every text ever written by, or attributed to, Montalbán'.[4] Moreover,

---

[1]   See Jack H. Parker, *Juan Pérez de Montalván* (Boston: Twayne, 1975), p. 118.

[2]   2 See Victor Dixon's review, *Bulletin of Hispanic Studies*, XLIX (1972), 186–87, at p. 186.

[3]   See Patricia Kenworthy, 'Juan Pérez de Montalbán (or Montalván) (1601/02–1638)', in *Spanish Dramatists of the Golden Age. A Bio-bibliographical Sourcebook*, ed. Mary Parker (Westport, Conn./London: Greenwood Press, 1998), pp. 1124–31, at p. 1128.

[4]   Kenworthy, p. 128. See Maria Grazia Profeti, *Per una bibliografía di J. Pérez de Montalbán* (Verona: Università degli Studi di Padova, 1976), and *Per una bibliografía di J. Pérez de Montalbán. Addenda e corrigenda* (Verona: Università degli Studi di Padova, 1982); Germán Vega García-Luengos, *Para una bibliografía de J. Pérez de Montalbán. Nuevas adiciones* (Verona: Università degli Studi di Padova, 1993). Profeti and Vega García-Luengos did not then know of several *comedias sueltas* associated with Montalbán, in Liverpool University. See my article, '*Comedia[s] de Lope Vol. II*. A Unique Volume of Early *comedias sueltas* in Liverpool University's Sydney Jones Library', in *The 'Comedia' in the Age of Calderón. Studies in Honour of Albert Sloman*,

greatly expanded microfilm and photocopying facilities and recent developments in information technology have made rare manuscripts and editions of
plays lodged in libraries in Spain, Austria, Italy, France, USA, etc. much
more readily available nowadays to scholars interested in Montalbán than
they were to Victor Dixon more than forty years ago, when he conducted his
thorough, personal researches in different libraries and archives for his,
regrettably still unpublished, doctoral thesis.[5] Although a few articles related
to Montalbán have appeared in recent years, there has been no truly detailed
book-length study of Montalbán's *comedias* published since the books by
Parker and Profeti appeared in the 1970s. Also, while Patricia Kenworthy
seems to have overlooked, for instance, Barrett's work on *Como padre y
como rey*,[6] she has not greatly exaggerated in asserting that 'no one play has
attracted sustained, serious scrutiny by modern critics', or that 'no modern
critical edition of any of his full-length plays' exists.

There is no doubt that Montalbán deserves much more scholarly attention
than he has to date received. His personal and literary relations with Lope de

---

ed. Ann L. Mackenzie, *Bulletin of Hispanic Studies*, LXX (1993), 17–35, especially pp.
19–21, 27–28; cf. my note 43.

   [5] See Victor F. Dixon, *The Life and Works of Juan Pérez de Montalbán, with special
reference to his plays*, Ph.D. dissertation, Cambridge University, 1959. I wish to express
my gratitude to Victor Dixon for making available to me photocopies of relevant pages
from his dissertation. While the thesis in its detailed entirety has never been published,
two chapters were reworked and published as key articles: Victor Dixon, 'Juan Pérez de
Montalbán's *Segundo tomo de las comedias*', *Hispanic Review*, XXIX (1961), 91–109, and
'Juan Pérez de Montalbán's *Para todos*', *Hispanic Review*, XXXII (1964), 36–59.

   [6] Kenworthy, pp. 126, 128. See Linton Lomas Barrett, *A Comparative Study of Six
Manuscripts of Juan Pérez de Montalbán's 'Como padre y como rey'*, ed. Carmen Iranzo
de Ebersole (Chapel Hill, NC: Hispanófila, 1976). For her edition of *Los amantes de
Teruel* (Valencia: Albatros-Hispanófila, 1983), Carmen Iranzo evidently relies on an
eighteenth-century *suelta*, rather than on the first edition. Profeti has, however, carefully
and scrupulously edited an *auto sacramental*: 'Il manoscritto autografo del *Caballero del
Febo*', *Miscellanea di Studi Hispanici*, XIV (Pisa: Università di Pisa, 1966–67), pp.
218–309. Scholars of the Golden-Age *comedia* are also indebted to Profeti for editing
Montalbán's *Índice de los ingenios de Madrid*, a rich source of information on his fellow
playwrights, in *Anales del Instituto de Estudios Madrileños*, XVIII (1981), 535–89.
Admittedly, several doctoral theses have been completed which deal wholly or partially
with Montalbán. See Guy Wallace Parker, *The Dramatic Art of Juan Pérez de Montalbán*
(University of California, Riverside, 1977); Hilda Angélica Morales de Rodríguez, *Philip
II in the Historical Comedies of Juan Pérez de Montalbán* (Pennsylvania State University,
1984); Jean Tena, *Les Noms de personnages dans les 'comedias' de Juan Pérez de
Montalbán* (Université de Montpellier, 1970); John William Van Kerk, *The Figure of Don
Carlos in Selected Plays of the Spanish Golden Age* (University of Georgia, 1978). For all
these references I am indebted to John J. Reynolds and Szilvia E. Szmuk, *Spanish Golden
Age Drama. An Annotated Bibliography of United States Doctoral Dissertations
1899–1992, with a Supplement of Non-United States Dissertations* (New York: The
Modern Language Association of America, 1998) (see Nos. 537–538, p. 259; No. 1452, p.
477; No. 188, p. 150).

Vega give, in themselves, sufficient reason to study his life and works in detail.[7] Not only was he Lope's first biographer,[8] and a fervent imitator of the master's dramatic practices, he even composed plays with Lope on more than one occasion. Montalbán himself testifies that he and Lope wrote *La tercera orden de San Francisco* together, for performance by the *autor de comedias*, Roque de Figueroa.[9] That they collaborated together is also confirmed by Lope himself who, in a letter to Antonio Hurtado de Mendoza, probably written in 1628, comments as follows:

> Estos días se decretó en el senado cómico que Luis Vélez, don Pedro Calderón y el doctor Mesqua hiciesen una comedia, y otra, en competencia suya, el doctor Montalván, el doctor Godínez y el licenciado Lope de Vega.[10]

Montalbán's relations with Calderón, with whom he also wrote plays, though scarcely studied to date, are likewise significant. Their collaboration with Antonio Coello produced *El privilegio de las mujeres*, destined to be the source-drama for Calderón's own *Las armas de la hermosura*. With Mira de Amescua they composed *Polifemo y Circe*, which was very possibly planned not by Mira, but by Montalbán.[11] *El monstruo de la fortuna*, a play of considerable dramatic value, in which Rojas Zorrilla was the third *ingenio* involved,[12] confirms Montalbán's interest in the *comedia de privanza*, a genre to which two of his most noteworthy historical tragedies also belong.[13]

---

7   Victor Dixon has told me, in a letter dated 17 December 1999, of his intention to write up some time what he has 'found out about his [Montalbán's] biography, especially his university career'.

8   See Juan Pérez de Montalbán, *Fama póstuma a la vida y muerte del doctor Frey Lope Félix de Vega Carpio* (Madrid: Imprenta del Reino, 1636). For a useful commentary on this work see Parker, *Montalván*, ch. 9, 'The First Biography of Lope de Vega: *Fama póstuma*', pp. 119–24.

9   For Montalbán's possibly rather exaggerated account of his collaboration with Lope in *La tercera orden de San Francisco*, see his *Fama póstuma*; the passage is quoted by Parker in 'Lope de Vega and Juan Pérez de Montalván: Their Literary Relations', in *Hispanic Studies in Honour of J. González Llubera*, ed. Frank Pierce (Oxford: Dolphin Book Co., 1959), pp. 225–35, at pp. 229–30.

10   See Agustín G. de Amezúa, *Epistolario de Lope de Vega Carpio* (Madrid: RAE, 1943), IV, p. 102. Neither of these *comedias* appears to have survived.

11   See Dixon's comments on this point, 'Montalbán's *Para todos*', p. 41, note 23.

12   For a detailed analysis see Ann L. Mackenzie, 'Examen de *El monstruo de la fortuna*: comedia compuesta por Calderón (I), Pérez de Montalbán (II) y Rojas Zorrilla (III)', in *Hacia Calderón. Tercer Coloquio Anglogermano. Londres 1973* (Berlin/New York: Walter de Gruyter, 1976), pp. 10–25.

13   *El fin más desgraciado y fortunas de Seyano* and *El mariscal de Virón* were published in the *Primero tomo de las comedias del doctor Juan Pérez de Montalván* (Madrid: Imprenta del Reino, 1635). There was a performance of *La historia [?] de Seyano*, probably *El fin más desgraciado* of Montalbán, by Andrés de la Vega, either in

The popularity of Montalbán's plays with Golden-Age audiences is well documented. His plays, in the repertoires of most of the leading *autores de comedias* (Roque de Figueroa, Bartolomé Romero, Andrés de la Vega), were regularly performed not only in the capital but in other parts of Spain.[14] *El mariscal de Virón* was in the repertoire of the company of Andrés de la Vega in 1632–33, figuring on a list of *comedias* from which three were chosen for performance in the village of Daganzo in 1633.[15] *No hay vida como la honra*, a play composed c.1627–28, performed in 1628 by Roque de Figueroa, and 'celebrated as being one of Montalván's best', was evidently performed simultaneously in both the *corrales* of Madrid, and over many days, presumably in that same year – an 'unprecedented distinction'.[16] In 1631–32 the same play was still being performed by Roque de Figueroa in Madrid, and his wife, Antonia Manuela, who took a leading role in it, was received with great applause.[17] Not only were Montalbán's plays popular in performance, there was an enormous demand for reading them in print which no doubt encouraged Montalbán to include four of his plays in *Para todos* and then to select twelve more for publication in his *Primero tomo de las comedias* (Madrid: Imprenta del Reino, 1635). Montalbán did not prepare this volume for press without being aware of the implications in doing so. As his Prologue to his readers reveals, the playwright knew that, as Profeti has succinctly put it, 'al ser impreso, el texto cambia de categoría'. Montalbán keenly perceived that what audiences had enjoyed, caught up in the immediate excitement of performance, they might, nevertheless, criticize in print, since they would have time, while reading, to think carefully about thought-content:

Madrid or at the Pardo, in 1627 (see N. D. Shergold and J. E. Varey, 'Some Palace Performances of Seventeenth-century Plays', *Bulletin of Hispanic Studies*, XL [1963], 212–44, at p. 238).

[14] Roque de Figueroa was noted for producing plays by Montalbán (see Hugo Albert Rennert, 'List of Spanish Actors and Actresses 1560–1680', in *The Spanish Stage in the Time of Lope de Vega* [New York: The Hispanic Society of America, 1909], p. 473).

[15] See Cristóbal Pérez Pastor, *Nuevos datos acerca del histrionismo español en los siglos XVI y XVII* (Madrid: *Revista Española*, 1901), pp. 225–26. A play called *El mariscal Cleverín*, which was almost certainly *El mariscal de Virón*, was performed at the palace by Francisco López on 8 June 1632 (see Jack H. Parker, 'The Chronology of the Plays of Juan Pérez de Montalván', *Publications of the Modern Language Association of America*, LXVII [1952], 186–210, at p. 191; Shergold and Varey, 'Some Palace Performances', p. 229).

[16] Parker, *Montalván*, pp. 29–30; Dixon, 'Montalbán's *Para todos*', pp. 40–41; Shergold and Varey, 'Some Palace Performances', p. 232. We do not need to rely only on Montalbán himself, but have more impartial sources for information about the play's success (see Montalbán's *Para todos* [Madrid: Imprenta del Reino, 1632] in which the text of this *comedia* was published; also Gutierre, Marqués de Careaga, *La poesía defendida y difinida, Montalbán alabado* [Madrid, 1639], fols. 17–18, cited by Dixon).

[17] See Rennert, *The Spanish Stage in the Time of Lope de Vega* (1909 ed.), p. 421.

Para desengañar a los curiosos y desmentir a los que profanan nuestros estudios me reduje a imprimir las mías [comedias] empezando por estas doce, que es el tomo, lectores míos, que os consagro, para que las censuréis en vuestro aposento, que aunque parecieron razonablemente en el tablado, no es crédito seguro, porque tal vez el ademán de la dama, la representación del héroe, la cadencia de las voces, el ruido de los consonantes, la suspensión de los afectos suelen engañar las orejas más atentas, y hacer que pasen por rayos los relámpagos, porque como se dicen aprisa las coplas, y no tiene lugar la censura para el examen quedan contentos los sentidos, pero no satisfecho el entendimiento.[18]

Unfortunately, Montalbán died before he could finish preparing a further volume of his plays. As a consequence, as Dixon has shown, at least three *comedias* that are not, in fact, the work of Montalbán, appeared in the volume entitled *Segundo tomo de las comedias del doctor Juan Pérez de Montalbán* (Madrid: Imprenta del Reino, 1638).[19] In addition, numerous plays either definitely or possibly by Montalbán were destined to be printed during the seventeenth century, either forming part of collected volumes, or repeatedly issued as *comedias sueltas*.

The playwright's popularity and influence, on stage and in print, were not confined to Spain. Some of his plays are known to have been adapted by seventeenth-century playwrights in France, and *El mariscal de Virón*, for instance, is thought to have influenced Italy's *commedia dell'arte*.[20] In the New World, to cite only two examples, *No hay vida como la honra* was performed in Peru as early as 1630,[21] and *El valor perseguido*, a play of doubtful authorship but 'probably his',[22] was performed in Mexico in 1682, where it was banned, because of perceived religious and other improprieties. All copies of both this play and its attendant *entremés* were ordered by the Inquisition to be collected and an edict issued 'prohibiting *in toto* the reading and performance of these works'. The fact that 'this devoted disciple of Lope

[18] Maria Grazia Profeti appositely quotes this passage in considering the dual function of the Golden-Age *comedia* as both performance work and literary text (see 'Comedias representadas/textos literarios: los problemas ecdóticos', in *Teatro, historia y sociedad [Seminario Internacional sobre Teatro del Siglo de Oro Español, AITENSO, Murcia, octubre 1994]*, ed. Carmen Hernández Valcárcel [Murcia: Universidad de Murcia/Mexico: Universidad Autónoma de Ciudad Juárez, 1996], pp. 205–16; see p. 210).

[19] The plays are: *El divino portugués, San Antonio de Padua*; *Amor, lealtad y amistad*; and *El sufrimiento premiado* (see Dixon, 'Montalbán's *Segundo tomo de las comedias*', pp. 98–109; my note 38).

[20] See Parker, *Montalván*, pp. 30, 45; Winifred Smith, 'The Maréchal de Biron on the Stage', *Modern Philology*, XX (1923), 301–38.

[21] See Rodrigo de Carvajal y Robles, *Fiestas de Lima por el nacimiento del Príncipe Baltasar Carlos* (Lima, 1632), ed. Francisco López Estrada (Sevilla: Escuela de Estudios Hispano-americanos, 1950), pp. 51–52.

[22] See Victor Dixon, '*La mayor confusión*', *Hispanófila* (1958), No. 3, 17–26, at p. 24, note 16; Dixon, *The Life and Works of Montalbán*, p. 357.

de Vega was popular in the Spanish Indies throughout much of that [seventeenth] century', as Irving A. Leonard has eloquently pointed out, 'is well attested by the frequent performances of his plays recorded and by the large numbers of his *comedias* and particularly of his miscellany, *Para todos*, which dot the ship-manifests and the inventories of colonial libraries and book-collections'.[23]

Researches into theatre-records and the preferences of Spanish printers have proved that Montalbán's plays continued to be performed and to be reprinted throughout the eighteenth and even into the nineteenth century in Spain, and not only in Madrid but in places such as Seville, Valencia, Valladolid and Barcelona.[24] In Seville during the eighteenth century, for example, as Vega García-Luengos' invaluable researches have shown: 'El autor más editado, con neta diferencia, es Calderón: 221 ediciones (15,1% del total), pertenecientes a 86 títulos distintos de comedias, 1 auto, 2 entremeses y 20 relaciones. Le sigue Moreto con 100 ediciones (7%): 28 comedias diferentes, 4 entremeses y 6 relaciones. A continuación se sitúa

[23] For both quotations see Leonard's article 'Montalbán's *El valor perseguido* and the Mexican Inquisition, 1682', *Hispanic Review*, XI (1943), 47–56, at pp. 50, 56.

[24] See Ada M. Coe, *Catálogo bibliográfico y crítico de las comedias atribuidas en los periódicos de Madrid desde 1661 hasta 1819* (Baltimore: The Johns Hopkins Press, 1935); J. E. Varey and Charles Davis, *Los libros de cuentas de los corrales de comedias de Madrid: 1706–1719. Estudio y documentos*, Fuentes de la Historia del Teatro en España XVI (London: Tamesis, 1992); Francisco Aguilar Piñal, *Sevilla y el teatro en el siglo XVIII* (Oviedo: Cátedra Feijoo, Universidad de Oviedo, 1974); Eduardo Juliá Martínez, 'Preferencias teatrales del público valenciano en el siglo XVIII', *Revista de Filología Española*, XX (1933), 113–59; Germán Vega García-Luengos, 'El teatro barroco en los escenarios y en las prensas de Valladolid durante el siglo XVIII', in *Teatro del Siglo de Oro. Homenaje a Alberto Navarro González* (Kassel: Edition Reichenberger, 1990), pp. 639–73; Alfonso Par, 'Representaciones teatrales en Barcelona durante el siglo XVIII', *Buletín de la Real Academia Española*, XVI (1929), 326–46, 492–513, 594–614. See also Lázaro Montero de la Puente, 'El teatro en Toledo durante el siglo XVIII (1762–1776)', *Revista de Filología Española*, XXVI (1942), 411–68. It is worth noting that Montalbán's *Despreciar lo que se quiere, El segundo Séneca de España* and *El mariscal de Virón* figure in the list of 'A Shipment of *comedias* to the Indies', dated 1713 (reproduced by Irving A. Leonard, *Hispanic Review*, II [1934], 39–50, at pp. 46–47); and that *La más constante mujer, De un castigo dos venganzas, Lo que son juicios del cielo* and *Los amantes de Teruel* were being performed in Portugal (Lisbon) in the first decades of the eighteenth century (see Tomás Pinto Brandão, *La comedia de comedias*, ed. Mercedes de los Reyes Peña and Piedad Bolaños Donoso, *Criticón* [1987], No. 40, pp. 81–159, at pp. 131, 136, 148). For information on performances of Montalbán in the nineteenth century see, for instance, Charlotte M. Lorenz, 'Seventeenth Century Plays in Madrid from 1808–1818', *Hispanic Review*, VI (1938), 324–31; Nicholson B. Adams, 'Siglo de Oro Plays in Madrid, 1820–1850', *Hispanic Review*, IV (1936), 342–57. Federico Carlos Sainz de Robles – though he overstates the case, since we cannot be sure of the precise numbers or titles of all Montalbán's authentic plays – contends that 'Todas las comedias de Montalbán fueron representadas con general aplauso . . . hasta muy entrado el siglo XIX' (see his *Teatro español. Historia y antología* [Madrid: Aguilar, 1943], IV, p. 507, in which is published Montalbán's *El segundo Séneca de España* [pp. 509–80]).

Pérez de Montalbán con 79 ediciones (5.6%): 25 comedias diferentes, 2 autos y 10 relaciones.'[25]

'Problems of authorship' as Victor Dixon has rightly commented, 'continue to befog and bedevil the study of Golden Age drama'.[26] In Montalbán's case, however, these problems appear to be extraordinarily numerous and peculiarly difficult to resolve. Like many successful and famous dramatists of the Golden Age, Montalbán suffered from the careless and unscrupulous activities of printers in Seville and elsewhere, who not only truncated his plays but printed them full of errors. In particular, they frequently omitted to print his name as the author, regularly assigning his works, out of ignorance or in hope of still better sales, to other playwrights, while often publishing under Montalbán's name *comedias* which he had not composed. Montalbán's complaints about such practices and misattributions are very much like those made, for instance, by Lope, Calderón and Rojas Zorrilla. In a prologue addressed to his readers in the *Segunda parte* of his *comedias* (1645) Rojas Zorrilla condemns in particular the printers of Seville for assigning plays to the wrong authors: 'Imprimen en Sevilla las comedias de los ingenios menos conocidos con nombre de los que han escrito más; si es buena la comedia usurpando a su dueño la alabanza; y si es mala quitando la opinión al que no la ha escrito'.[27] Ten years earlier, describing in the 'Prólogo largo' to his *Primero tomo de las comedias* how badly he had been treated by printers of his *comedias*, Montalbán expressed his indignation in remarkably similar terms: 'salen llenas de errores, barbarismos, despropósitos, y mentiras, hasta en el nombre, atribuyéndome muchas [comedias] que no son mías, vanidad muy enojosa para mí, porque si son buenas les usurpo la gloria a sus dueños; y si malas, me desacredito con quien las compra'.[28]

In addition to these typical problems, however, Montalbán seems to have had exceptional difficulties to contend with, for he appears to have acquired an unenviable reputation among his contemporaries for habitually putting his name to *comedias* that had been written by other dramatists. The allegation that he had stolen or plagiarized from Jerónimo de Villaizán in composing *De un castigo dos venganzas* may or may not have had some basis in truth.[29] It is

[25] Germán Vega García-Luengos, 'Lectores y espectadores de la comedia barroca. Los impresos teatrales sevillanos del siglo XVIII', in *Estado actual de los estudios sobre el Siglo de Oro. Actas del II Congreso Internacional de Hispanistas del Siglo de Oro*, eds Manuel García Martín, Ignacio Arellano, Javier Blasco and Marc Vitse (Salamanca: Ediciones Universidad de Salamanca, 1993), 2 vols; II, pp. 1007–16, at p. 1012.

[26] See Dixon, 'Montalbán's *Segundo tomo de las comedias*', p. 91.

[27] See Rojas' address 'Al lector', in *Segunda parte de las comedias de Don Francisco de Rojas Zorrilla* (Madrid: Francisco Martínez, 1645).

[28] See Bacon, p. 8; and Dixon, 'Montalbán's *Segundo tomo de las comedias*', p. 92.

[29] For useful information on Montalbán's bitter disputes with Villaizán, Quevedo and others, and illuminating comments on the disputed authorship of *De un castigo dos venganzas*, see Dixon, 'Montalbán's *Para todos*', pp. 44–52; Parker, *Montalván*, pp.

clear that the rumours by no means stopped there, however, and, judging by Montalbán's own comments on the topic, he was regularly accused of not being the true author of plays that were definitely his works. In the Prologue of *Para todos* (1632), addressed to 'Al que ha de leer', Montalbán makes plain that he bitterly resented such accusations, which, he tells us, were partly responsible for his decision – made in or about 1631 – to cease writing plays for a period. He also openly admits how profoundly rumours of this nature disturbed his peace of mind:

> está el vulgo tan novelero, que con que se le antoje a uno decir por chanza que no es mía la comedia que estoy escribiendo, no faltará un piadoso [*sic*] que lo apoye, y un apasionado que lo crea; y mientras se averigua la verdad, yo me vuelvo loco y mi opinión padece.[30]

Nor is *Para todos* the only work composed at this period in which Montalbán expresses his resentment towards those who damaged his reputation by alleging he was not the author of his own *comedias*. *La doncella de labor*, evidently composed about 1632,[31] and a *comedia* of which he himself had a particularly high opinion, concludes with the following words which Montalbán, wittily but in meaningful reproach, addresses to the audience:

> Y aqui acaba la doncella
> de servir a doña Elvira,
> y la comedia también,
> cuyo poeta os suplica
> que os parezca tan gustosa,
> alegre y entretenida,
> *que se diga que no es suya,*
> *aunque mienta quien lo diga.*[32]

114–16. Dixon comments that it is possible that Montalbán's play 'was deliberately modelled on one by Villaizán, and could be regarded, according to one's allegiances, as a parody, as an original *refundición*, or as a shameless piece of plagiarism' (p. 48).

[30] See *Para todos* (Madrid: Imprenta del Reino, 1632), fols 6–7. Montalbán also indicates in this book (fol. 29), that he stopped writing plays 'por algunos meses' to complete *Para todos* (Dixon, 'Montalbán's *Para todos*', pp. 51–53). As Dixon comments, 'if his plays are to be separated, as suggested by J. H. Parker, *Chronology*, 193 ff., into "early" and "late" periods, the crisis of 1631 might be taken as the watershed between them, in preference to Parker's 1629' (Dixon, p. 57, note 62).

[31] The play was included in the *Primero tomo de las comedias* (1635), but Parker believes it was written about 1632 ('Chronology of the Plays of Montalván', pp. 187, 191–92).

[32] I quote from the text in *Dramáticos contemporáneos de Lope de Vega, II*, ed. Ramón de Mesonero Romanos, *BAE*, XLV (Madrid: Rivadeneyra, 1858), pp. 587–604, at p. 604 (my italics).

Whatever the full explanation for the remarkably numerous 'uncertainties of the Montalván canon in drama', these, as Jack H. Parker has observed, 'remain legion', and 'to a great extent it is only a guess as to which ones of the many [*comedias*] attributed to Montalbán in other collections and in separate publications (*comedias sueltas*) are really his'.[33] A general result of these uncertainties is that scholars of Montalbán to date, while accepting that he was a prolific playwright, perhaps too persistent 'in aping Lope's fluency',[34] have significantly different views about the number of plays he wrote, or might have written. Bacon declares 'we can account for fifty-eight dramas, – of eight only the titles are found', believing that there were, besides that number, 'thirty supposititious dramas and four in which he collaborated'.[35] In discussing, in 1952, the 'Chronology' of Montalbán's plays, Parker took into account '47 *comedias*, 3 *autos sacramentales*, and 4 *comedias* in collaboration'. By 1975, however, when he produced his monograph on Montalbán, Parker was disposed, in view of Dixon's researches, to discount a number of plays he had previously regarded as authentic. In *Montalbán: un commediografo dell' età di Lope*, also no doubt influenced by Dixon's convincing opinions, Profeti limits herself to studying around forty plays. Dixon, whose calculations are probably still the most accurate available to us, believes that there are a hundred-odd plays in existence that have been attributed to Montalbán. It would appear therefore that at least fifty and possibly as many as sixty of that number are plays about whose authorship, given the present state of Montalbán researches, we are far from being confident.[36]

A significant number of the plays sometimes printed as by Montalbán have also been attributed to the master dramatist whom Montalbán particularly revered and imitated: Lope de Vega. Montalbán himself complains that some of his plays were deliberately misattributed to Lope.[37] It has to be said, on the other hand, that several *comedias* published as by Montalbán were definitely Lope's works. As Dixon has pointed out, 'at least two plays published as his – *Lucha de amor y amistad* (*La amistad y obligación*) and *Sin secreto no hay amor* – were certainly Lope's'. Moreover, Dixon has proved beyond any reasonable doubt, that 'the same is surely true' of *El sufrimiento premiado*, 'an entertaining example of early Lope comedy', which Dixon 'rescued from the oblivion of Montalbán's *Segundo tomo*'

---

33 Parker, *Montalván*, p. 26.

34 See Dixon's review of Profeti, *Montalbán: un commediografo*, p. 187.

35 See Bacon, p. 16. According to Bacon (note 6), Schack states that Montalbán wrote about a hundred plays, while Ticknor gives the number as about sixty, and Mesonero Romanos mentions seventy-one titles.

36 See Parker, 'Chronology of the Plays of Montalván', p. 186; Dixon, 'Montalbán's *Segundo tomo de las comedias*', p. 91.

37 In his *Sucesos y prodigios de amor en ocho novelas ejemplares* (Madrid: Juan González, 1624); mentioned by Bacon, p. 11.

through his splendid critical edition of that drama.[38] Nevertheless, like Victor Dixon, 'I have no faith in the critical tradition that Montalbán shamelessly put his name to works in fact by Lope'.[39]

Thorough researches into the many *comedias* variously printed as the work of either Lope or Montalbán, and sometimes appearing under the name of other dramatists besides, have still to be undertaken. When these are completed they might well reveal, so I suspect, a surprising number of plays to which Montalbán has the best claim. Among these *comedias* three in particular would merit careful study by scholars interested in the dramatic art and output of Montalbán. *El dichoso en Zaragoza* – which is also known as *El premio en la misma pena* and *La merced en el castigo* – is attributed in some early seventeenth-century editions to Lope, in others to Montalbán, and in others, implausibly, to Moreto. A good play with an excellent *gracioso*, *El dichoso en Zaragoza* interestingly explores the theme of 'del rey abajo, ninguno' and the conflict, as experienced by King Alfonso of Aragón, between royal duty and human passion.[40] *El valor perseguido y traición vengada*, despite its extravagant and disorganized plot, is not devoid of dramatic interest and merit. Irving Leonard wrote in 1943 that 'no systematic study of the problem [of its authorship] seems to have been made as yet' – a comment that is still correct –, 'but the weight of the evidence appears to point to Montalbán rather than to Lope'.[41] Likewise, sometimes ascribed to Lope and sometimes to Montalbán, *Los desprecios en quien ama*, though it has received regrettably little attention from critics to date,[42] is, as I shall illustrate, an excellent *comedia palaciega*.[43]

Similarities of theme, subject-matter and plot-development, too striking to

[38] See Dixon, 'Montalbán's *Segundo tomo de las comedias*', *passim*, especially pp. 98, 109. In his critical edition Victor Dixon has established beyond doubt Lope's authorship of *El sufrimiento premiado, comedia famosa, atribuida en esta edición, por primera vez, a Lope de Vega Carpio* (London: Tamesis, 1967). As Jack Parker rightly says, 'Victor Dixon's evidence and arguments are overwhelmingly convincing, and critics will agree with him that we ought to accept *Suffering Rewarded* as not Montalván's but Lope de Vega's' (*Montalván*, p. 72).

[39] See Dixon, 'Montalbán's *Segundo tomo de las comedias*', p. 109.

[40] Victor Dixon says of *El dichoso en Zaragoza* that 'nothing in the play . . . suggests to me that Montalbán may have been the author' (*The Life and Works of Montalbán*, p. 296) – an opinion with which I disagree.

[41] See Leonard, 'Montalbán's *El valor perseguido* and the Mexican Inquisition, 1682', pp. 47–48, note 2. Dixon comments: '*El valor perseguido* . . . is probably Montalbán's; it may have been a relatively early play' (*The Life and Works of Montalbán*, p. 357). Profeti's comments on the play are essentially contained in a single paragraph (*Montalbán: un commediografo*, p. 65).

[42] Bacon, as is his practice, offers little more than an admittedly detailed plot-summary (pp. 111–15). Parker offers no information at all other than its title (*Montalván*, p. 63).

[43] A monograph by Don W. Cruickshank and Ann L. Mackenzie, *The 'Comedia' in Seville 1620–1650. Researches into a Unique Collection of Early 'Comedias Sueltas'*

be coincidental, suggest that the author of *Los desprecios en quien ama*, whoever he might have been, was influenced (c.1625) by Lope's *El perro del hortelano*, written at least ten years previously (c.1613–15), and that his work influenced, in its turn, Moreto's *El desdén con el desdén*, composed nearly thirty years afterwards (c.1653–54).[44] The playwright of *Los desprecios en quien ama* follows Lope's lead in dramatizing the predicament of a certain 'Condesa de Belflor' who falls in love with her secretary, but, adoring also her position and reputation, cannot bring herself to marry beneath her station.[45] It is not inconceivable that in choosing to give his heroine, Claudia, exactly the same title as the one which Diana, Lope's famous Condesa de Belflor, enjoys, the playwright was hoping for a favourable reception comparable to that which *El perro del hortelano* must surely have received from Golden-Age audiences.

Los desprecios en quien ama could well have been composed in or about 1625, for it is known to have been performed at the royal palace by the company of Andrés de la Vega on 22 September in that year. A play referred

(Liverpool: Liverpool University Press, forthcoming), discusses *El dichoso en Zaragoza*, *El valor perseguido* and *Los desprecios en quien ama* in detail.

[44] For the date of *El perro del hortelano,* I rely on S. Griswold Morley and Courtney Bruerton, *The Chronology of Lope de Vega's 'Comedias'* (New York: The Modern Language Association of America, 1940), pp. 228–29. While the exact date of composition of *El desdén con el desdén* is unknown, it was published in the *Primera parte de comedias de D. Agustín Moreto* . . . (Madrid: Diego Díaz de la Carrera, 1654), and shows the significant influence of the same author's *El poder de la amistad*, of which the signed autograph manuscript survives, dated 25 April 1652 (BN MS No. Vitr.ª 7–4). Although *El perro del hortelano* and *Los desprecios en quien ama* were both plays taken into account by Mabel Harlan during her extensive researches into 'The Relationship of Moreto's *El desdén con el desdén* to Suggested Sources' (*Indiana University Studies*, X [1924]), she was disposed to exclude them, in my view mistakenly, as 'possible sources for Moreto's masterpiece'. Ruth Kennedy agrees essentially with Harlan, in discounting them (*The Dramatic Art of Moreto, Smith College Studies in Modern Languages*, XIII [1931–32, Nos. 1–4; reprinted Philadelphia, 1932], p. 167). Dixon, on the other hand, describes *Los desprecios en quien ama* as 'a real forerunner, if not a source, of *El desdén con el desdén* (*The Life and Works of Montalbán*, pp. 293–94). I have commented briefly on the likely influence of *El perro del hortelano* on *El desdén con el desdén* in my book, *Francisco de Rojas Zorrilla y Agustín Moreto: análisis* (Liverpool: Liverpool University Press, 1994), p. 156, note 7. I discuss in detail the relationship of *Los desprecios en quien ama* to *El perro del hortelano* and *El desdén con el desdén* in another study (see my note 43).

[45] Interestingly, Lope's *El perro del hortelano*, when it was printed as a *suelta* with the title *La condesa de Belflor* (possibly through confusion with *El desdén con el desdén* and its similar theme), was wrongly attributed to Moreto. See C. A. de la Barrera y Leirado, *Catálogo bibliográfico y biográfico del teatro antiguo español desde sus orígenes hasta mediados del siglo XVIII* (Madrid: M. Rivadeneyra, 1860; facsimile edition, Madrid: Editorial Gredos, 1969), p. 431; and William A. McKnight, *A Catalogue of 'Comedias Sueltas' in the Library of the University of North Carolina* (Chapel Hill, NC: University of North Carolina Library, 1965), p. 51.

to as *El nuncio fingido*, which was performed at the palace earlier that same year, and by the same theatre company,[46] might also have been, in fact, *Los desprecios en quien ama*, for it was sometimes known and printed by the title *El embajador fingido*.[47] While no manuscripts of the play appear to have survived[48] there are a number of undated but seventeenth-century *sueltas*, variously titled *Los desprecios en quien ama* and *El embajador fingido*, which attribute the *comedia* to Lope de Vega.[49] *Sueltas*, attributing the play, under the title *Los desprecios a quien ama*, to Pérez de Montalbán appear to be significantly later, most of them dating from the middle to late eighteenth century.[50] Although this fact might seem to strengthen marginally Lope's

[46] For information on these early performances see Shergold and Varey, 'Some Palace Performances', pp. 223, 232.

[47] An evidently modern (? nineteenth-century) manuscript of *Acertar errando*, in the Biblioteca Nacional, Madrid (MS 15.443[4]), carries the comment 'idéntica a la del Embajador fingido', and Paz and La Barrera, evidently on the basis of this description, believed the two plays were the same work (A. Paz y Melia, *Catálogo de las piezas de teatro que se conservan en el Departamento de Manuscritos de la Biblioteca Nacional* [2nd edn (by Julián Paz) Madrid: Blass, 1934–35], 2 vols; I, pp. 5, 68; La Barrera, p. 523). *Acertar errando*, usually accepted as Lope's work, has nothing in common with *Los desprecios en quien ama*.

[48] An early eighteenth-century manuscript of a *loa* of *Los desprecios en quien ama* exists in the Biblioteca Nacional, described as follows by Paz (*Catálogo*, I, p. 307): 'Loa para la comedia *Los desprecios en quien ama*, que se representó en el convento de Santa Catalina de Zafra, en ocasión de elegir priora' (Ms S 14.611[8]). The play continued to be performed into the eighteenth and nineteenth centuries. There is a record of its performance in Valencia in the first half of the eighteenth century (Juliá Martínez, *Preferencias teatrales*, p. 127). In the Biblioteca Municipal de Madrid (see Carlos Cambronero, *Catálogo de la Biblioteca Municipal de Madrid* [Madrid: Imprenta Municipal, 1902], p. 335) there are three manuscript copies of a *refundición*, dated 1829, of *Los desprecios en quien ama* – which, interestingly, still associate the play with Montalbán, and prove that the play was thought worth recasting for performance in Madrid some two centuries after it was written.

[49] The earliest of these *sueltas* may well be the *suelta* of *El embajador fingido* in the volume entitled *Comedia[s] de Lope Vol. II*, Sydney Jones Library, Liverpool University. Don Cruickshank has proved that this *suelta* was printed in Seville by Francisco de Lyra, probably as early as 1632–34. (Interestingly, the *sueltas* of *El dichoso en Zaragoza* [*El premio en la misma pena*] and *El valor perseguido* in this same volume were, according to Cruickshank's researches, likewise printed c.1632 by Francisco de Lyra [cf. note 43 above].) Two early *sueltas* entitled *Los desprecios en quien ama* and another called *El embajador fingido* (evidently identical to the 'Liverpool' *suelta*), all attributing the play to Lope, which were previously part of the Harrach collection, are now in the library of the University of Pennsylvania (see José M. Regueiro, *Spanish Drama of the Golden Age. A Catalogue of the 'Comedia' Collection in the University of Pennsylvania Libraries* [New Haven, Conn: Research Publications Inc., 1971], pp. 9, 43; and Profeti, *Per una bibliografia di Montalbán*, p. 418).

[50] See Regueiro, p. 8; Profeti, *Per una bibliografia di Montalbán*, pp. 416–18, and *Addenda e corrigenda*, 38. For a description of the *suelta*, *Los desprecios en quien ama* in the British Library, see M. C. Pérez y Pérez, *Bibliografía del teatro de Lope de Vega*, *Cuadernos Bibliográficos*, XXIX (Madrid: CSIC, 1973), p. 90a.

claim to the drama, other evidence indicative of Lope's authorship is insufficient to undermine the case for Montalbán as the playwright responsible. Nor is the debt that *Los desprecios en quien ama* undoubtedly owes to Lope's *El perro del hortelano* a convincing reason for favouring Lope rather than Montalbán as author. With plays like *El perro del hortelano* and *Los milagros del desprecio* – the latter probably, as McKendrick has commented, 'one of the earliest plays to deal in depth with the *mujer esquiva*' – Lope 'created a genre',[51] influencing many different playwrights to write *comedias* illustrating, in varying degrees, the effectiveness of treating 'disdain with disdain', as a means to overcome a lady's resistance to love.[52]

The few critics who have ventured an opinion on the authorship of *Los desprecios en quien ama* express different and uncertain views. La Barrera, though he comments that 'se ha impreso como de Lope', attributes it to Montalbán.[53] Perhaps significantly, Morley and Bruerton did not include this play among the works studied in their *Chronology of Lope de Vega's 'Comedias'*. Morley had considered its versification in an earlier article and, unfortunately, had concluded that 'the metrical analysis offers in this case no decisive answer'.[54] Consideration of Montalbán's preferences in versification has caused Victor Dixon to comment that 'no authentic play has less than 25% *romance* or – except for *El mariscal de Virón*, with 47.2% – more than 40% *redondillas*'. By this reckoning the proportion of *romances* (23.9%) in *Los desprecios en quien ama* is rather low for a play by Montalbán, and the proportion of *redondillas* (63.5%) is certainly too high. On the other hand, although he notes the uncharacteristic percentages of *romances* and *redondillas* in *Los desprecios en quien ama*, and also the presence of six-syllable *redondillas* (not utilized in any definitely authentic play), Jack Parker reaches the conclusion that 'the play is by Montalván'.[55] Less

[51] See Melveena McKendrick, *Woman and Society in the Spanish Drama of the Golden Age. A Study of the 'mujer varonil'* (London: Cambridge University Press, 1974), pp. 146, 148.

[52] The genre is one to which Montalbán's *Despreciar lo que se quiere* might also be said to belong. This work (published in Montalbán's *Segundo tomo de las comedias*), was performed at the palace by Roque de Figueroa in 1633, but was probably written c.1624 – that is, close to the date of composition of *Los desprecios en quien ama* (see Varey and Shergold, 'Some Palace Performances', pp. 222–23; Parker 'Chronology of the Plays of Montalván', p. 195). *Despreciar lo que se quiere* is a different play entirely (for a plot-summary, see Parker, *Montalván*, pp. 59–60), but it is always a possibility that their similar titles simply misled printers into assuming that *Los desprecios en quien ama* and *Despreciar lo que se quiere* were one and the same play, by Montalbán.

[53] See La Barrera, p. 541.

[54] S. Griswold Morley, 'Notes on the Bibliography of Lope de Vega's *Comedias*', *Modern Philology*, XX (1922–23), 201–17, at p. 208.

[55] See Dixon, 'Montalbán's *Segundo tomo de las comedias*', p. 106; Parker, 'Chronology of the Plays of Montalván', pp. 202, 204. Parker's study of Montalbán's versification practices, though necessarily tentative, is still the most comprehensive available to us.

convinced than Parker of Montalbán's authorship, Dixon points to several features in *Los desprecios en quien ama* that he considers to be uncharacteristic: 'Untypical of Montalbán, to my mind, are the *gracioso*'s impersonation of an "ambassador", and the hero's assumption of the role of secretary to the heroine; the situation, with its suggestion of Love *versus* Social Inequality . . . recall[s] plays like Lope's *El perro del hortelano* more readily than any of Montalbán's works.' Yet, Dixon also identifies 'a few episodes – Alberto's *relación*, for instance, which recalls one in *Cumplir con su obligación* – and occasional ideas or turns of phrase [which] might remind us of Montalbán'. Dixon concludes, therefore, that while 'there is no clear confirmation of his authorship in the play', equally, 'we cannot affirm that it is not his, especially since in any case it seems to have been performed when he was only twenty-three or twenty-four'.[56] Initially, Profeti (*Montalbán: un commediografo dell'età di Lope* [1970]) had been inclined to accept Montalbán's authorship, while not judging it to be among 'le più caratteristiche' of Montalbán's plays. But in *Per una bibliografia di J. Pérez de Montalbán*, published six years later, she explains that 'ad un più maturo esame, l'attribuzione a Lope appare tutt'altro che da scartare'. Therefore, she prefers to reserve final judgement in this matter: 'Allo stato attuale della documentazione riteniamo ragionevole nutrire dubbi circa la legittimità dell'inserimento di questa commedia nella produzione di Montalbán.'[57]

Dixon's and Profeti's expressed uncertainties indeed seem reasonable in view of the shortage of documented evidence available to date to substantiate Montalbán's claims. Nevertheless, certain internal indications perceived within the play have encouraged me to believe (though, as yet, belief stops short of conviction), that Montalbán rather than Lope de Vega composed *Los desprecios en quien ama*.

Interested scholars, like Victor Dixon and Peter Evans, seeking to discredit further the once commonly held view 'that Golden-Age dramatists had little taste or aptitude for characterization',[58] will find evidence in rich supply in this play. All the main characters in the play – aptly described by Dixon as a 'comedy of character'[59] – are skilfully portrayed. Whoever characterized the heroine, Claudia, had a good knowledge of feminine psychology. No better knowledge, of course, than that repeatedly displayed in his *comedias* by Lope de Vega. Montalbán, too, however, had an unusual

---

[56] See Dixon, *The Life and Works of Montalbán*, pp. 293–94.

[57] See Profeti, *Per una bibliografia di Montalbán*, p. 419; cf. Profeti, *Montalbán*, p. 65.

[58] See Peter Evans, '*Peribáñez* and Ways of Looking at Golden-Age Dramatic Characters', *Romanic Review*, LXXIV (1983), 136–51, at p. 136; Victor F. Dixon, *Characterization in the Comedia of Seventeenth-century Spain*, Manchester Spanish and Portuguese Studies, 3 (Manchester: Department of Spanish and Portuguese, University of Manchester, 1994).

[59] Dixon, *The Life and Works of Montalbán*, pp. 293–94.

insight, enabling him to dramatize convincingly the workings of the female mind, as more than one scholar has pointed out.[60] As I show in another study, Claudia has a distinct resemblance to Diana, the 'dog-in-a-manger' heroine of Lope's famous play. Much as she loves her secretary, she considers marriage to him to be impossible because of the difference which she perceives (in Claudia's case, mistakenly) in their status. Yet, when she believes that another woman might win the love of the man she herself adores, she refuses to give him up. Interestingly, Claudia is sufficiently self-analytical to recognize the contradictions in her own behaviour. So when she believes that she has no choice but to send Alberto far away from her household, in order to protect his life, she confesses to him:

> Cuando no juzgase,
> que podía perderte,
> podré aborrecerte,
> ¡ay, qué mal pensé!
> Mas ya en tu partida,
> pues sin alma quedo,
> negarte no puedo,
> que eres tú mi vida.   (III, fol. 78)[61]

The hero, Alberto, Duque de Florencia and the *gracioso*, Yepes, are also characterized skilfully and in depth. Alberto is a creative thinker and consummate strategist. Personally he devises and carries out a strategy of pretended disdain, while also utilizing, as needed, a variety of other deceptions, until he succeeds in overcoming the resistance of his lady. With these deceptions he is constantly assisted by his *gracioso*-lackey Yepes/Carlos, 'el embajador fingido' referred to in the play's alternative title. The *gracioso*, as Parker says, is usually well drawn in Montalbán, and, in its importance, Yepes' role is in keeping with that played by his counterparts, the 'fully developed' *graciosos* observed by Dixon 'in every authentic play of Montalbán'.[62]

Perhaps in part because of his admiration for Lope, Montalbán had a particular fondness for naming his *graciosos* 'Tristán'. Lope used 'Tristán' as the name for the lackey in *La francesilla* (1596), a play which Lope dedicated to Montalbán when he published it in *Parte XIII* of his *comedias* (1620).[63] Lope was to use the name 'Tristán' not infrequently thereafter, and perhaps

[60] See, for instance, Bacon, p. 56; Parker, *Montalván*, p. 133.

[61] All quotations are taken from the *comedia suelta* printed, with the title *El embajador fingido*, by Francisco de Lyra (Seville, c.1632–34) (in *Comedia[s] de Lope Vol. II*, Sydney Jones Library, University of Liverpool).

[62] See Parker, *Montalván*, p. 30; Dixon, 'Montalbán's *Segundo tomo de las comedias*', p. 108.

[63] See Américo Castro and Hugo A. Rennert, *Vida de Lope de Vega (1562–1635)* (Salamanca: Anaya, 1968), pp. 463–64.

most famously for the *gracioso* in *El perro del hortelano*. This demonstrates the truth in Dixon's comment that 'in questions of attribution, the very names of the characters of a play do not fail to have their importance, since each author had his own criterion of selection'.[64] However, whereas *graciosos* called 'Tristán' are easily encountered, for instance, in Montalbán's *No hay vida como la honra*, *Como padre y como rey* and *La doncella de labor*, I can think of none who is called 'Yepes', the true name of the *gracioso*-envoy in *Los desprecios en quien ama*. Yet, that unusual choice of name, if, as I suspect, it was made for a particular reason, might provide an additional clue to the authorship of *Los desprecios en quien ama*. The play is, of course, set in Italy, in and near Florence. But the *gracioso* makes a point of telling the audience that he is from Spain, and, to be precise, as he repeatedly reminds them, from Seville. Yepes is called Yepes, because he is, in fact,

> de Yepes, lugar famoso,
> que alinda con la gran mesa
> de Osuna, patria mia.
> [. . .]
> En Yepes nací, mi nombre
> es Yepes.   (I, fol. 63)

While Yepes is the only authentic Spaniard, and *sevillano*, in the play, no fewer than two other major characters, Alberto, Duque de Florencia, and Federico, Duque de Ferrara, choose to pretend to be natives of Spain. What is more, in adopting their falsely Spanish identity, each to pursue their amorous interest in Claudia, Condesa de Belflor, each opts, independently, for the same choice of *patria* – which is, like the *gracioso*'s, Seville! Thus, when he seeks asylum in Claudia's household, pretending to have incurred the anger of the Duque de Florencia (who is, as the audience is well aware, himself!), Alberto introduces himself to Claudia as follows:

> Yo soy, hermosa condesa,
> un caballero de España,
> [. . .]
> Mi nombre es don Juan Manrique,
> la gran Sevilla es mi patria.   (I, fol. 65)

Federico similarly insists that he is 'de Sevilla' which produces an entertainingly argumentative exchange between him and Yepes. The *gracioso* clearly does not believe for a moment that Federico is a fellow *sevillano*, and questions him closely – for instance, about Seville's most famous monument:

---

[64] See Dixon's prologue to his edition of *El sufrimiento premiado*, p. xix.

Yepes:	¿De dónde sois?
Federico:	Soy de España
[. . .]	
Yep:	¿De qué lugar?
Fed:	De Sevilla
Yep:	Es octava maravilla
	del mundo, lugar famoso:
	¿qué hay en la Torre, soldado?
Fed:	Es fábrica hermosa, y bella,
	y es muy alta.
Yep:	¿Qué hay en ella?
Fed:	Hay un chapitel dorado.
Yep:	¿Qué hay en la Torre?
Fed:	No vi
	hombre tan preguntador.
Yep:	Ves como os cogí señor,
	¿la Giralda no está allí? (I, fol. 67)

So much entertaining emphasis and positive comment on Seville, its surroundings and its identifying features, indicate that the play's author might well have had a special relationship with that part of Spain. There were many Golden-Age dramatists who were from the South of Spain, and some of these (Cristóbal de Monroy y Silva, Luis Vélez de Guevara) were from Seville, or, like Andrés de Claramonte, had connections with that province or city.[65] Montalbán was, of course, an 'hijo de Madrid'. Some time before 1635, however, he is known to have spent a period in Seville, for his father had business interests there.[66] The inclusion of so many references to Seville certainly points to a first or early performance of the play there, perhaps by the same company of Andrés de la Vega that performed the play at the palace in Madrid in 1625, since that *autor de comedias* is known to have been in Seville, with his company, in 1624.[67]

According to Rennert, Montalván often asked for a *vítor* in the final verses of his *comedias*, whereas 'Lope de Vega never stooped so low as this'.[68] Probably Rennert exaggerated Lope's abstinence in this regard. Even

[65] Claramonte was from Murcia, but is known to have been in Seville during, though not necessarily throughout, the period 1617–24. He was certainly there in 1623–24, when his *autos* were being performed by the company of Andrés de la Vega (see José Sánchez-Arjona, *El teatro en Sevilla en los siglos XVI y XVII* [Madrid, 1887; new edition, Sevilla: Centro Andaluz de Teatro, 1990], pp. 231–34, at p. 232; Vern G. Williamsen, *The Minor Dramatists of Seventeenth-Century Spain* [Boston: Twayne, 1982], p. 41).

[66] See Parker, *Montalván*, p. 18.

[67] See Rennert, *The Spanish Stage in the Time of Lope de Vega* (1909 ed.), pp. 621–22; and cf. my note 65.

[68] See Rennert, *The Spanish Stage in the Time of Lope de Vega* (New York: Dover Publications, 1963), pp. 122–23.

so, he is correct about Montalbán, for there are, indeed, in the closing lines of
Montalbán's definitely authentic plays many requests to the audience for that
traditional sound of acclaim. As the last verses of *Cumplir con tu obligación*,
Como padre y como rey, *La toquera vizcaína* and *La más constante mujer* all
serve to demonstrate, Rennert is also correct to suggest that Montalbán
usually made his request for a *vítor* in terms chosen with ingenuity. In *Los
desprecios en quien ama* the *gracioso* helps to bring the *comedia* wittily to an
end in a fashion wholly characteristic of Montalbán, asking the audience, on
the playwright's behalf, to voice their approval:

Alberto:	Tus cuidados
	premien doce mil ducados.
Yepes:	Vítor, ya no ha sido escasa
	la merced, iré a gastarlos
	a España, y me llamaré
	a dondequiera que esté,
	el embajador don Carlos:
	esta grandeza la fama
	publique.
Alberto:	Y en bien tan cierto
	canten con glorias, Alberto,
	los desprecios en quien ama. (III, fol. 78)

As early as 1962, when still only at the beginning of his distinguished
career in research, Victor Dixon already perceived clearly the fundamental
need 'to determine so far as possible which of the hundred-odd plays attributed to Juan Pérez de Montalbán were in fact written by him'.[69] To accom-
plish such a huge enterprise will require the dedicated endeavours of
numerous *comediantes* working internationally in collaboration. The initiative needed to realize a team project of this magnitude should logically be
taken by scholars within Spain itself, many of whom are currently completing
important researches on the drama of the Golden Age. Not until the
numerous plays which have been attributed to this transitional dramatist are
edited and studied in depth will it be possible for scholars to ascertain where
and how Montalbán stands, or falls, between the two great schools of dramatists dominated respectively by Lope and Calderón. Only then will Juan Pérez
de Montalbán be adequately understood as 'a dramatist in his own right and a
figure of significance in the development of the *comedia*'.[70]

[69] See Dixon, 'Montalbán's *Segundo tomo de las comedias*', p. 91.
[70] Dixon, review of Profeti's *Montalbán: un commediografo*, p. 186.

Constructions of a Scapegoat: Calderón and the Anglo-Spanish Demonization of Anne Boleyn

MELVEENA MCKENDRICK

The attraction for Calderón of writing a play about the schism of England is, both in dramatic and theological terms, obvious. It is a striking historical anticipation of the Faust theme that he was to tackle more directly in *El mágico prodigioso* ten years or so later – the true story of a man who had sold not just his own soul but the soul of his country for the possession of a woman he desired. Anne Boleyn had been Eve incarnate – the Fall had been replayed.

The schism must be one of the most spectacular consequences of human passion in history. Not only did Henry's irritation and impatience with Rome lead to the withdrawal of a major European political player – England – from the universal Church, but that rejection of papal authority and the separation from Rome which followed it gave a crucial added impulse to the permanent division of Christendom into two camps. Passion, of course, was by no means the only cause. Indeed it can more accurately be seen as the catalyst of events rather than the cause itself. A nexus of political intrigue, dynastic anxieties, family rivalries and personal interests in fact led to the English Reform. There is little doubt now that what drove Henry along his chosen path was his conviction that Catherine's inability to provide him with a male heir was a divine punishment for marrying his brother's wife. Certainly his fascination with Anne Boleyn hardened his resolve, but his desire to marry her rather than keep her as his mistress was crucially determined by his lack of a son. Had a healthy boy been born to Catherine it is almost inconceivable that he would have scandalized most of Europe by repudiating his much admired and much loved queen. Similarly, Wolsey's own ambitions for himself, as well as for his king and his country, certainly played their part in the divorce. Eager for it while it seemed that it might lead to a French union that would further his own campaign for the papacy, he retreated into ambivalence only upon discovering Henry's desire to replace Catherine with Anne.

Anne Boleyn is seen now as the occasion rather than the instigator of the events which followed. When it became obvious that Catherine, by this time in her mid-forties, was unlikely to conceive again, Henry began to think of an alternative solution, and at some stage in this process a courtly dalliance with one of her ladies-in-waiting began to turn into something more serious, probably encouraged by her refusal to become his mistress. Anne certainly held out for marriage, supported Henry in the ensuing battle with Rome and, although doctrinally orthodox, became genuinely interested in reform, showing herself to be an astute and determined politician.[1] However, the picture of her as a malicious, manipulative schemer who led Henry astray from the path of marital and religious fidelity has now been relegated to the scrapheap of historical interpretation, a creation of her Spanish and many English enemies. Henry was far too wilful a man to be persuaded to do anything he did not wish to do, least of all by a woman.

The demonization of Anne Boleyn is in itself an extraordinary story. It seems to have its origins not in any spontaneous Spanish animosity towards her for usurping a Spanish princess and supposedly detaching England from Rome, but in a concerted campaign launched early on by Catherine's supporters to try and provoke Charles V into action over a matter in which he was understandably reluctant to intervene: overt Spanish hostility, after all, might drive the English into the arms of the French. A *consulta* from his council on 31 May 1533 pointed out that his concern over his aunt's honour was a private matter and placed no public and political responsibilities upon him.[2] In the event he did nothing, in the vain hope that diplomatic pressure would change Henry's mind. However, the campaign of defamation initiated by the Imperial Ambassador, Íñigo de Mendoza, and Eustace Chapuys, the Spanish Ambassador and Anne Boleyn's most resolute enemy, was extremely effective in laying the groundwork for the construction closer to home of Anne's composite image of witch, heretic and wanton, an image which fulfilled its purpose of contaminating the King's perception of her and bringing about her destruction.

There is no doubt that, although sallow-skinned and not formally beautiful, Anne was handsome, graceful and sexually seductive, with a comely figure and, according to the Venetian ambassador, beautiful black eyes. She was also highly intelligent, strong-willed, independent and unconventional – dangerous things for a woman to be in the sixteenth century. These qualities made her the inevitable scapegoat in a crisis where blame had to be laid somewhere and where, for political reasons at home and diplomatic reasons abroad, it could not readily be laid upon the King. It was for her a misfortune that Catherine, who had been so loved a queen, proved so steely an opponent

---

[1] Peter Ackroyd in his *The Life of Sir Thomas More* (London: Vintage, 1999) points out that 'Anne had grown up in the society and culture of French humanists and may already have espoused what could be called a "reformist" attitude towards church matters based upon an intense reverence for the New Testament. She was by no means a Lutheran, and was indeed much closer to Erasmus; but, in the climate of the time, her position was significant' (p. 264).

[2] See David Loades in his excellent reassessment of Anne Boleyn in *Henry VIII and His Queens* (Stroud: Sutton Publishing, 1996), pp. 63–64.

(for religious as much as personal reasons), and that she and her daughter Mary strove so successfully to appear ill-used and to cast Anne in the role of wicked stepmother. Through her refusal to conform to prevailing expectations of what it was to be a woman in a situation where powerful vested interests wanted her gone, Anne provoked unpopularity and suspicion, and herself partly created the conditions for her own downfall. Since the ambitious Boleyn family were politically active and influential at court – Anne's father Thomas Boleyn, Earl of Wiltshire, was Lord Privy Seal – Henry's heresy and his tyrannical excesses, including in due course the executions of John Fisher and Sir Thomas More, were only too easily attributed to the Queen's influence. When time went by without the appearance of a live male heir after three pregnancies in as many years, recent history almost inevitably repeated itself. With Jane Seymour hovering in the wings, Henry's sexual and dynastic anxieties led him to doubt the legitimacy of his second marriage in turn and to choose once more to see in his lack of male issue a sign of divine disapproval. Fatefully for Anne, who not long before had been delivered of a still-born child, she miscarried in January 1536 a premature male foetus that was rumoured to have been defective and almost certainly was.[3] Thomas Cromwell, a former supporter who had recently turned his coat for political advantage and was now an implacable enemy, had no difficulty in encouraging Henry to see in this a sign of sexual deviance – still births and malformations were associated at the time with witchcraft and illicit sex and the last thing Henry would have wished to admit to was the paternity of such a child. On 2 May Anne was arrested and taken to the Tower.

The charges brought against her were comprehensive and grievous. She was accused of having committed serial adultery with five lovers between October and December 1535, one of them her own brother George, Lord Rochford, who appears to have been given prime responsibility for her aborted pregnancy.[4] For good measure she was also accused of poisoning Catherine and attempting to poison Mary, of causing the King bodily harm (it is assumed that the allusion here was impotence) and of conspiring against his life.[5] All those implicated were found guilty. These charges were crucial in the vilification of Anne Boleyn, transforming her as they did from a scheming seductress into something infinitely more sinister. She was not technically charged with witchcraft, but incest and sexual depravity were associated during this period with witches, and Henry himself made up his

[3]   Retha M. Warnicke persuasively argues that Anne did miscarry a deformed foetus. See her illuminating revisionist study, *The Rise and Fall of Anne Boleyn. Family Politics at the Court of Henry VIII* (Cambridge: Cambridge University Press, 1989), pp. 3–5.

[4]   Warnicke suggests that the implication of so many men was intended to rule out the likelihood of Henry's being the father of the aborted foetus (pp. 191–232).

[5]   Her supposed lovers were reputed libertines suspected of illicit sexual acts, two of them of sodomy. See Warnicke, pp. 3–5.

mind, once his course became clear to him, that he must have been literally bewitched by Anne into marriage. There seems little doubt that he convinced himself of Anne's guilt. She was not only dispensable, but she was the sacrifice necessary for Henry to come to terms with his repudiation of Catherine and move on. She therefore became the repository and ultimately the expiator of Henry's own sins. After some moments of panic during which she unwisely tried to defend herself with explanatory talk of courtly gallantries, thereby implicating several more unfortunate courtiers, Anne conducted herself with remarkable steadfastness and dignity, eloquently denying all charges to the last.[6] Impressed by her testimony as they were, the judges could do little in the face of the King's conviction that he had married a depraved monster. Before her death, Anne swore upon the Eucharist that she was innocent. Many, even the Imperial Ambassador who desired her downfall, believed the charges to be false, and the fickle public, who had colluded in her destruction with their tongues, now muttered indignantly of injustice. The damage to her reputation, however, had been done. In Catholic Europe at large, the woman of whom her confessor Archbishop Cranmer was brave enough to say to his king at the time of Anne's arrest, 'I never had better opinion in woman, than I had in her; which maketh me to think, that she should not be culpable', became a devil figure. In Spain Ana Bolena would appear as a demon in carnivals down until the twentieth century and do long service as a bogey invoked by parents to frighten naughty children into obedience.

Such, in brief, are those circumstances of Anne Boleyn's part in the schism of England which concern us here. Calderón, of course, when he wrote *La cisma de Inglaterra* was separated from these terrible events not only by almost a hundred years but by religious perspective and by a long history of Anglo-Spanish hostility. While retaining this narrative as our fixed frame, therefore, we have to turn to the source material actually available to Calderón in order to identify the choices he made in his dramatization of Anne Boleyn and to understand why he made them. These choices are revealing and not a little surprising. It goes without saying that what appears at first sight to be historical specificity is compounded not only of religious and national perspectives but also, like Anne Boleyn's reputation itself, of contemporary attitudes to women. At the same time an examination of Calderón's likely sources reveals an active and deliberate selection process at work in the play text, a process that discriminates against some of the very ingredients that might have been thought to suit his purpose. News of the sensational aspects of Anne's trial certainly reached Spain, although how long and in what sort of detail the memory of the charges against her lasted it is impos-

---

[6]   As David Loades points out, the antics of courtly love could be a dangerous game if things went wrong (p. 83).

sible to tell. What is clear is that Calderón relied neither on the prejudices of the ignorant nor on the superstitions of the gullible for his Ana Bolena.

Three works figure in the construction of the events of the schism of England available to Spaniards by the late sixteenth century: the anonymous *Chronica del Rey Enrique Otavo de Inglaterra,* which appears to have been started in 1550 with the earliest surviving copy dating from 1556;[7] the Catholic priest and polemicist Nicholas Sander's *De origine et progressu schismatis Anglicani*, published posthumously in Cologne in 1585;[8] and the Jesuit Padre Pedro de Rivadeneyra's *Historia Eclesiástica del Scisma del Reino de Inglaterra* of 1588.[9] Calderón's principal source was Rivadeneyra, whose principal source in turn was Sander. However, Rivadeneyra reproduced the *Chronica's* version of events in at least two places (describing Anne's coronation and Henry's deathbed farewell to Mary), and there is some evidence that Calderón too might have had access to this text. In chapter II the *Chronica* ascribes the following words to Wolsey as he first broaches the legitimacy of Henry's marriage to Catherine: 'Sir, your Majesty must know that for many days I have wished to say something to you, but I do not dare for fear you should be angry with me' (Hume, op. cit. p. 3). While Rivadeneyra and Sander make no mention of this, Volseo (Act II, p. 159a) says something very similar: 'Mil veces ha querido/ mi lealtad, que te adora,/ decirte lo que ahora;/ pero no me he atrevido;/ que, por injustas leyes,/ no se dicen verdades a los reyes.' Again, only the *Chronica* and Calderón attribute Wolsey's downfall to Anne Boleyn. It is therefore legitimate to consider all three texts as potential grist to Calderón's mill when he came to write his play.

Although the dedicatory epistle of the *Chronica* refers to the author as being a Valencian lawyer or man of letters who lived in England at the time of the events described, Hume concluded that the writer was more likely to have been a resident merchant or interpreter, so imprecise and crude is the narrative. Since the author claims to have been the only foreigner present at Anne Boleyn's execution in the Tower, I think we can assume that his account is a mixture of some witness and much hearsay. The fact that he wrote his account years later, possibly from exile during the persecutions, no doubt encouraged a certain indeterminacy and inflation of recall. He was certainly not politically informed. Chapuys in his despatches to Charles V between 1529 and 1536, which are a mass of contradictions, represented Anne as both flirtatious and evil, a she-devil and desecrating concubine who he was

7   *Chronicle of King Henry VIII of England*, translated and edited by Martin A. S. Hume (London: George Bell & Sons, 1889).

8   See *Rise and Growth of the Anglican Church*, translated by David Lewis (London: Burns and Oates, 1977).

9   *Obras escogidas del Padre Pedro de Rivadeneira*, Biblioteca de Autores Españoles, 60 (Madrid: M. Rivadeneyra, 1868), pp. 177–357.

convinced used witchcraft to achieve her ends. Exploited by Catherine and Mary for their own purposes, fed misinformation by his sources, and ready to put a malicious spin on everything, he it was who initiated the fateful reinvention of Anne's life. But none of this seems to have percolated through to our anonymous chronicler. He presents Wolsey as the prime cause of events, and although he gives Anne the responsibility for Wolsey's downfall when he inconveniently changed his mind and decided that the marriage with Catherine was after all valid (p. 9), there is no criticism of Anne at this stage. When he gets to Anne's coronation he does upbraid her for keeping the purse of 2000 nobles she received by tradition on her way to be crowned, instead of dividing it amongst her retinue as Catherine had done, and he states that 'not ten people wished her well as she passed', observing that the common people always disliked her (pp. 12–13), which was true, very largely because they were so devoted to her predecessor. As the narrative proceeds, he becomes more censorious. The information that at the French court she had been said to be 'not averse to the Admiral of France' (possibly the inspiration for Carlos in Calderón's play and a coy accusation in comparison with Rivadeneyra's Sander-inspired claim that she was known by the French as 'la yegua inglesa' (p. 193), is followed by 'Anything may be believed of her, for she acted as will be related presently' (p. 32). This judgement, which inadvertently puts its finger on the creative role played by credulousness in the confection that became Anne Boleyn's history, expands by and by into 'No man could imagine or think of all the wickedness which Anne invented, or the pleasure she took in doing harm to the blessed Queen Katherine' (p. 44). The *Chronica* was the first account to claim that Sir Thomas Wyatt, later ambassador to Charles V, had been Anne's lover, but where it goes into extraordinary detail is in its account of Anne's alleged adultery with Mark Smeaton, the low-born groom of the privy chamber whom it makes the central figure in the sexual scandal.[10] The author of the *Chronica* says nothing of the Queen's miscarriage just before this, but reports that Rochford, Anne's brother, was arrested on the basis that he had been seen entering Anne's chamber on several occasions dressed in night clothes. He dutifully relays Rochford's protestations of innocence – he claims to have been just talking to his sister who had been unwell – and he himself neither asserts that any of the charges were valid nor accuses anyone of guilt. Anne's sin for him was pride, her crime persuading the King to leave Catherine.

---

[10] Smeaton confessed, under duress and on the promise of a pardon, to adultery with the Queen – he was the only one of the five to do so – but he was executed nonetheless. The *Chronica* holds that it was Henry Percy, by now Earl of Northumberland, who had earlier been betrothed to Anne, who reported the affair to Cromwell out of jealousy. Warnicke, arguing that all five alleged lovers were chosen for their role on account of their dubious sexual reputations, suggests that Smeaton might have been Rochford's catamite (pp. 191–232).

The *Chronica*'s portrait of Anne Boleyn, in other words, is a relatively sober, relatively objective account of her character and behaviour which implicitly accepts the truth of events and reports as its author recounts them but without any of the indignant denunciations and outraged moralizing that characterize the narratives of Sander and Rivadeneyra, as we shall see. There is no mention of Lutheran tendencies, no mention of her physical appearance, which was to play so large a part in Anne's demonization, no suggestion of witchcraft, and no mention of still births or miscarriages. Indeed it is tempting to see in this restrained portrait of Anne the model for Calderón's own Ana, particularly since, as we have already seen, unlike Rivadeneyra who presents Wolsey as the victim of political rivals, both the *Chronica* and Calderón give Anne the prime responsibility for the Cardinal's downfall. Like the anonymous chronicler's Anne Boleyn, Calderón's Ana Bolena is never larger than life, never more than human.

Nicholas Sander, unlike the author of the *Chronica*, had an obvious axe to grind. He was a ferocious enemy of Elizabeth I and his aim in blackening Anne Boleyn was to denigrate her daughter and promote resistance against her. Born in 1530, he settled in Madrid in 1573 as a spokesman for English Catholic refugees and it was there he committed to public record the Medean version of Anne Boleyn that best suited Catholic interests – by now there existed a wealth of written material and rumour on which he could draw.[11] He was the first to report information about Anne's alleged sexual habits as a child, to claim that Anne's mother had been Henry's mistress, and that Anne was his own daughter. Even an invitation in 1512 from Margaret of Austria, Regent of the Netherlands, to Anne's father, then envoy in the Netherlands, for Anne to join the schoolroom of her four wards – the children of Philip of Burgundy and Juana la Loca, including the future Charles V – was rewritten as a decision to send her away from home because of her sexual involvement (at the age of five) with the Boleyn household's chaplain and butler.[12] Although he had never seen her, Sander also painted a grotesque and entirely false picture of Anne as extremely tall (height in a woman was taken at the time as a sign of lustfulness), sallow, with a tumour on her neck, a projecting tooth, and six fingers on her right hand, all features associated with witchcraft and none of them reported by more reliable commentators who knew her well.[13] He goes on to give credence to the rumour of the malformed

---

[11] See Warnicke, p. 243.

[12] Two years later in 1514 Henry VIII's sister Mary, recently wed to Louis XII of France, asked to have 'la pettite Boulain' with her in France and she remained there after Mary was widowed seven months later. Her father finally asked for her return in 1521. See Warnicke, pp. 1–28.

[13] See Warnicke, p. 3. The most lurid reports gave her witches' teats on her neck. Presumably Anne's sexual appeal in spite of this extremely ill-favoured appearance was put down to witchcraft. Henry himself, after all, came to explain his 'bewitchment' by Anne in this way.

foetus in a tendentious manner heavy with unspoken accusations of witchery and sexual depravity. All the sensational elements in Anne's stigmatization were therefore brought together in this text, which was published in French, German and Italian translation before the end of the century and republished in Latin in Cologne in 1610 and 1628. It was considered the leading Catholic indictment of the English Reformation and the demonization of Anne was central to its argument and to its purpose. It is not at all improbable that Calderón would have known Sander's work. He would certainly been very familiar with its contents at one remove because Rivadeneyra, his principal source, closely reproduced Sander's account, as he had every reason to do. When Mary Tudor fell ill in 1558 Rivadeneyra accompanied Philip II's representative, the Duque de Feria, to England, arriving in time to be present at her death. Rivadeneyra stayed on for four months, spending his time protecting the Duke's household from contagion by Protestantism, which was already beginning to flourish again, and combating heterodoxy wherever he encountered it. His history of the schism went into numerous editions and remained Spain's prime source of information about the Reformation for two hundred years.

Calderón retains the general image of Anne presented by Rivadeneyra as arrogant, ambitious and wanton, but he tones down considerably the sexual and other sensationalist claims taken from Sander. Whereas Ana Bolena has only the one old flame whom she genuinely loves – the French ambassador Carlos whom she got to know in France, a conflation perhaps of Anne's original betrothed Lord Henry Percy and the Admiral of France referred to by Chapuys[14] – Rivadeneyra repeats the lurid accusations of an insatiable sexual appetite and hints at depraved practices, although he like Sander carefully avoids direct mention of witchcraft.[15] Calderón is clearly using the fact of Anne's long stay in France before her arrival at the English court as a basis for his fiction. His scenario is that of an ambitious woman in love who sacrifices love for ambition, allows passion to surface again, thinking she can indulge both desires, and pays the price. In pursuit of that ambition she ruins a saintly queen and destroys an arm of the Catholic Church. Calderón is also more realistic in his presentation of Anne's sexual appeal. Rivadeneyra is as unflattering as Sander about Anne's appearance although both concede that 'el resto del cuerpo era muy proporcionado y hermoso' (Rivadeneyra, p. 193).[16] The strained attempt to make her simultaneously attractive (and

[14] Anne became secretly engaged to Henry Percy, but royal permission was of course needed for such a marriage and Wolsey put a stop to it for political reasons.

[15] The nearest Calderón comes to the suggestion of witchcraft is in Carlos's mythologized description of Ana as a 'bellísima sirena,/ que aduerme a su encanto los sentidos/ ciega los ojos y abre los oídos' (Act I, 146b).

[16] It has been suggested that it was Anne's fondness for the French ruff and for sleeves which came down over the hand that gave the malicious food for their conclusions.

hence seductive) and repellent (to suggest the witch) has its amusing aspect. Calderón's Ana, by contrast, is not only an exceptionally graceful dancer – which most reports conceded – but is unqualifiedly beautiful, without any of the blemishes and deformities supplied by her detractors. This was not just *comedia* convention asserting itself here but practical psychology – on stage Ana's attraction for the King needed to be convincing, and common sense dictated that, had the descriptions of Anne been true, Henry would have run a mile from her.[17] Rivadeneyra, interestingly, scarcely refers to the royal miscarriages and births other than those of the 'monstruo' Elizabeth (who is not allowed even a mention in Calderón's play), choosing to omit Sander's reference to 'a shapeless mass of flesh', and not even mentioning the need for, or anxieties about, a royal heir. But he does make insistent accusations of incest. He maintains that since Anne's mother, as well as her sister, had been the King's mistress, Anne married her own father.[18] He argues both that the purpose of her sexual activities was to produce a male heir when Henry proved unable to give her one, and also that she committed incest with her own brother in order to make sure that that heir was a Boleyn through and through (the illogic of this, if Henry rather than Thomas Boleyn was her father, does not seem to have bothered him). While there is no doubt that family ambition formed a large part of Anne's motivation in first insisting on marriage to Henry and then wanting to provide him with an heir, the attempt to make Anne's supposed sexual depravity more convincing by applying political motives to it does suggest a certain lack of confidence in the charge of sexual depravity itself.

Calderón, for his part, does not deploy even a hint of incest to blacken Ana's character, although he might well have done given the presence of an incest motif in others of his plays.[19] There is however, I think, a suppressed echo of it in Tomás Boleno's hostility to his daughter in the play and in his involvement in the organization of her trial and execution – both taken from Rivadeneyra. Calderón's Thomas is in fact very much more hostile than Rivadeneyra's, who is disapproving rather than hostile, and who is considerably affected by the execution in spite of supposedly having been one of the trial judges.[20] Tomás Boleno's unnatural hostility, explicitly put down to his

---

[17] Henry indeed is known to have had a superstitious horror of the slightest physical blemish.

[18] Mary Boleyn, Anne's sister, was for a while Henry's mistress and she seems to have been the one with the reputation for loose morals. See Warnicke, pp. 45–46.

[19] It would not have served his purpose to mention the charge that Anne was actually Henry's daughter since that would have demonized too much the husband of one Spanish queen and the father of another, but Anne's alleged incest with her brother, if only hinted at, could have served very well indeed to blacken her character. A few years later the incest motif would become central to *La devoción de la cruz*.

[20] In fact Thomas Boleyn acted as judge only at the trials of the four men accused of adultery with Anne and not at those of his daughter and son. Since Calderón is more accu-

daughter's ambition and arrogance, is used, I suggest, by Calderón as a way of keeping his portrait of Ana within the bounds both of decorum and normality, as a way of demonizing her without recourse to lurid accusations of witchcraft and sexual depravity. Even Rivadeneyra's accusation that she was a covert Lutheran who refused confession before her death (which is untrue – she died a Catholic) inserts itself only tentatively, first in Henry's dream when the woman in his room threatens to erase what he is writing and later when Carlos, the French Ambassador and Ana's admirer, gives what he suspects are her Lutheran sympathies as his reason for wanting her for a mistress rather than a wife (Act I, p. 147b). What more convincing condemnation of a child than the testimony of its own parent? And yet there is something curiously disproportionate about it. It is infused with a distaste and a contempt that have their source in a distant chorus of accusation and whisper inaudible within the world of the play itself.

Calderón's characterization of Anne Boleyn, therefore, is not only remarkably restrained in the context of her scurrilous reputation in Catholic Europe, but it is extremely moderate in comparison with the outraged tone of his major source, the sober and learned Rivadeneyra. His streamlined version may be the thoughtful construct of a man wary of the excesses of scandal-mongering and superstition, even in relation to a woman perceived as having been so destructive to the Faith, and with a surer grasp of the plausible. But it is also the considered strategy of a playwright intent on producing a workable theatrical action – as distinct from the pageant play that constitutes Shakespeare's *King Henry VIII* – to serve as an effective vehicle for his own dramatic purposes.

Shakespeare's purpose was largely political.[21] Written in 1612–13, and possibly connected with the marriage celebrations of Princess Elizabeth and Prince Frederick, the Elector Palatine (a leading champion of Protestantism in Germany) on 14 February 1613, his play owes much to masque and romance and deals with power and politics at court, with the disruption and restoration of national order. Anxious to avoid offending both Protestant and Catholic sensibilities, its version of events is carefully selective, avoiding any explicit reference to the schism and the relevance to it of Henry's marriage to Anne. It is tolerant and reconciliatory, ending as it does with Elizabeth's christening and Cranmer's vision of a new and glorious age under her and James. Wolsey's role in the divorce from Katherine is ambiguous and Shake-

rate in involving Thomas Boleyn judicially in the affair without actually making him the judge of his own daughter's case, it is conceivable that he had an alternative and more reliable source of information on this point.

[21] For a bibliography of criticism of *La cisma de Inglaterra* and of comparisons between it and *King Henry VIII* see *The Schism in England*, translated by Kenneth Muir and Ann L. Mackenzie, with an introduction and commentary by Mackenzie (Warminster: Aris & Phillips, 1990), pp. 258–59.

speare's treatment of him makes some attempt at being even-handed, but he still comes across unequivocally as scheming, manipulative and power-hungry – a great but deeply flawed and dangerous man playing a complicated and devious game for very high stakes. Katherine herself is portrayed as a courageous, honest and saintly woman, clear-sighted and resolute in her op-position to royal absolutism. Anne is beautiful and blameless, loved by the people (a blatant piece of historical rewriting that illustrates her protean availability to vested interest), and described even by Wolsey as a woman of moral quality 'virtuous / and well-deserving'.[22] Both women are presented as victims but, whereas Anne is little more than a cypher of hope and rebirth whose story is not yet over when the play ends, Katherine's rôle as the tragic figure at the centre of that part of Henry's reign covered by the play is much more fully developed. The schematic configurations of rôle here are Wolsey as effective villain, Henry as contributory victim and Katherine and Anne as blameless victims. Calderón, as one would expect, reshuffles the parts, casting Ana and Volseo as first and second villains in that order, Enrique as contributory victim, with Catalina of course as blameless victim. This scapegoating of Ana, like the highly selective nature of her characterization, is determined by the thrust of Calderón's purpose. This is not sectarian, for all that it is inevitably informed by a sectarian perspective, but moral albeit with a political application. For him Ana and Volseo are cast in the same mould. He rejected the sensationalist version of Anne Boleyn because it would have distracted from his immediate preoccupation: the monumentally destructive effects in two people (Ana and Volseo) of overweening pride and ambition, and their fall into ignominy and disgrace, and in one of them (Ana) of overwhelming sexual passion. Ambition and passion, the unrestrained indulgence of personal desires and the individual will – at the highest level – are his palpable theme. Its political dimension is absolutism: the will of a monarch to pursue his own wishes in the face of natural justice, right thinking, and the temporal and spiritual welfare of his kingdom, and the attendant danger of partisan and self-serving counsellors, of whom Ana here is one – another familiar scapegoat role in which she was cast by Sander and Rivadeneyra. The shades of Henry VIII and Elizabeth I haunt the succession of anxious treatises on kingship subsequently produced by Spanish political philosophers over the following century, one of the most influential of course being Rivadeneyra's own.

Witchcraft, incest and sexual excess would not have been easy subjects to handle on the seventeenth-century stage particularly all in one package, but other plays circumspectly broached such subjects and got away with it. The fact that Calderón chose not even to hint at such well-known matters suggests

---

[22] See *King Henry VIII*, ed. John Margeson (Cambridge: Cambridge University Press, 1990), pp. 97–98.

a determined exploration of a concentrated set of motives grounded firmly in the soil of larger, recurrent moral patterns rather than in the bizarre. He needed a human villain whose motivation fell within the more normal spectrum of psychological motivation and moral values. As a result Calderón's Anne is very close to the picture of her given by most modern studies until very recently – an ambitious, aggressive woman who through an irresistible combination of sex appeal and political manipulation persuaded Henry into abandoning both Catherine and Catholicism. He deals with the problem of reducing a hugely complicated set of circumstances to manageable, comprehensible size by utilizing his favoured device of the prophecy/omen. Volseo, unable to resist augury and to trust in Providence and the evidence of Catalina's goodness, becomes convinced that she is the woman who will destroy him and turns against her.[23] Enrique's vision of Ana in his room simultaneously prepares him psychologically for events to come and to some extent exonerates him from responsibility for what happens. It may also be intended to suggest that his is a mind already troubled and predisposed subconsciously to religious reform, for all his devout writings. Ana then becomes the embodiment of these troubled thoughts. Whichever way round it works, Enrique falls instantly for her sexual attractions and it his passion for her that triggers the events that follow.

Calderón's characterization for the three main players in his drama is unambiguous. The King is portrayed as the all-round Renaissance prince, a gifted, multi-talented leader, a thinker and theologian committed to the Church and its defence, and unquestioning of his marriage until he falls for Ana Bolena. Whether Calderón knew it or not, Henry was indeed a man prey to superstition and emotional impulse, and he presents Enrique as a man so bowled over by sexual infatuation that he is prepared to accept any consequence it might bring despite the terror of the visionary dream in which Ana threatens to erase what he is writing (an anti-Lutheran tract). The idea that the marriage is not legitimate, however, here comes not from him but from Volseo. Volseo is accordingly presented as an ambitious, vain, insecure upstart obsessed with the prophecy that a woman will prove his downfall. His historical opposition to Spain in favour of France is expressed in terms of a personal animosity towards Catherine, for whom he is entirely transparent (Act II, p. 154b). Ana from the start of the play is the villain designate, a latter-day Lucifer in ambition, arrogance, rebelliousness and unwillingness to bow down to authority, a second Eve in her seductive female sexuality, the downfall of men and mankind itself. By the end, an appropriate biblical paradigm has been supplied for her in the figure of the infamous Jezabel, the queen who encouraged idolatry and the killing of the prophets of Israel (Act III, p. 171b). Like all scapegoats she has sins and faults heaped upon her and

---

[23] His source Rivadeneyra states that it was claimed by some that Wolsey had been warned by an astrologer that a woman would ruin him.

what better scapegoat than one who epitomizes at once destructive pride and disruptive sexuality. Like Catholicism and popular history at large, Calderón casts her in the role of first cause in that it is the King's desire for her that renders him open to Volseo's opportunistic suggestion that his marriage to Catherine was illegal from the start. Ana even speaks *aparte* to the audience like the Devil in an *auto* or saint's play to ensure that the audience makes the correct identification of her character and what she stands for:

REY	A mis plantas has caído.
ANA	Mejor diré que a tus plantas
	(pues son esfera divina)
	me he levantado. . . . [Ap] (Tan alta
	que entre los rayos del sol
	mis pensamientos se abrasan
	más remontados). (Act II, p. 155a)[24]

Volseo, too, talks in this Luciferian way, admitting and relishing the evil he intends (Act II, p. 157a), acknowledging at the last that he has fallen from the heights into the abyss (Act III, p. 166b). And this cosmic self-analysis is part of a distinctive, larger textual patterning whereby the play constantly anticipates its own resolution. All three main characters are purposefully endowed with prophetic thoughts, suspicions and dreads which simultaneously stimulate and confirm the expectations of an audience already in possession of the broad facts of the matter. The audience consequently is always ahead of the characters and never behind. Aware that he could not ignore the familiarity of his material, Calderón chose to exploit it instead, constructing an interaction between play story and real (hi)story, between the unfolding and the finished, for purposes both moral and artistic.

For Ana, Calderón invents a lover, Carlos the French ambassador, whose passion can bear witness to her effect on men but who can be abandoned at the drop of a hat as soon as Volseo presents his proposal to her, in order to illustrate her woman's inconstancy, her ambitiousness, her veniality.[25] Ana again condemns herself out of her own mouth:

> Carlos, perdona
> si tu firme amor ofendo,
> cuando hoy aspirar pretendo
> al lustre de una corona.
>   Mujer he sido en dejar

---

[24] *Obras Completas*, I, *Dramas* (Madrid: Aguilar, 1969).

[25] It is possible that behind Carlos there lies the shadow not only of Henry Percy and the Admiral of France but of Sir Thomas Wyatt himself, for the fact that England's ambassador to the court of Charles V was thought by some to have been Anne's lover would have attracted particular interest in Spain.

que me venza el interés:
séalo en mudar después,
y séalo en olvidar.
    Que cuando lleguen a ver
que el interés me ha vencido,
que he olvidado y he fingido,
todo cabe en ser mujer.   (Act II, p. 157b)

Carlos is then used to precipitate her downfall, a single representative of the
multiple lovers with whom the real Anne was accused of committing adultery. The terms of Ana's self-condemnation configure her as the archetypal
woman of misogynist tradition, yet by putting head before heart she is also,
according to an allied set of traditional assumptions, behaving like a man.
The measure of her monstrosity here is not sexual depravity or physical
deformity but gender hybridity. She is 'hic mulier', both what woman is
expected to be (inconstant, vain, venial, selfish) and what woman is expected
not to be (forceful, ambitious, proud, political). She loves Carlos but places
advancement before her feelings for him; it says everything for her vanity that
she thinks she can have both. She is presented as a woman competing in a
man's world at the highest level and for the highest stakes – a portrayal strikingly close in this respect to the modern revisionist view – by using the usual
male ploys of political intrigue in combination with her sexual power over the
King. Desire, in the event, proves her downfall because she cannot resist
responding to Carlos's accusations on his return with the hint of a promise to
renew their affair. So ambition is ultimately betrayed by illicit sexuality, in a
woman the most culpable and dangerous of failings. According to the traditional characterization of woman, therefore, every sin is hers, even those that
are virtues when present in men. Ana's father, significantly, whose antago-
nism towards her is manifest from the start, is repelled precisely by her arrogance and ambition, masculine traits she shares with her co-villain Volseo.
While the plan actually to replace Catalina is Volseo's, Ana is first his indispensable partner and then ultimately his adversary, the *sine qua non* of the
entire enterprise, and the relationship's dynamic is that they share the same
goal – power. Although Calderón schematizes a very complicated political
situation as a personal struggle between Volseo and Ana, it is Ana who
eventually engineers Volseo's downfall and who plots against Catalina and
María – she claims, indeed, to want the deaths of all three of them (Act III, p.
165a), an echo of the charges brought at Anne's trial. She is the designated
devil figure, the scapegoat made to carry the burden of a shared guilt and
eliminated in order to expel the pollution, because that is how the rôle of the
real-life Anne was construed at the time. It is the legacy of the sensationalism
which in its detail Calderón was careful to reject. In the play, Ana is, as she
was in life, the one who departs most from the model of what she ought to be,
the hardest to understand therefore and the easiest to hate. In Volseo's case

the prophecy explains and to some extent excuses behaviour born of fear and insecurity. In Ana's there are no mitigating factors. The anti-feminism of Ana's speech is not Calderón getting at women but part of the necessary process of heaping upon the scapegoat sufficient ignominy to justify her selection for the role. Ana is given what the time would recognize as all the vices of her sex as well as those of her own character, and the fact that, like the Devil, she admits to them is merely a sign of greater wickedness.[26] Any sense that in doing so she is hiding behind her sex compounds the guilt.

The play, of course, in dramatizing the downfall of three great figures, can be seen as a striking multiple example of the turn of Fortune's wheel. It is inflected not in terms of the historical and contingent, of sectarian, factional or family politics, or dynastic concerns reinforced by superstitions about childbirth and witchcraft, but in terms of the unchanging moral failings of ambition, greed and lust for power – the Church is scarcely mentioned until the play's end and the controversy over the marriage of Henry and Catherine is acknowledged only by stressing its legitimacy. Calderón did not need to resort, as Henry had done, to the idea of supernatural power for a convincing explanation of events because he saw in them the only too plausible workings of passion and the absence of reason. Passion is presented as something ungovernable even in a devout and exceptionally gifted king. The King's instant desire for Ana is accompanied by an instant fatigue with Catalina, and although he sees through both Volseo and his own motives he immediately yields to Volseo's suggestion that he repudiate Catalina because that is the direction in which passion drives. Unlike the historical Henry, he is clear that his marriage is legitimate and this makes his subsequent actions a wilful rejection of scriptural exhortation and natural law as well as of papal authority (p. 160a). The King is the one who allows sexual passion to rule his head, but passion, as the unfettered appetite for a desired object, is also involved in the pursuit of self-interest at the expense of reason, and Ana, Volseo and Enrique are all guided and betrayed by it, for all that Ana regards it as a feminine trait.

Calderón knew only too well how court politics worked but he was not interested in the political complexities that informed the events he drama-tized. Nor was he interested in blackguarding Henry and the Protestant cause, in spite of the fact that by 1627, when the play is thought to have been written, Spain and England were at war again after a period of improved diplomatic relations dominated by negotiations for the Spanish Match between the future Charles I and the daughter of Philip III.[27] For Calderón the

---

26 In *El mágico prodigioso* the Devil refers to himself as 'soberbio, altivo, ambicioso', Act II, ed. McKendrick with A. A. Parker (Oxford: Oxford University Press, 1992), line 1710.

27 Ann Mackenzie suggests that Philip IV might have suggested to Calderón that he write a play about these events on the grounds that he had read Rivadeneyra's history and

loss to the Catholic Church was a tragedy and what attracted him above all to his material was its potential as a very powerful parable. He was not even interested in vilifying Ana beyond the requirements of the play because this would have been counterproductive to his purpose. He required Ana to be beautiful and he required her to be plausibly villainous, but no more. Calderón was only too aware that human beings can achieve the Devil's ends all on their own. This is why he edits out Rivadeneyra's excesses and adopts instead the more sober tone of his other likely Spanish source, the *Chronica del Rey Enrique Otavo*. All three guilty characters get their comeuppance according to an appropriate scale of culpability. The King discovers Ana's relationship with Carlos and her continuing feelings for him, is racked with guilt at Catalina's death, and appalled by the consequences of his actions. Volseo, reduced to beggary and full of remorse, escapes an ignominious death by the desperate and sinful act of taking his own life (Act III, p. 168a).[28] The disgraced Ana is eagerly escorted to her execution by her own father, her last words a bitter, unrepentant invocation of the mutability of fortune and the vanity of life (Act III, p. 170b). Visually the play's ending is appropriately emblematic and triumphalist, with the enthronement of Enrique and María and the decapitated corpse of Ana serving as cushion for their feet. The play's last words artfully put history to the service of both irony and the Faith as a chastened Enrique persuades his daughter to concede the principle of freedom of conscience in order to obtain the people's oath of fealty, in the knowledge that, once she is queen, María can deal with heterodoxy with all the rigour she pleases. Enrique thus makes what restitution he can, with what is tantamount to a promise that England will be reclaimed for Spain and Catholicism. Playwright and audience were perfectly well aware that historically events had taken a different course, but parables have their own imperatives. The closure of this great *tragoedia morata*, with its insistence, to use Victor Dixon's words in relation to *Los cabellos de Absalón*, on 'the exemplification of a poetic justice which mirrors the divine',[29] has to offer new beginnings consistent with the play's doctrinal and moral universe. The moral turpitude that had led to the schism, to the downfall of a saintly queen and to the spiritual damnation of a brilliant king, could not possibly within the world of poetic justice be punished by anything other than a restoration of the *status quo*. The merest hint that Protestantism had prevailed would have unravelled Calderón's purpose, to show human failings – passion,

took seriously his duty to learn about kingship from the lessons of history. See *The Schism in England*, pp. 3–6.

[28] The Aguilar edition's 'ha de acabar' is clearly an error. It is corrected in Ann Mackenzie's edition of the Spanish text in *The Schism in England*.

[29] 'Prediction and its Dramatic Function in *Los cabellos de Absalón*', in M. McKendrick ed., *Golden-Age Studies in Honour of A. A. Parker*, *Bulletin of Hispanic Studies*, 61 (1984), 304–16, p. 313.

ambition, self-interest – having momentous historical consequences. As for the notion of la Bolena's daughter becoming Queen of England, reigning for forty-five years and being Spain's most formidable enemy, any concession that the villainous Ana's part in the scheme of things did not end with the play would have been unthinkable.[30]

Calderón rewrote history not only to produce a tighter dramatic plot but, more importantly, to distil the contingent complexities of historical narrative into those universal passions and desires which motivate human beings and lead them astray from rational, selfless behaviour. Indeed so intent is he on identifying and magnifying these motives that Ana Bolena and Volseo are conceived essentially as elaborate and sophisticated versions of the devil-figure in a morality play, their sins constantly reiterated. Enrique fares better as an outstanding figure led astray by the malice of others and by sexual desire, always more venial in a man than other passions. The play in this respect accurately reflects both the double sexual standard of tradition and the historical reality, rooted as this standard was in dynastic anxieties – Enrique's very real philandering is regrettable whereas Ana's flirtatious exchange with a former admirer carries the death sentence. It is significant that when first Sander and then Rivadeneyra felt the need to explain Anne's alleged serial adultery they ascribed it to her desire to increase her chances of presenting Henry with a male heir.[31] This at once suggests the assumptions, firstly that no queen, not even the lascivious Anne Boleyn, would otherwise be so foolish as to risk her life in this way, and secondly, that the possibility of dynastic pollution was adequate reason for regarding sexual impropriety in a queen to be *lèse majesté*. Calderón's restraint in depicting Ana's sexual misdemeanours, in view of Rivadeneyra's extravagant denunciations, is testimony to his desire to avoid particularization through sensationalism. It was her overweening ambition he wished to stress, not her errant sexuality, and he was clearly fascinated by the symbiosis between Ana and Volseo and the idea of a self-destructive pairing that ended up destroying an arm of the universal church as well. His preference not to introduce even a hint of those other demonizing factors, rumours of which had swept Europe and were embedded by now in public consciousness, is another indication of his chosen focus.

---

30 For A. A. Parker the ending, with the King counselling moderation and his daughter insisting on repression, is shaped by the circumstance that Spain in 1627 had not yet entirely given up hope, encouraged by the recent marriage negotiations, that England might be brought back to the Catholic fold. But Calderón in fact presents Enrique's counsel as strategic, his real goal the return to religious uniformity that would assuage his guilt, an approach that fits more closely both with the play's moral and artistic shaping and with its presentation for its audience, as Parker so expertly argued, of Henry as a sympathetic and tragic figure. See *The Mind and Art of Calderón. Essays on the Comedias* (Cambridge: Cambridge University Press, 1988), pp. 250–87.

31 It is curious how this chimes with the recent suggestion by behavioural scientists that female adultery is connected with in-built programming to increase the gene pool.

Where sexuality was concerned, he was interested in the effects of passion on the King and not in sexual excess or deviance in Anne Boleyn. In other words, he was interested in the representative not the bizarre, in historical example not in the historically unique. And, as if with some sixth sense for what was likely to have been the human reality behind the scandalous myth, in the process of pursuing this vision he came nearer than did either his sources or hearsay to what is now thought to be the truth about Anne Boleyn. She was not physically blemished, she was not sexually depraved, she was not a witch, but she was indeed ambitious for herself and her family and eager for the power and influence marriage to Henry could bring. In the bald words that we saw Calderón put into her mouth, passion did yield to ambition, albeit not in the wilful way the play would have it – forced by Wolsey and others out of her clandestine betrothal to the man she seems to have loved she responded to the King's interest in her by insisting on marriage.

Where Calderón's portrayal moves away from the truth is in sacrificing for the sake of art and moral purpose the unwieldy nexus of dynastic and political issues that necessarily complicate, attenuate and blur the role in these events of individual responsibility and guilt. He needed a villain for his piece, Ana Bolena was the scapegoat preselected for him, and Calderón did a thorough job. The respective sins of Enrique and Volseo, inappropriate sexuality and unbridled ambition – both doubly culpable in a woman – are found together in her. Their sins are revealed to be tragic in their consequences through the working of their consciences; and the King's belated resolve to put things right and Volseo's suicide rescue them for tragedy in a way that leaves Ana to stand alone as the unredeemed and unredeemable Machivellian figure. Unlike Henry and Volseo, Ana is given no scenes or even words of remorse. Her regret at the end is for her own fate and not for the part she has played in it, and this is her ultimate condemnation.[32] In both history and play, she is the woman who tried and failed to play the male game of power politics and fell prey to her enemies. In history she was the victim of factional politics in complicity with her inability to deliver a healthy male child, but Calderón did not conceive of events in these terms and here she is the victim of her own arrogance and sense of invulnerability. He does not demonize her as he could so easily and with respectable authority have done, but his condemnation of her is none the less absolute.

---

[32] Ana's dignified reaction to her downfall, which is historically faithful, has been cited by Ann Mackenzie (*The Schism in England*, p. 33) as indicative of Calderón's willingness to accord her some finer feeling, but since there is no sign of contrition or self-knowledge in her words (Act III, p. 170b) they convey only anger and bitterness.

Stages of History and History on Stage: On Lope de Vega and Historical Drama

ALAN K. G. PATERSON

Over the last fifty years our home-based *Comedia* criticism has shown limited interest in history. I do not, of course, refer to the work on texts (bibliocritical above all) and archival records, but to literary critical studies. The long period of A. A. Parker's influence over Golden-Age studies was characterised by and encouraged an essentially ahistorical methodology, designed to elicit moral 'universal' meanings which were detached from any serious cultural and historical context. The paradox was that while Golden-Age historians in Britain were moving into the vanguard of history writing and opening up new perspectives on political and social history, the interdisciplinary contact between the historian and the literary scholar was feeble.

Then post-modernist trends, which opportunistically and as a matter of routine dismantled previous orders of literary authority, did nothing to correct this bias against historically informed reading. On the contrary, as a point of principle, the post-modernist denied the possibility of bringing historical awareness to bear on seventeenth-century texts by defying the reader's capacity to move outside the synchronicity of language. An exception was made for applying versions of social history written by Foucault, which it must be said were chronologically and spatially quite arbitrary over major issues of importance for the *comedia* such as gender and law. New Historicism itself was not conducive to reviving a lost historical instinct, partly because of its restricted preoccupation with the nature of power. The New Historian's vision of how state authority usurps language for its own ends essentially deprived art of the freedom to make statements other than those which served a monopolistic and oppressive authority.

Oddly, the student of Golden-Age theatre had been there before. I refer to the extensive critical corpus of José Antonio Maravall, who carried out an exegesis of seventeenth-century literature very similar to the New Historians'. In his view, the arts served the interests of a *dirigiste* state that was bent on eliminating voices which may be construed as being in opposition to the ruling culture.[1] Maravall doubtless thought out that position in Franco's

---

[1] I refer above all to Maravall's *La cultura del Barroco* (Barcelona: Editorial Ariel, 1975).

Spain sooner than the New Historians did elsewhere because of his own oppositional role as the intellectual dissident in an actual *dirigiste* state. He was a curiously divided writer. On the one hand he had a wide and deep reading of the age and on the other he basically spun the stuff of Golden-Age writing into one, self-repeating narrative of oppression, emptying it of other voices in which we could detect the dissenting attitude, the alternative view, the other's interest. In the studies of Renaissance theatre, the New Historicism proved as opposed as Maravall to the idea that theatre could be seen as an arena of conflict, where diverse interests from outside the theatre could represent themselves, and where dramatists could fashion drama from the unresolved competition of ideas and attitudes in their own society.[2] Such allegiances as were formed with an epistemic view of social and political history meant that by and large there was scarcely any dialogue between literary exegetes and professional historians, to the serious impoverishment of Golden-Age studies. A hermeneutical project directed towards the *comedia* and history could profitably address two areas of study: the location of the theatre within the coordinates of its own seventeenth century and the vision of the past the *comedia* placed before the community it entertained.

Here, I wish to ask questions that have a bearing on the second of these enquiries. First, was there a developed historical awareness in the Golden Age, in other words a historiography, and, if so, what did it consist of? The second question, out of recognition of Professor Dixon, the scholar who has done much to deepen our understanding of a contextualized Lope de Vega, is whether Lope de Vega can be said to have held a governing sense of the past in his drama.

Juan de Mariana's *Historia general* is a key text for providing evidence of a developed historical awareness in the early seventeenth-century cultural agenda. Attitudes expressed towards the publication give important insights into the science of History and the way it was being regarded by contemporaries of Mariana well before the inclusion of the discipline into the official curriculum of an important educational institution such as El Colegio Imperial (see note 11). The *Historia* met with some hostile comment, and Tamayo de Vargas came to its defence, marshalling a formidable if curiously mixed bag of intellectuals: Ribadeneira, Bernardo Aldrete, Góngora, González de Salas and Quevedo, all of whom testify to the value of the *Historia* for its elegance and style. Tamayo himself claims that thanks to the *Historia general* Spaniards have gained a knowledge of who they were, referring to 'Mariana, por quien los españoles sabemos lo que fuimos, i sin cuia aiuda estuuieran en perpetuo oluido nuestras cosas, como hasta que este nueuo Sol deste Emispherio las dio su luz, mouido del zelo que en la dedicación de su historia

---

[2]   See the lucid account in their introduction to *New Historicism and Renaissance Drama*, edited and introduced by Richard Wilson and Richard Dutton (London and New York: Longman, 1992).

latina descubrió a la Magestad del II Philippo'.[3] So the historian imparts a sense of national identity by remembering the Spaniards' collective possession of a past that is otherwise in constant danger of being forgotten. Tamayo describes how the nature of the historian's work is putting the documents into order: 'el intento del Padre no fue derechamente hazer historia, sino poner en orden i estilo lo que otros auían recogido, como materiales de la fábrica que pensaba levantar',[4] giving the writing of history a centripetal motion, that of gathering in the documents and assembling them in an order that corresponds to the new 'fábrica' the historian intends to create, as Mariana's papers make clear he himself did. History has lessons to teach us, argues Tamayo, not only from the virtues it records but from the vices as well.

In his *Historia general* Mariana himself amplifies some of these points. He sees his mission as a historian in terms of a national enterprise, devoted to the 'grandezas de España', 'nuestra España', and indeed its ultimate justification is to preserve these from the ravages of time. Asserting how states are subject to change and decay, a premiss that may well come directly from the neo-stoic and historian Justus Lipsius, Mariana writes:

> La historia en particular suele triunfar del tiempo, que acaba todas las demás memorias y grandezas. De los edificios soberuios, de las estatuas y tropheos, de Cyro, de Alexandro, de César, de sus riquezas y poder, que ha quedado? La vejez lo consumió, y el que haze las cosas las deshaze. El Sol que produze a la mañana las flores del campo, él mismo las marchita a la tarde. Las historias solas se conservan, y por ellas la memoria de personages y de cosas tan grandes. Lo mismo quiero pensar será desta historia.[5]

The historian thus provides us with a memory of the past. But equally, History instructs us in the present and future, and Felipe III is urged to make use of the knowledge of the past, a counsel that Mariana conveys in the image of the pilot and his chart. History enables the King 'a guisa de buen piloto tener todas las rocas ciegas, y los baxíos peligrosos, de un piélago tan grande como es el gobierno, y más de tantos reinos, en la carta de marear bien demarcados'.[6] We note how the trope of the history book as a sea chart is expanded to illustrate how the composite realms of the Spanish crown need

---

3   Tomás Tamayo de Vargas, *Historia general de España del P. D. Juan de Mariana defendida por el Doctor Don Thomás Tamaio de Vargas contra las Advertencias de Pedro Mantuan* (Toledo, 1616).

4   Tomás Tamayo de Vargas, op. cit., xxxix.

5   P. Juan de Mariana, *Historia general de España compuesta primero en Latin, despues buelta en Castellano por Juan de Mariana . . .*, Toledo, 1601, ¶ 4r. Lipsius's grandiose image of cosmic and political decline is found in Book 1, Chapter XVI of *De Constantia*.

6   P. Juan de Mariana, *Historia general,* ed. cit., ¶ 4v.

an understanding at the centre that is acquired from the accounts of the past. These various glosses on the nature of history confirm that among its purposes were seen that of forming and maintaining a national identity by giving the present nation-state an ancestry in a past that was its own possession, that of providing a frame of reference for the contemporary governance of a composite state with complex origins, and that of inculcating lessons on behaviour through the historical record of virtuous and vicious actions.

Such functions of history receive interesting refinements in a primer for writing and reading history by Luis Cabrera de Córdoba. In particular he gives history a part in an anthropology of man, for History gives us a present without which we are as animals: 'aun a penas lo presente pareciera, si no supiéramos lo passado, y fuéramos como las bestias, porque no se pudiera discurrir, ni inquirir las causas. . . . El que la [historia] aborrece no es hombre',[7] and being man in this context refers to the civil state of *homo civilis*, here distinguished from the world of beasts precisely by his knowledge of the past. This claim that the knowledge of History marks out human civilisation from the animal world provides a key text for an understanding of the cultural importance that the discipline was acquiring in civic life. Cabrera makes two further points which may prove useful contemporary markers when we move to the *comedia*. First, he identifies a hybrid mix of history and poetry: 'Sale bien el mentir al Poeta quando mezcla lo verdadero con lo verosimil, y llámase Mythistoria, de los Griegos, según Lipsio.' The authority of the great Dutch historian is named, to sanction the mixing of history and poetry.[8] Cabrera also has an interesting line on theatricality and history: 'Si las figuras y simulacros hechos por mano de artífices despiertan para imitar lo representado en ellas (causa porque hizo Augusto César el teatro de las estatuas de los héroes de su República) quanto mejor mouerá la historia que muestra la compostura y delineamiento del cuerpo, facciones del rostro, virtudes y passiones del ánimo, que hizieron a los claros varones dignos de inmortal memoria.' Here, Cabrera applies a function and method to history that are akin to those of rhetoric. Both aim to move their readers, and hence Cabrera promotes eidetic features of history that suggest performance in the theatre ('compostura y delineamiento del cuerpo', 'facciones del rostro', 'passiones del ánimo'). This association between History and theatre is curiously reinforced in the preliminaries where the normal address 'Al Lector' is

---

7   *De Historia, para entenderla y escribirla . . .* (Madrid, 1611), f. 22v.
8   Cabrera will be referring here to Lipsius's letter on historiography, where Lipsius makes the first distinction: 'summa ejus divisio est, *Mythistoria & Historia*: illa, quae fabulas vero mixtas; ista quae purum & merum verum habet. In illa poetae sunt, & id genus: qui oblectamenta auribus aminisque quaerunt, & florida ista veste ornant & augent corpus hoc veritas'; quoted from *De Historia Iusti Lipsii Epistola*, ed. Wittenberg (1604), 4r.

substituted by 'Al Teatro'. This is an appropriate point to move to Lope de
Vega and history.

A substantial part of Lope's theatre consists of history plays, in the sense
that their anecdotal material is set into a time and an environment which his
audience could recognize as belonging to a period of the past through certain
coordinates established by characters and events. That preceding qualification made to the term 'history play' required care, for characteristically a
dialectic goes on in such plays between local anecdote and national history
that is more complex than the common models of 'foreground–background'
or 'story and setting' can handle. Take the case of *El mejor alcalde el Rey*. In
this play we have the advantage of seeing how Lope adapted a narrative from
a given source, the *Crónica general* of Alfonso el Sabio, no doubt from its
standard edition by Florián Docampo. Comparison between Lope's plot and
the *Crónica* gives us the opportunity to speculate with reasonable confidence
on how Lope read a historical record, noting what he kept and what he
altered, and thus deducing what motives guided him in the process of
adapting a historical narrative to a piece of theatre. The *Crónica* tells of a
Galician farmer whose inheritance, i.e. land, was taken from him by force by
a local lord. The farmer goes to Toledo and complains to King Alfonso who,
after various rebuffs to his authority, goes clandestinely to Galicia and hangs
the local magnate at his front door. Lope changed the original subject of
dispute, a land inheritance, into a stolen bride. No doubt the level of human
interest and audience attention are both raised by this change, for Lope, like
any dramatist of his age, knew that love and sex form a staple ingredient of
all *comedias*. But no doubt, too, Lope understood that what the *Crónica* was
demonstrating was the exemplary defence by the just King of a feudal right
of custom. By the same token, by engaging the King with the moral issue of
abduction and rape, Lope gave him a distinctive judicial role, namely that of
the judge entrusted with his subjects' moral well-being and moral rights,
these being matters of conscience not of custom. The original issue thus
changes into one that is in resonance with the juridical-moral notions of
Kingship in Lope's own time.

Comparing further the source and the dramatization, we find two features
from the original that are conserved and emphasized: these are the geographical theatre of action and the identity of the King. The distance and the
tension between remote Galicia and León forms a significant and emphatic
geopolitical motif throughout the play. As to the King's identity, the *Crónica*
promotes Alfonso as Alfonso el Emperador on account of the concord and
unity he brought to the divided kingdoms of Castile and Aragón. On account
of the way he transformed the place of internecine struggle between its kingdoms into 'España', he was called el Emperador de las Españas, a title further
refined into el primer Emperador de España.[9] This imperial identity is duly

[9] The motif of how warring Christian kingdoms were brought into agreement domi-

folded into Lope's characterisation of Alfonso. Both these aspects of adaptation contain significant historical signposting for the audience to take note of.
They not only, of course, project the play back in time, providing it with
historical markers, but define the historical circumstances that it recreates:
Lope locates his play temporally at a point of crisis. An old order wielded by
don Tello, feudal in the rights it assumes over the individual and secure in its
remoteness, is challenged by the nascent power of the nation state. Alfonso
must prove his fitness by asserting his legal and moral authority over the lord
in Galicia. At the moment of fulfilling his sovereign duty to do justice,
Alfonso synthesizes the monarch's unitary authority in the formulaic
first-person, familiar to all decrees emanating from the King and with which
he reveals himself to the *infanzón*: 'Yo'. If the King must prove himself by
extending his might and right to the remotest corner of Galicia, so those who
look to the sovereign for justice must put their faith in him to the test, to trust
and be prepared to face uncertainty before being released into the security of
a new order. By the end a new order is indeed found between the one who has
power and those who live under it, an order that safeguards moral well-being,
for central authority is exercised with a sense of justice. This is not an old
order restored but a new order gained.

The same configuration of breakdown of an old order, followed by uncertainty and then by release through the attainment of new order recurs in other
plays of the type referred to as *comedias de comendadores*, perhaps Lope's
most coherent dramatic enquiries into the historical process. In *Fuenteovejuna*, the crisis is reached at a local level in the violence that ensues upon
the unbridled tyranny of feudal authority, and at a national level in the war
between representatives of the old martial values of the Military Orders and
the new order of the Reyes Católicos. The community of Fuenteovejuna is
placed on the dangerous cusp of change, living out the dangers of being in a
divided world, descending into the anarchy of desperate, animal fury,
emerging into the new order that judges them with both justice and mercy and
which, in the final act of the great process of history, inaugurates the sovereign state of a Spain united under Isabel and Fernando. It is indeed the final
act of a process, because history deemed it to be that same unitary sovereign
state, with its advanced theoretical framework that bound power, law and
justice, if not into the practice, certainly into the ideology of government, in
which Lope's audience lives.

In *Peribáñez*, the crisis lived in Ocaña coincides with the confrontation of

---

nates the account of Alfonso VII's reign in the *Crónica*, '. . . y de allí adelante se llamo
siempre don Alfonso emperador de las Españas; e segun que las estorias cuentan este fue
el primer emperador de España'. *Las cuatro partes enteras de la Cronica de España que
mando componer el Serenissimo rey don Alfonso llamado el sabio . . . Vista y enmendada
mucha parte de su impresion por el maestro florian Docampo . . .*, Zamora, 1541, 4ª
Parte, f. ccclviii[v]–f. ccclxxvi.

Catholic Castile with the enemy Islam. Once again, Lope shapes a perception
of a nation being proved at two levels, at the local level of its humble citi-
zenry sorely tried by a failure of the mutual bond it once enjoyed with an
overlord, and at the level of national events which is represented by the
crusade that will set out from Toledo as part of the process of territorial and
religious reconquest. Before the great events can materialise, however, the
quality of the King's justice has to be proven in the way he exercises the
demands of justice towards Peribáñez. The testing of the King is sharply
focused in the public event succeeding the explosive private act of violence
that leaves Peribáñez to answer for three murders. The stage space is prepared
for this event – the trial of Peribáñez – by emblematic image-making, as has
featured previously in the play by the use of decorative hangings that signal
socially-defined space. The motif is the Cross, which in its former appear-
ances on costume and in the stage space had illustrated the status of the
Comendador. At this point of the play, however, the dialogue glosses the
emblem into an expression of justice, not social identity. The quotation reads
from the entry of the secretary before the King and Queen with a banner:

*Entre un Secretario con un pendón rojo, y en él las armas de Castilla, con
una mano arriba que tiene una espada, y en la otra banda un Cristo
crucificado.*

SECRETARIO	Este es, señor, el guión.
REY	Mostrad. Paréceme bien;
	que este capitán también
	lo fue de mi redención.
REINA	¿Qué dicen las letras?
REY	Dicen
	'Juzga tu causa, Señor.'
REINA	Palabras son de temor.
REY	Y es razón que atemoricen.
REINA	Desotra parte ¿qué está?
REY	El castillo y el león,
	y esta mano por blasón
	que va castigando ya.
REINA	¿La letra?
REY	Sólo mi nombre.
REINA	¿Cómo?
REY	'Enrique Justiciero':
	que ya, en lugar de Tercero,
	quiero que este nombre asombre. (2980–95)[10]

---

[10] The text is quoted from Lope de Vega, *Peribáñez y el comendador de Ocaña y La
dama boba* (Madrid: Clásicos Castellanos, 1963), checked against Lope's *Quarta parte*,
Madrid, 1614, for accuracy.

We observe how precisely Lope orders language and staging to the point that a powerful dramatic conceit is achieved. The emblematic banner reinforces the theme of geopolitical unity that had always glossed the location of the action in Toledo. The banner introduces the motif of justice ('una mano arriba que tiene una espada'), focused on the person of the King by his resolving to be what his historic title claims he is, Enrique Justiciero. Justice on earth has its model in divine justice, figured in the banner's Crucified Christ with the Biblical quotation from Psalms LXXIII, 22, 'Iudica causam tuam', and whose divine leadership the King acknowledges: 'este capitán [referring to Christ]/ lo fue también de mi redención'. By this captaincy the King means military leadership associated with the crusade, the setting in the Alcázar and indeed reinforced by how captaincy has been impressed on our attention by the promotion of Peribáñez to that rank. However, there is also the martial-spiritual metaphor of Christ the King whose banners go forth in the form of the Cross. The King and Queen sit in judgement ('Señora, tomemos sillas' – 3008) and Peribáñez, restored to his peasant self, presents himself for justice. The Judge's answer is swift upon learning the petitioner's name: sentence of death, without trial. But the Queen, whose patient questioning of the banner now turns out to have been more than just a pretext for prompting a gloss on its meaning, calls the judge to order, and the ensuing process, again with her intervention, vindicates Peribáñez. The Queen's part in the trial is an interesting complication, for it suggests a flaw in the man's justice that the woman corrects by tempering punitiveness with the spirit of compassion, as the emblematic banner unfurled above the place of judgement promises. This is the new order of a justice informed with divine mercy that heals the disorder that has divided class against class, and in this new-found unity the Crusade will set forth.

There is a pattern which we see repeated in the historical configuration of these plays. All three are examples of how a historical vision is formed of a Spain evolving towards the unitary sovereign state, one that is sanctioned by the needs of universal justice as well as by the prerogatives of royal authority. The desire to reach that state of political and moral fulfilment is at one and the same time felt and expressed by the common folk as a common yearning and by the monarchs as a mission. The monarchs have a historic identity to prove, a test to pass, in how well they answer that yearning on the part of their subjects. Lope seems to have been guided by an underlying pattern in contemporary history writing, which did not divide the past into the now familiar periodicities (that is a form of ordering that later historians were to discover) but which rather looks into the past for prefigurations of the order that would eventually emerge as the modern state, as if the nature of that state were continually being exposed and pre-enacted at critical junctures in its past. It is on such a view of history, not dissimilar to the prefigurative readings that were made in Scriptural exegesis, that the exemplarity of the past is based; history holds lessons because our own present is being rehearsed in the past, and hence the importance of the historian to his contemporaries for recording these prefigurations of their times.

Can we then relate these readings from Lope's theatre to the historiographies of his times? There are significant points of contact. Lope uses theatre to convey themes that are concerned with national identity, that is with the building of a nation and with the lapses that obstructed the attainment of that goal. His plays thus present history as an evolutive process, a movement towards a desired end. His concept of nation is centralist, located in a Castile that is the centripetal point of Spanish identity. His plays are lessons whose material is taken from the past and which inform his audience of the relationship between the past and their present. This enterprise he shares with the fundamental didactic mission that is undertaken by contemporary historians. That relationship with the past is seen in terms of how the individual is related to authority and of what binds figures of authority to the citizen; the moral and political lessons of today are contained in the events of yesterday. Finally, Lope creates what contemporary historiographers called 'mithistoria', combining the many voices of poetry, his theatrical inventiveness and historical reconstruction. As we have seen, this was the concept recognised as a cognate field of history by Lipsius, no doubt the most influential of contemporary thinkers on the nature of history

There is a missing question; can we refine the contemporary interests that Lope's historical plays served in the community? If we look further than a self-evident monarchism and an evident distrust of the aristocrat, whose ideology does he privilege? The circumstances of his family are not known well enough for us to isolate his class allegiance by birth in the Madrid to which his parents migrated. It may be, though, that the frequent identification of his Madrid with its *hidalgo* class is relevant to attributing a set of urban social and political values to Lope, yet it is to be remembered in this respect that his unusual career as intellectual, secretary and writer makes him hard to fit into a firmly recognised class ethos. Given the relative paucity of information about Lope's own education, it is problematic to look to his schooling for an answer. We would need to know more than we currently do about the early Colegio de San Isidro and particularly with reference to a history curriculum.[11] Even with that knowledge, the span of Lope's creative life would put into question whether his early intellectual formation at school is directly relevant to the understanding of his work many decades later. Similarly, it would be unusual if Lope's reading of past and present were not being modified by the actual political events that took place over the three reigns that he lived through. After all, shifts in the writer's political and social sensi-

---

11 The study by Mario Góngora 'El Colegio Imperial de Madrid en el Siglo XVII y los orígenes de la enseñanza de Historia en España' in *Cuadernos de Historia de España*, 29–30 (1959), pp. 231–43, dealing as it does with the Colegio Imperial and from c.1625, covers too late a period.

bility in response to events are germane to a project of reading the *comedia* historically. However, there is a way in which we can detect a manner of thinking about and exposing the historical process on stage that carries his special hallmark; it is the consistency with which he shows the process of History as one that is engaged with the aspirations of a people. His individual and collective local heroes do not make history, but together they will the goals that other exceptional figures realise for them. It is Lope's form of populism, his way of placing characters who are representative of community in the stream of history, experiencing its crises through their suffering and ultimately shaping the future by their wholesome goodness and their just hopes, that give his historical vision a very special and lasting originality.

Lost Lady Found:
The Countryside as Redemptive Space
in Tirso de Molina's *La República al revés*

N. G. ROUND

For Victor Dixon
and in memory of Louise Fothergill-Payne

Perhaps the most immediately striking feature of Spain's seven-teenth-century playwrights was their extraordinary productivity. Even if we count only those limited *corpora* which have survived, the output of Lope de Vega, of Calderón, of Tirso de Molina, remains very large indeed. By contrast, the canon of accepted masterworks, claiming that sustained critical attention which we accord even to middle-ranking Shakespeare, constitutes a relatively brief list. One obvious explanation for this is the constant pressure to produce, generated by the turnover of plays in the *corrales de comedias*: clearly, this state of affairs did not favour the honing of finished master-pieces. Yet conditions in the London theatres of the time cannot have been ideal in this regard either. There are also problems of perspective at work. Critical and public reception has not dealt even-handedly between English and Spanish classic theatre. Nor has it been easy for anyone – even among the splendidly erudite *comediantes* of North American Hispanism – to become familiar with the whole array of available (and not-so-available) texts. Non-specialists like myself would hardly know where to start. Yet even they can sometimes stumble on a play with more claim to importance than has so far been acknowledged. Such was my own experience with Tirso de Molina's *La república al revés*: drawn to it first of all by a powerful, though ill-informed, curiosity about its Byzantine setting, I soon came to think it an impressive piece of theatre, deserving more critical attention than it usually got. The paper which follows seeks to make the case for that view.[1]

---

[1] An eighteenth-century *suelta* (Madrid: Teresa de Guzmán, 1733) calls the play 'Comedia sin fama'. For a summary of its modern reputation (admired but not edited by Hartzenbusch; regarded as 'mediana' by Cotarelo y Mori, and as attractive but flawed by Blanca de los Ríos; emphatically approved by Vossler and by Carmela Hernández García) see John B. Wooldridge, 'The Topsy-Turvy World of Tirso's *La república al revés*' in *Tirso*

Three main elements go to make up the conventional critical profile of *La república al revés*. It is known as a play about the Empress Irene who ruled in Constantinople around AD 800, saw off the Iconoclast movement in the Eastern Church, and after a protracted power-struggle with her son Constantine VI, had him deposed and blinded. Byzantine subjects are uncommon in the *comedia*, but this one is recognized as having been available to Tirso through Boccaccio's *De mulieribus claris*.[2] The play is widely identified, too, as an early one, a prototype for the much better-known *La prudencia en la mujer*, about the fourteenth-century Castilian Queen Regent, María de Molina.[3] There is also a general awareness that its theme is 'the world turned upside-down', about which Helen Grant and Dawn Smith, for example, have written perceptively.[4] On all three topics more might be said.

Tirso's remaking of Byzantine history is, in many ways, extravagantly free. His characters call themselves 'Greeks' and not, following the invariable usage of the Eastern Empire, 'Romans'. Their enemies include the Persians (some centuries too late in AD 800) and the Turkish Sultan (two centuries early), as well as Tartars, Hungarians, Poles, and needless to say, the Moors.[5] A wholly fictitious client-king, father of Constantine's ill-used bride, rules over Cyprus. At the end of the play, father and daughter contemplate a voyage to China. Another unhistorical personage, the rebel Leoncio, moves from near the capital to the Armenian frontier and back again in little more time than it takes Constantino to organize a hunting-party. At first sight this play seems as little tied to Byzantine realities as *A Winter's Tale* is to the

---

de Molina: vida y obra. Actas del I Simposio Internacional sobre Tirso, eds José María Solá-Solé and Luis Vázquez Fernández (Madrid: Revista «Estudios», 1987), pp. 155–65, at pp. 155–56.

[2]   Giovanni Boccaccio, *Tutte le opere*, X, ed. Vittorio Zaccaria (Verona: Arnoldo Mondadori, 1967), pp. 418–23: 'De Yrene costantinopolitana imperatrice'. This is a more detached and political account of Irene than is presented in Tirso's drama.

[3]   See Blanca de los Ríos, *Preámbulo* to *La república al revés* in Tirso de Molina, *Obras completas dramáticas*, I (Madrid: Aguilar, 1946), p. 375; also Dawn L. Smith, 'Women and Men in a World Turned Upside-Down: an Approach to Three Plays by Tirso', *Revista Canadiense de Estudios Hispánicos*, 10 (1985–86), 247–60, at p. 249; Melveena McKendrick, *Theatre in Spain 1490–1700* (Cambridge: University Press, 1989), p. 118.

[4]   Helen F. Grant, 'The World Upside-Down', in *Studies in Spanish Literature of the Golden Age Presented to Edward M. Wilson*, ed. R. O. Jones (London: Tamesis, 1973), pp. 103–35, at pp. 120–21; Smith, pp. 249, 251–54.

[5]   Tirso de Molina, *La república al revés* in *Obras completas dramáticas*, ed. Blanca de los Ríos, I, pp. 382–428, at I, ii, p. 383a (Persians; Moors), I, ix, p. 390b (Turkish Sultan) III, xi, p. 421b (Tartars, etc.). All textual references here refer (by act, scene, page-number, and column) to this widely available but unsatisfactory edition – which does not, for example, number lines. Account has been taken, however, of the textual corrections suggested by Xavier A. Fernández, *Las comedias de Tirso de Molina. Estudios y métodos de crítica textual* (Pamplona: Universidad / Kassel: Reichenberger, 1991), III, pp. 117–28.

history of Sicily or the geography of Bohemia – neither play, of course, being any the worse for that.

Yet *La república al revés* actually takes in rather more of authentic history than this might suggest. The rivalry between Constantine and Irene, his Iconoclasm and her anti-Iconoclasm, are all historical. But Irene was never the general of armies which Tirso makes her out to be: rather, her support lay in anti-militarist quarters.[6] Her exile – perhaps no more, in practice, than exclusion from power and from the imperial Palace – ended some years before the internal coup in which she deposed and blinded her son. The link, underlined by Tirso, between this last atrocity and the offence of Constantine's Iconoclasm was less of an issue at the time than was his marital history. He had put away his wife Maria of Paphlagonia and married, with much pomp and a dispensation from the Patriarch of Constantinople, Theodote, a lady of the court. The ensuing scandal swung opinion behind Irene at a crucial moment of their struggle for power. Tirso changes names – the wronged bride is now Carola of Cyprus, and her rival is her waiting-maid Lidora – and adds much romantic detail, but retains the main outline here. He even preserves the key institutional item: the dispensation from the Patriarch (II, vi, p. 400b).

He has other institutional matters roughly in place too. The ninth-century Empire did still have a Senate, its function of advising the Emperor not quite extinguished – which is more or less the state of affairs represented by Tirso.[7] By contrast, there were no 'Armenian legions' for Leoncio to rally in revolt: the Byzantine army was organized in territorially-based 'themes'; but the 'Armeniakon theme', raised on the border with Armenia, did play a role in the events of Constantine's reign. Originally it had helped him to oust Irene from power; but, after he had degraded and blinded their commander, the Armenian troops rebelled against him.[8] There is another name, too, which Tirso appears to have right. Tarso the shepherd, loyal to Irene in her adversity, is rewarded by being made her *Secretario Mayor*, with the promise of further advancement. Tarso is conventionally seen as the representative of his near-namesake Tirso, intervening in his own play. And so, in some ways, he doubtless is. But the historical Irene did have a secretary, whom she later

6   See Henri Grégoire, 'The Byzantine Church' in *Byzantium: An Introduction to East Roman Civilization*, ed. Norman H. Baynes and H. St. L. B. Moss (Oxford: Clarendon, 1949), pp. 86–135, at pp. 106–107. For the history of Irene and Constantine see George Ostrogorsky, *History of the Byzantine State* (Oxford: Blackwell, 1989; 1st English edn 1956), pp. 176–80.

7   It was Leo VI (886–912) who finally extinguished the residual powers of the Senate (Ostrogorsky, p. 245.)

8   For the system of military themes see Ostrogorsky, pp. 96–98; ibid., pp. 179–80 for the role of the Armeniakon theme in Irene's history. Boccaccio, pp. 410–11 mentions their part in ousting Irene from power, but not their involvement in her restoration; Tirso, who ignores the former, presumably knew about the latter from some other source.

made Patriarch of Constantinople. His name was Tarasius.[9] Again, though no Leontius ever rebelled against Constantine VI, there had been a Leontius two centuries earlier, who briefly seized the Empire from Justinian II.[10]

None of this, it is true, does much for the documentary value of Tirso's account; but it does suggest that he looked at things Byzantine a little more seriously, and over a somewhat wider range, than would be implied by the simple response to Boccaccio's *exemplum* of a notable woman ruler. In particular, and despite his use of 'Greek' in consistent preference to 'Roman', he seems conscious that he is dealing with an Empire, the Christian successor to the power and authority of Rome. That awareness may well be relevant to the play's original conception, and thus to its date.

Blanca de los Ríos put it as early as 1611, alleging a reference to it in the form of a 'juego de palabras' in Cervantes' *Novelas ejemplares* of 1613. I have not been able to identify this, nor do the annotations in the Schevill/Bonilla or Avalle-Arce editions offer any help.[11] In any case it is hard to see how an oblique allusion of this kind could prove conclusive as evidence. The 'world upside-down' topos was too much of a commonplace to make the reference to Tirso certain. Nor does Tirso's apparent borrowing of certain names from Lope de Vega's *Arcadia* underwrite any particular *terminus ad quem*; still less does his failure to comment, in a play about ninth-century Byzantium, on life in contemporary Madrid. As so often happened with Doña Blanca, the clinching argument seems to be a strong subjective impression: that *La república al revés is* early Tirso, offering a virtuoso display of his erudition and talent for verse. Ruth Lee Kennedy, by contrast, argues that Tirso revised the text in 1621, adding the passage about Tarso's preferment as part of a campaign to secure a post for himself on the royal payroll.[12] That argument is weakened, of course, if we assume that he was aware of the historical Tarasius. Yet there are still grounds for questioning the supposed immaturity of the piece.

In clear contrast to both history and Boccaccio, Tirso has Irene condemn

[9]   Ostrogorsky, p. 177 describes him as 'a cultivated layman with sound theological training'. Wooldridge, p. 158 was the first to suggest a link between Tarasius and Tarso, speculating that Fray Gabriel Téllez might have adapted the Greek name into this, the earlier version of his eventual pseudonym. For Tarso as the author's representative on stage see Blanca de los Ríos, I, p. 380; Karl Vossler, *Lecciones sobre Tirso de Molina* (Madrid: Taurus, 1965), pp. 35, 44; André Nougué, *L'Oeuvre en prose de Tirso de Molina* (Paris: Centre de Recherches de l'Institut d'Études Hispaniques, 1962), p. 457n.

[10]   Ostrogorsky, pp. 140–41.

[11]   Blanca de los Ríos, pp. 375–76; cf. Miguel de Cervantes Saavedra, *Novelas ejemplares*, eds Rodolfo Schevill and Adolfo Bonilla, 3 vols (Madrid: Gráficas Reunidas, 1922–25); *Novelas ejemplares*, ed. Juan Bautista Avalle-Arce, 3 vols (Madrid: Castalia, 1982).

[12]   Ruth Lee Kennedy, 'Tirso's *La república al revés*, its Debt to Mira's *La rueda de la fortuna*, its Date of Composition and its Importance', *Reflexión*, 2 (1973), 39–50.

Constantino to be blinded in terms directly linked to his Iconoclasm. 'Juez de la causa de Dios/ he de ser', she declares, accepting it as her obligation 'que quede vengado todo/ el mundo, Dios y los Santos' (III, xx, p. 427b). By making the Emperor's wronged wife Carola plead against this for mercy, Tirso keeps alive the notion that such rigour might not, after all, be the only way, but the connection thus made had an obvious logic: the man who denied believers the visible supports of their faith was himself to be deprived of sight. Yet why, one wonders, the concern with Iconoclasm at all? Spanish theatregoers hardly required reminding of the claims of sacred images to be treated with respect: they, of all peoples in Europe, were perhaps the most forthcoming with such respect. The play's possible lesson for them lay, rather, in its carefully-drawn distinction between orthodox reverence for images and their heretical worship:

> la adoración que se aplica
> a la imagen [. . .]
> no es por ella o su materia,
> mas por lo que significa.   (III, v, p. 417a)

This echoes the position adopted in 787 by the Council of Nicaea, at which Irene and Tarasius broke the hold of Iconoclasm in the Church.[13] The echo is no coincidence: the Council of Trent, in its twenty-fifth session, had reaffirmed the Nicaean teaching on images. The issue remained a defining one between Catholics and Protestants, especially Calvinists. Yet there was nothing topical or urgent about exhorting Madrid audiences to beware of falling into Calvinism. Tirso and his public, though, might for a time have shared a degree of anxiety about just such a development at the other end of Catholic Europe.

To their Spanish cousins and to the people over whom those cousins ruled, the Austrian Habsburgs had long seemed unsatisfactory paladins of their common faith. The old Emperor Rudolf II, eccentric and depressive, sometimes looked to be at risk of heresy simply because it was hard to tell what he believed about anything. His brother Matthias had an actual record of threatened rapprochement with north-European Protestants.[14] In the first dozen years of the seventeenth century it had been the need to stiffen Hungarian loyalties against the Turks which had led Matthias into formal compromises with the Magyar gentry; later, the building of support for his own claim to the

---

[13] Ostrogorsky, pp. 178–79; see also Alfonso Rodríguez G. de Ceballos, 'Arte religioso de los siglos XV y XVI en España' in *Historia de la Iglesia en España*, III–2º, *La Iglesia en la España de los siglos XV y XVI*, ed. Ricardo García Villoslada (Madrid: Biblioteca de Autores Cristianos: 1980), p. 659.

[14] On the Emperor Matthias see Geoffrey Parker, *The Thirty Years' War* (London: Routledge, 1984), pp. 9–11, 38–41; also David Maland, *Europe at War 1600–1650* (London: Macmillan, 1980), p. 60.

imperial succession impelled him towards similar courses among the Czechs and Austrians. Local toleration for Protestants figured largely in these deals. When, after giving all these political hostages, Matthias finally achieved the Empire in 1612, Spanish foreign policy saw this development with the liveliest alarm. Matthias was old and childless; those with the strongest claims to succeed him – Philip III of Spain, and the man on the spot, Archduke Ferdinand of Styria – were staunchly Catholic, but for the moment they were faced with a situation not unlike that of *La república al revés*: what was to be done when the Emperor – the bearer of God's secular sword – was himself disposed to favour heretics? The dilemma eased in 1617, when Matthias acknowledged Ferdinand as his heir, thereby opening up a decisive breach with the Protestants of Bohemia; but for the five years after 1612, the theme of the heretic-Emperor would have resonated topically in Madrid.

It was necessary, even so, to treat it obliquely. Tirso's Constantino is no portrait of Matthias, no merely suspect trimmer. He is both a full-blown heretic and a tyrant. As to what ought to be done with tyrants, there existed a well-developed body of recent thinking. A few years earlier, the Jesuit Juan de Mariana had offered in his *De rege* a powerful defence of Jacques Clément, the assassin of Henri III of France, and of tyrannicide in general.[15] His arguments had helped to inspire the similar murder of Henri IV in 1610. Mariana had defined the tyrant as a ruler ruled by passions, a subverter of the state and mocker of its laws, who brought public safety and sound religion into jeopardy. All that is true of Constantino; yet Irene tells the rebel Leoncio that:

> no hay ley
> ni razón ninguno hallo
> con que despoje un vasallo,
> por malo que sea, a su rey.   (III, xix, p. 426b)

She concedes, it is true, that 'un hereje Emperador/ a aquesto pudo obligarte', but Leoncio's treason must still be punished. In the event, however, he escapes even gaol. The signs point to a good deal of uncertainty on Tirso's own part as to what the right response to the 'heretic-Emperor' dilemma was: politically, to rise in revolt, or to wait patiently on providence; theologically, stern justice as proclaimed by Irene, or free forgiveness as advocated by Carola.

---

[15] Juan de Mariana, *Del rey y de la institución real (de rege et regis institutione) con la biografía del célebre jesuita por el Doctor D. Jaime Balmes, presbítero* (Barcelona: La Selecta, 1880); see especially pp. 116, 128, 129–50. Mariana saw such action as a last resort, when less drastic measures had been exhausted: 'Quod si omnis spes sublata est, in periculum salus publica, religionis sanitas vocatur, quis erit tam inops consilii qui non confiteatur tyrannidem excutere fas fore, jure, legibus et armis?' (p. 149). This fits Constantino's case, but hardly Leoncio's motives.

However, the Iconoclast issue had other overtones. A broadly iconoclastic hostility towards all products of the artistic imagination was extremely common among religious moralists. Many, going beyond the Tridentine insistence that images must be decorous, truthful, and transparent, saw all painting as (in Caro Baroja's words) 'sinónimo de engaño'.[16] As Barry Ife has shown, the old Platonist charge that all poets were liars still challenged literary creativity along similar lines. In the tradition of anti-theatrical polemic, these concerns fused with more practical anxieties about lax moral examples on the stage. This is a current that can run closely parallel to the Iconoclasts' objections to 'materiality' – as in Father Mariana's complaint that the displays put on by disreputable actors are unworthy vehicles to honour the saints. At other times, licentious plotting, or the Lopean theatre's refusal of Aristotelian discipline may be to the fore. But Tirso, the playwright who was also a professed friar, had more reason than most to be aware of that tradition. Throughout his active career as a dramatist he strove against it, and the relevance of the Iconoclast precedent was unlikely to have escaped him. Behind his refutation of Iconoclasm one senses an implied defence of his own art: the art of making one thing stand powerfully – and, indeed, beneficially – for another.

That defence is more directly stated in *El vergonzoso en palacio*, where theatre is described as a 'de los sentidos banquete [. . .]/ que mata de hambre a los necios/ y satisface a los sabios'.[17] That play does seem to be tied in date to 1611. Yet Tirso's use of the Iconoclast motif seems subtler and more reflective, and could well be the outcome of a more mature return to the same theme. The link with the Emperor Matthias offers us 1612 and 1617 as terminal dates for this; the playwright's departure in April 1616 for two years' work with the Mercedarians in Santo Domingo narrows the latter of these limits a little. Rather tentatively, I would seek to place *La república al revés* late in the period thus defined: in 1615 or early 1616.[18] Much still turns on the more subjective estimate of its artistic maturity.

[16] Julio Caro Baroja, *Las formas complejas de la vida religiosa. Religión, sociedad y carácter en la España de los siglos XVI y XVII* (Madrid: Akal, 1978), p. 113. See also B. W. Ife, *Reading and Fiction in Golden-Age Spain: a Platonic Critique and Some Picaresque Replies* (Cambridge: University Press, 1985). On objections raised against the theatre see Caro Baroja, pp. 101–06 (p. 102 for Mariana, *Contra los juegos públicos*, VII); also Nougué, p. 351n for the strictures of the Mercedarian Alonso Remón, *Entretenimientos y juegos honestos* (1623); more generally, J. T. C. Metford, 'The Enemies of the Theatre in the Golden Age', *Bulletin of Hispanic Studies*, 28 (1951), 76–92.

[17] Tirso de Molina, *El vergonzoso en palacio*, II, lines 776–82 in *Comedias*, I, ed. Américo Castro (Madrid: Espasa-Calpe, 1967; 1st edn 1932), p. 75; see also Nougué, p. 351.

[18] This would coincide with Kennedy's proposed dating for the first recension of the play (see above, n. 12). For April (not June) 1616 as the date of Tirso's departure for Santo Domingo see Luis Vázquez Fernández, 'Apuntes para una nueva biografía de Tirso' in *Tirso de Molina: vida y obra*, pp. 9–50, at p. 34.

It is, one has to admit, theatrically ambitious, and at some risk of seeming over-ambitious. There are thirty-five speaking parts – eighteen of them named, and at least ten of these distinctively characterized, with assorted soldiers, senators, shepherds, sailors, huntsmen and courtiers making up the rest. There is a coronation, a state visit, a village fiesta, and an attempt at bride-swapping – and that only takes us to the end of Act I. Act II includes a fatal stabbing and a comic manhunt, an attempted rape (which turns out to be unwittingly transvestite), and a *caso de honor* whose blood-revenge is rigged to go awry, but does so in a wholly unexpected direction. The final Act takes in a shipwreck, a courtroom farce, a magic mirror, a military coup, a royal hunt, and a tableau of Fortune's Wheel. There are no scenes of Heaven, Hell, or nudity, but these apart, it is difficult to see what else Tirso could have gone out of his way to include. Yet if one shaping impulse for this play was the desire to vindicate the claims of theatre, a real case existed for making it, deliberately, as theatrical as possible. We have no compelling reason, then, to set it all down as an immature display of theatrical effects for their own sake.

Nor need we take that view of the play's intricate plotting. The succession of events, certainly, can seem bafflingly diverse, but it is not ineptly handled: this is a proliferation, not a confusion, of narratives. The overarching story is that of Constantino and Irene: his elevation, misrule, and fall; her abdication, trials, and restoration. On either side subplots soon appear; these in their turn ramify into subordinate plot-lines. The play, increasingly, develops from the interaction of them all. Not far into Act I, for example, the Constantino/ Carola/Lidora plot begins, as the Emperor rejects his bride, and seeks to have her replaced in his marriage-bed by Lidora. This plot-line is crossed almost at once by what might be called 'the Leoncio plot', in which that ambitious courtier bids to rival Constantino for his empire and his mistress. He deliberately frustrates the bride-swapping plan – disastrously for Carola, made pregnant by a husband who persists in believing that he has slept with Lidora and not with her. Constantino's attachment to Lidora deepens; his persecution of his wife (and of his mother) grows more extreme. But Leoncio's flight and rebellion help to advance events leading to Irene's restoration.

Still in relation to Constantino, two further plot-lines are followed out in Act II. Lidora's lover Clodio arrives from Cyprus and, presented by her as her brother, wins instant advancement at court. Carola's father and brother also arrive, and are shocked when Constantino charges her with infidelity: each one lets himself be incited to avenge the family honour. The Emperor's plan is that they should waylay and kill each other in the dark; in fact, they fall upon Clodio, on his way to visit Lidora, and kill him. A final subplot – the tale of Constantino's Iconoclasm – belongs wholly to Act III.

On Irene's side, meanwhile, plot-lines are similarly, though rather less profusely, elaborated. There is one main subplot: that of the faithful shepherd Tarso, with whom she renews an old friendship on her retirement to the country in Act I. He protests at her detention then, frees her in Act II, and in

Act III befriends both her and Carola at the lowest point of their fortunes. Two minor plot-strands emerge from Tarso's story. He is loved by the shepherdess Melisa, to whom he is rather callously indifferent, but this attracts the jealousy of another shepherd Italio, who in an assault on Tarso is himself killed. At a slightly later stage, Irene's gaoler Andronio determines to rape her before discharging Constantino's order for her execution. What he does not know is that his prisoner is now Tarso, who has exchanged clothes with Irene while visiting her cell. He soon finds this out, in a scene which moves abruptly from brooding, lustful violence to something much more like *Charley's Aunt*.

At this and other key moments, different plot-lines converge to impel the story in unexpectedly positive directions. Thus, Leoncio evades capture by changing clothes with the murdered Italio; the King of Cyprus and his son, bent on avenging Carola's supposed dishonour, kill Clodio rather than each other; meeting Leoncio in the wilds, they are brought to a sounder view of her story; Irene in her lonely exile meets first Tarso and then the shipwrecked Carola. These interactions and the accompanying shifts of mood are deftly and often movingly handled, but they are not the kind of plotting which the *comedia* at its most effective typically exhibits. All this ramifying and reunifying, drawn providentially onward towards a good end, seems rooted, rather, in another genre altogether: the romance.[19] It was, of course, normal for the *comedia* to borrow motifs and incidents from that genre, but the large-scale adoption of a romance-like form was another matter. It might seem natural to associate this with a young Tirso, still uncertain of what can or cannot properly be put on stage.

Again, though, there are other ways of seeing it. Elsewhere, at about this date, another playwright was trying to fit the plotting of the romance into the conventions of his own theatre. And while *Pericles, Prince of Tyre* arguably does it less well than *A Winter's Tale*, we cannot credibly set that down to immaturity or dramatic inexperience on William Shakespeare's part. Almost contemporaneously, again, Cervantes was opting for this form of narrative for his own last work of all, the *Persiles*. We might just as plausibly link it, then, with a certain ripeness of experience – or if not yet with that in Tirso's case, then with a developed sense of needing a form which could encompass

---

[19] Guido Mancini, 'Caratteri e problemi del teatro di Tirso' in *Studi Tirsiani* (Milan: Feltrinelli, 1958), pp. 11–89, at p. 21, suggests that Tirso's plotting in general is indebted to the pastoral novel, but not to chivalresque or picaresque fiction. Serge Maurel, *L'Univers dramatique de Tirso de Molina* (Poitiers: Université, 1971), pp. 244–45 suggests that this play may owe something to the Italian *novellieri*. David H. Darst, 'La muerte y el matrimonio en el teatro de Tirso de Molina' in *Tirso de Molina: immagine e rappresentazione*, ed. Laura Dolfi (Naples: Edizioni Scientifiche Italiane, 1991), pp. 219–31, at p. 225, sees *La república al revés* as one of a rather heterogenous group of 'Comedias históricas', reworking historical narratives. The fictional model of the romance is relevant to all these assessments.

(still within a providentialist vision and design) the vicissitudes of a 'world turned upside-down'.

Strictly speaking, Tirso's title refers not to an upside-down world, but to *la república*, the State. Yet the notions are never entirely separate, either as treated by Tirso in this and other plays, or in the much wider currency of the 'world upside-down' topic.[20] Any form of social dissidence or disturbance could be characterized as subverting the natural order of the world, and ridiculed in terms of the young instructing the old, domesticated men and warlike women, the reversal of animal and human roles, and so forth. In the historiography – and to some degree in the reality – of the seventeenth-century English revolution, 'the world turned upside-down' would become something of a badge of honour; Spanish history has no equivalent tradition.[21] Yet there existed, in Tirso's background as in that of the most radical English sectary, a complex of theological and other associations with this topic – by no means all of them being negative in their implied representations of it.

'Turning the world upside-down' did often imply challenging hierarchies which, with some assumed scriptural warrant, were seen as God-given. More generally, the Scriptures told of an original divine ordering, turned upside-down by human misconduct in man's Fall (and often since). But they also repeatedly displayed God's intervention in the world shaped by that misconduct as his own turning of that world upside-down: 'putting down the mighty from their seat and exalting the humble and meek'; a divine foolishness 'wiser than the wisdom of men'. These notions interacted with more secular

---

[20] On this aspect of the play see the articles, already cited, of Smith, Wooldridge, and especially Grant, whose 'The World Upside-Down' begins the placing of Tirso's use of the topic in its fuller context. Henry W. Sullivan, *Tirso de Molina and the Drama of the Counter-Reformation* (Amsterdam: Rodopi, 1976) points out its importance in his theatre as a whole, as well as in Quevedo, Gracián, and Cervantes. For Carmela Hernández García, *El tópico del mundo al revés en Tirso de Molina*, New York University Ph.D. dissertation, 1976 (*Dissertation Abstracts*, 37 (1976), 1593A) its presence implies an Erasmian influence, but the European resonances are very much wider. For more on the iconography of the topic see Helen F. Grant, 'El mundo al revés' in *Hispanic Studies in Honour of Joseph Manson* (Oxford: Dolphin, 1972), pp. 119–37; for more recent Hispanic uses, Stephen M. Hart, 'Some examples of the *Topos* of the World Upside-Down in Modern Hispanic Literature and Art', *Revista Canadiense de Estudios Hispánicos*, 12 (1987–88), pp. 459–72. The theme is traced in some of its early literary instances by Ernst Robert Curtius, *European Literature and the Latin Middle Ages* (London: Routledge, 1953), pp. 94–98, and contextualized as an aspect of early modern cultural history in Peter Burke, *Popular Culture in Early Modern Europe* (revised edn, Aldershot: Ashgate, 1978), pp. 185–91.

[21] See Christopher Hill, *The World Turned Upside Down. Radical Ideas during the English Revolution* (Harmondsworth: Penguin, 1975; 1st edn 1972). These contrasting cultural histories create an immediate problem for the translator: in my own unpublished version I have tried to avoid misleading overtones by rendering Tirso's title as *A State of Disorder*.

themes. Fortune, on whose wheel individual destinies rose and fell, could be viewed as turning the world upside-down, whether in expression of its inherent instability, or as agent of God's designs. There was, too, a widely-shared sense that some measure of turning upside-down was essential to the proper balance of things. This sense was more or less disreputably expressed in magic and folk-custom; it assumed more conventional and tolerated forms in such phenomena as Carnival, or the temporary 'misrule' of Christmas and Twelfth Night festivities.[22] Theatre, with a similar licence, habitually set one thing in the place of another. It could lay out the terms of the 'world upside-down' topic to illustrate and reiterate the claims of good order. Or it could do so in ways which made it far less certain which the right way up was.

To an extent *La república al revés* does present Constantino's tyrannical regime as an 'upside-down' condition, and Irene's restoration as setting it in proper order. The Emperor's descent into corruption observes a clear, objective progression. In Act I he is ruled by his own passions, making him an undutiful son and husband, and a negligent Emperor but, as yet, nothing worse. In Act II he rejects counsel from the Senate, orders Irene's death, persecutes Carola, and plots the death of her father and brother: all this is clearly tyrannical. Act III compounds his offences with perverse lawgiving, heresy, and the atrocious project of hunting down his own wife and mother. To call that a descent into disorder was merely to give it its right name. Irene does so call it, in different but closely-related terms, in a moment of foreboding just before she goes into retirement: '¡Dios, griego imperio, te guarde, / que vas a dar al través' (I, ii, p. 384b). Honorato the Senator, punished for giving that *consilium* which is his duty, exclaims '¡Ay República al revés!' (II, ii, p. 399b), and Andronio excuses his planned rape of Irene as conforming to the usages of 'un Reino al revés' (II, xxii, p. 410a).

Yet the most conformist of such references – those linking that *república al revés* with the flouting of social hierarchies – whilst emphatic enough in themselves, are contextualized in a way which seems to restrict their resonances. They are all voiced by Carola, in shocked reaction to Lidora's rise to favour. When the latter boasts that she might become Empress, Carola replies:

> Como el mundo anda al revés
> no es mucho que en eso des,
> y que suba tu bajeza
> a coronar tu cabeza.   (I, xiv, p. 395b)

---

[22] See the chapter 'The World of Carnival' in Burke, pp. 178–204. For links between the Madrid theatre and the revels, burlesques, and masquerades of Carnival time see N. D. Shergold, *A History of the Spanish Stage* (Oxford: Clarendon, 1967), pp. 244–45, 265–66, 287–92, etc.

The exchange leads to a violent quarrel: Lidora (under some provocation of insult) strikes Carola, who reflects bitterly that 'para que con razón/ todo en aquesta ocasión/ ande al revés, no me espanto' (I, xv, p. 396a). Put under arrest by Constantino, she ends Act I lamenting:

> ¡Qué bien anda el mundo ahora!
> Despreciada la señora;
> antepuesta la criada [. . .]
> La que descalzó mis pies
> entronizada en el puesto
> del Imperio. Mas poco es
> en la República aquesto
> que es República al revés. (I, xvi, p. 396b)

From this point on that broad linkage between social privilege and right order virtually disappears from the play. When Carola returns to the theme in Act II, it is to reflect sadly on her prostration before Lidora – 'Ves aquí al revés el mundo: / a tus pies postrada estoy' (II, viii, p. 402b) – as part of a plea for death as a merciful release from her suffering. For Carola is now launched on a trajectory that is made strikingly visible as the play unfolds. First seen as the richly-arrayed Princess of Cyprus, she was bound, in Act I, to feel her loss of status. Now, however, her humiliation has turned to an authentic humbling, and her concern is no longer for her social station: it is for her moral claim on Constantino, as a rightful (and loving) bride, who carries his child. Fleeing the Palace at the end of Act II, she knows that the world has taken more from her than rank alone:

> ¡Qué de cosas he perdido
> juntas, mundo burlador!
> Imperio, esposo y honor,
> padre, hermano y el vestido.   (II, xxviii, p. 412b)

She plunges into the sea, hoping that what is upside-down on earth may prove *derecho* – both 'right' and 'right-way-up' – there. We meet her next, shipwrecked and frail, and glad enough of Tarso's improvised kindness. Prior to her last appearance in the play, she has been running through the woods, clad in skins; her son, now born, is hidden in an oak tree. The glittering creature of Act I has undergone a *kenosis*, an emptying of privilege. And that makes her final role as the advocate of mercy – for Constantino, for Leoncio, for Lidora – significant indeed. If Irene, 'Juez de la causa de Dios', speaks for the first person of the Trinity, Carola, having laid her majesty by, plays the part of the second.

There is no obvious way of completing this female Trinity: the text of the play permits us to identify no Paraclete – not even, as one might very much wish, Tirso's own Muse, but it is still striking how this conformist element in the 'world upside-down' topic leads us away from its immediate resonances and towards more radical perspectives. Tirso knew well that the motif formed part of the defence which those in power – however much their power might contribute towards the world's botched ordering – habitually put forward in their own interest. Constantino, after all, does just that. '¿Él ha de regirme a mí?' he rages when the Senate offers him unwanted good advice, '¿Es este el mundo al revés?', and as he rails against the cult of images, he denounces Greece as truly 'la república al revés' (III, vi, p. 417b). The commonplace, Tirso seems concerned to remind us, is not automatically to be trusted: we need to know who is using it, and in what interest.

One area where Constantino appears supremely self-confident in its use is in the designation of spheres of activity proper to men and to women. For him, Irene as Empress is self-evidently out of place: his examples in relation to this are part and parcel of the 'world upside-down' topic:

> Semíramis querrás ser
> y hacerme a mí infame Nino
> [. . .]
> holandas, madre, dibuja
> que a la mujer el aguja
> le está bien, mas no la lanza.   (I, ii, p. 383a)

His idea of condign punishment for the Senators who petition him for Irene's release – 'yo haré de su vil Senado/ un senado de mujeres' (II, ii, p. 399a) – is further elaborated in terms of the traditional topic:

> y con basquiñas y tocas
> para que el vulgo provoques,
> les pon ruecas por estoques
> que sus pretensiones locas
> declaren [. . .]
> porque soy de parecer
> que como mujeres vean
> los que el Imperio desean
> que gobierne una mujer.   (II, ii, p. 399b)

The woman ruler correlates with the 'distaffs for swords' motif as an instance of subverted order, but Constantino remains unconvincing in his own terms. Irene has already noted that she was obliged to take up the imperial burden herself in time of crisis because no man was forthcoming to do so: 'por huir sus intervalos/ hilaran como mujeres/ y fueran Sardanapalos' (I, ii, p. 383a). When Constantino speaks a sonnet, justifying his subjection in love to Lidora, two of his chosen precedents are heroic (Samson and Hercules), but the third is – Sardanapalus (I, viii, p. 390a). More generally, Tirso leaves us in no doubt, in this or in other plays, of the potential rightness of a woman's

involvement in royal rule. In the case of Irene here, as in that of María de
Molina in *La prudencia en la mujer*, the feat of successfully transcending a
conventional gender-role emerges as heroic and wholly admirable.

Other reversals of male and female roles, arising involuntarily – often as a
result of disguise – could only appear as comic catastrophes. It happens, for
example, when Andronio visits the disguised Tarso's prison cell, to press his
attentions (as he thinks) on Irene:

> ANDRONIO   Ea, respondedme, pues
>   veis a lo que estoy dispuesto.
> TARSO   ¡No faltaba más que aquesto
>   para andar todo al revés!
>   Ya no puede durar nada,
>   habiendo luz, mi disfraz;
>   ánimo, ciego rapaz,
>   quitarle quiero la espada.   (II, xxiv, p. 410b)

Tirso's theatre offers a good many misunderstandings of this sort; it is by no
means clear what we should make of them psychologically. In dramatic
terms, such ineptly-targeted sexual desire offers a compelling comic metaphor for confusion. Once Tarso does get hold of his assailant's sword, matters
will be rapidly and effectively clarified. Yet the implied challenge to the
expected persists and is exploited in other ways. The prison guards see only a
woman; Andronio only a 'vil pastor', but Tarso defies them on either hand:
'con el traje de Irene/ me ha vestido su valor' (II, xxiv, p. 411a). Irene's
courage – the courage of a *mujer valiente*.

That scene, to which Tirso's independent reading of the 'world
upside-down' motif so plainly matters, is one of two decisive turning-points
in *La república al revés*. The second (its direct consequence in plot terms) is
the opening of Act III. Irene, alone on a wild hillside above the sea, laments
to the desolate landscape:

> que el mundo y su gobierno está de modo
> que, andando al revés todo,
> del hijo la madre huye,
> porque su vida, bárbaro, destruye,
> hallando aunque te asombres,
> en tus fieras piedad, mas no en los hombres.   (III, I, p. 413a)

Here are yet wider-ranging images of violated order: the order of nature and
the codes of civilized life; but for Tarso, who now echoes Irene's theme, yet
more is at stake:

> Trocad, brutos, los nombres
> por ellos, que por más brutos confieso
> los que hombres llama el engañado mundo.   (III, ii, p. 413a)

It is the integrity of the entire system of naming – of language – which is here seen as corrupted. Yet just at this point where the topic of the 'república al revés' assumes its deepest and most pessimistic sense, Irene's meeting with Tarso (and, a moment later, with Carola) decisively initiates a counter-movement. To make sense of that movement, we must take up another theme: the running contrast in this play between Court and country.

Even more than the 'world upside-down', that contrast, with its implicit valuation of the country at the Court's expense, and its strong message that the passage from one to the other can initiate a process of change and renewal, was a literary commonplace.[23] Once again, Tirso's handling of the topic goes well beyond the merely conventional. Of the play's three protagonists – Irene, Carola, Constantino – it is Irene who spends most time in the country, and who is changed least by it. She is, from the outset, presented to us as the ideal Christian ruler: devout, prudent and militarily successful. And she remains that: though the Empire loses her services for a time, it cannot become stable again until it gets her back. In that sense, and in that sense alone, her name (meaning 'peace' in Greek) has the allegorical resonance which Karl Vossler once claimed for it.[24] Yet her initial withdrawal from Court to village is framed in a way which suggests that she still has something to learn:

> que ya me enfada el palacio;
> y dando a Marte la mano,
> imitaré a Diocleciano,
> que tuvo por vituperio
> la púrpura del Imperio
> hecho en Dalmacia hortelano.   (I, ii, p. 384a)

The tale of the Emperor Diocletian's early retirement was, Gibbon tells us, widely known.[25] Yet it seems strange that the heroine of a play about heresy

---

[23] Any overall view of this topic would have to take account of the entire pastoral genre in verse and prose, and of the extensive literary progeny of Horace's *Beatus ille*, in addition to the more immediately relevant examples discussed by Noël Salomon, *Recherches sur le thème paysan dans la 'comedia' au temps de Lope de Vega* (Bordeaux: Institut d'Études Ibériques et Ibéro-Américaines de l'Université de Bordeaux, 1965) and J. E. Varey, 'La Campagne dans le théâtre espagnol au XVIIe siècle' in *Dramaturgie et société*, ed. Jean Jacquot (Paris: CNRS, 1968), I, pp. 47–76.

[24] Vossler, p. 35

[25] Edward Gibbon, *The Decline and Fall of the Roman Empire*, ed. Oliphant Smeaton (London: Dent, n.d.), I, pp. 377–78: invited by his former Imperial colleague to resume charge of the Empire, 'He rejected the temptation with a smile of pity, calmly observing that, if he could show Maximian the cabbages which he had planted with his own hands at Salona, he should no longer be urged to relinquish the enjoyment of happiness for the pursuit of power.' Irene, of course, does return to power – a characteristically Tirsian anomaly.

overcome should compare herself with that ruler who was, above all others, a persecutor of Christians (and the antithesis of the *Christian* Emperor, the first Constantine). It is as if Tirso did not mind letting it be seen that these traditionally exemplary instances were, to a degree, arbitrary. Something of the same doubt, inevitably, is cast on that other traditional motif which is in play at this point: the *menosprecio de Corte y alabanza de aldea*.

It is to a village, specifically, that Irene retires in order to escape the rapid pace of life at Court, and the perils of falling from any high position there. Within minutes of her arrival, she reflects on the contrast of lifestyles: the villagers wish her long life among them, and she responds:

> En la quietud
> del campo que viste Abril
> sí tendré, que en el palacio
> donde la ambición se bebe,
> la más larga vida es breve.   (I, xi, p. 392b)

Tarso's rejoinder – 'Acá vivimos despacio' – confirms the point. He has not sought her out at Court, he explains, because he would not expect her to recall their earlier friendship:

> Muda el mandar la costumbre
> y la púrpura imperial
> no hace caso del sayal.
> [. . .] acá
> más tiempo y lugar habrá.   (I, xi, p. 392b)

The topic is given body, then, in terms of the one element which seems to address real experience: the sense of expanded time. In other respects, though, its presentation remains commonplace: the basic institutional life, so important in Spanish versions of the bucolic idyll – 'Alcaldes, Concejo y gente / del pueblo' (I, xi, p. 391b); the rustic bounty carried in processional homage; the claim that such gifts have the value of an untutored sincerity, 'pobre en obras, rico en fe' (I, xi, p. 392a); and, for the streetwise audience in the urban *corrales*, no doubt a good deal of broad linguistic and gestural comedy.

As Cyril Jones observed some decades ago, Tirso was alert to the ironic possibilities of this kind of thing – more obviously exploited, perhaps, in the parallel scenes of *La prudencia en la mujer*.[26] But even in Irene's ideal retreat, country realities of a less elevating kind are disconcertingly evident. The Tarso-Melisa-Italio entanglement does not seem to be a particularly decorous

---

[26] C. A. Jones, 'Tirso de Molina and Country Life', *Philological Quarterly*, 51 (1972), 197–204, at p. 199; see also p. 203.

affair: she wants Irene to make Tarso love her 'por justicia' (I, xi, p. 392b). Dinampo the Mayor knows just what is to be expected when real soldiers enter a real village: 'si nos echan soldados/ no hay mujeres ni ganados' (I, xii, p. 393a). For all their simple loyalty, too, the villagers must stand impotently by while Irene is hauled off to prison.

Thus far – and Act I gets us no further – we have the village in traditionally exemplary contrast with the Court, in a perspective which seems distinctively Tirsian in being (to quote Cyril Jones once more) 'complex and questioning'. The country is different in its social and ceremonial styles, and in its typical virtues of loyalty and duty. Its scenes are sharply demarcated metrically, being wholly in *redondillas* (not used elsewhere in Act I). But they occupy only about a quarter of that Act, and have little effect on the course of events there. They merely elaborate Andronio's decorative trope on Irene's retirement:

> Aquí dicen que ha de estar,
> trocando en florido campo
> el campo armado.   (I, xii, p. 393a)

Act II, again, alternates Court and country scenes, the latter taking up about a quarter of the whole, but this is a different kind of country, where very different things go on. The village of Act I was a couple of leagues from the capital; the distance here seems vaguer, and the environment less settled. There is a village mayor here too – Damón – but he is a bumpkin, grotesquely ill-informed, for instance, about what it means to serve in the Emperor's 'cámara' (II, xii, p. 405a). The setting which offered Irene a temporal space to 'live slowly' is now a physical space, through which Tarso, bent on her release, and Leoncio, now a fugitive, can wander. Its one fixed point is the tower where Irene lies imprisoned, and Andronio broods on his lust. The *redondilla* form has ceased to function as a marker of the rural: it now occurs in Court settings too.

Yet the country scenes are still contrasted with those of Court life, insofar as they relieve the tensions of the latter. Constantino's ever more abusive treatment of Carola gives place to the innocently scatological fooling of Damón's rustic posse; the dark passions of the blood-revenge plot, echoed in another mode in Andronio's obsessive desire, are broken into by the transvestite farce of Tarso's escape. Where Court intrigue involved a multi-layered hypocrisy, these rural scenes exploit the more explicit stratagems of physical disguise. It is true that corruption, radiating from the imperial centre, has its effect here too. That point is established through Andronio, who conceives his monstrous plan in the conviction that 'andando como anda el mundo todo/ necedad es andar a lo derecho' (II, xvi, p. 407a). But even as he speaks, Tarso is proving his fidelity to Irene as 'entre tantos malos/ [. . .] un hombre que es tan bueno' (II, xvii, p. 407b). Through the key figure of Tarso, the rural

scenes of Act II develop a running thread of counterplot and escape: first
Leoncio's getaway; then Irene's release; and finally Tarso's own defiance. It
may not amount to much as yet, but it does show the countryside to be a
space substantially outwith Constantino's control.

That is important for what it becomes in Act III, where rural settings at last
come to predominate. They are still described as being 'en los montes más
cercanos/ de Constantinopla' (III, x, p. 421b), and Constantino, for example,
is able to organize a day's hunting there with minimal notice. But the landscapes are wilder and stranger now. The imagined scene where, at the start of
the Act, Irene and Tarso lament the disorder of the whole human world is
plainly the world of nature as *another place* – its wildness the guarantor of its
remoteness from human evil. Almost at once, though, it becomes a place of
human recognition. Irene's 'en tus fieras piedad, mas no en los hombres' (III,
I, p. 413a) is echoed in the first line of Tarso's own soliloquy, and when, a
moment later, the two recognize one another, Irene acknowledges this as a
turning-point in her affairs: 'cese el rigor; piadoso Cielo, ayuda' (III, ii, p.
413b). Another voice, in turn, repeats her words: it is Carola, whom we last
saw at the end of Act II, casting herself on the mercy of the waves. She now
appears, rescued from shipwreck by a sailor, and recognizable to the other
two from her cry of '¡Ay, perseguida y desgraciada Infanta!'

Unhappily for her, the sailor has recognized her too; he hurries off to claim
his reward from the Emperor. With the incursion of human beings, it seems,
betrayal and exploitation come back into the world of nature. Yet the final
emphasis of this scene is firmly on the other things that are brought back
there too. Carola, persecuted, in pain, and heavily pregnant, is in a state of
collapse. And Tarso offers her what help he can:

> Pues ten, señora, esfuerzo y no le pierdas,
> y vamos, que en lo espeso de este monte
> haremos chozas de sus verdes ramos,
> y aunque groseras, camas de sus hojas.
> Mi pedernal y yesca dará lumbre;
> con que enjugar las ropas y abrigarte;
> y aunque en peligro ponga aquesta vida,
> iré al lugar y pueblo más cercano
> a traer de comer, aunque el vestido
> en trueco deje.   (III, iii, p. 414b)

There is a moving concreteness about this, recalling the 'flax and whites of
eggs' with which the servants of the blinded Gloucester in *King Lear* seek to
soothe his injured eyes. At the extreme of what human beings can do to one
another, it is a reminder that this too is something which only human beings
can do. As such, it places, better than anything else, the positive element
which Tirso located in the life of the country, and the energies of renewal
which stem from that. The whole scene is about recognition – recognition of

individuals who have been lost, and of a humanity that has been too long abused – seen as a condition of renewal. In terms of traditional drama-criticism, it is an anagnorisis, and it is to the country that people must go (or be driven) to find it.

Act III furnishes a whole series of such moments of recognition. The King of Cyprus and his son encounter Leoncio wandering in the wilds (III, vii, pp. 418a–419a): his disclosure of the true facts of Carola's case cements their alliance with him in a plot which will be politically crucial to Constantino's downfall. Here again, a portion of the truth is revealed to those who have taken their quest far enough into desert places. The revelation which attends Constantino's hunting trip is rather different. On one level this is a routine incursion of Court into country, answering to that sense of their relationship which led Irene, early in the play, to speak of retiring to 'una aldea y recreación' (I, ii, p. 384a). The Court comes out to use the countryside as it needs and pleases. But this hunt has worse motives: an obsessive desire to be rid of Irene and Carola; an undertone of sexual excitement, linking Constantino and Lidora in that murderous chase as a *folie à deux*. The mix is all the more disturbing because some of Tirso's most evocative description of rural nature (a relatively rare element, as it happens, in the play as a whole) occurs here:

> El apacible sitio [. . .]
> de aquella zarza con taray funesto
> y parras enlazada y retejida.   (III, xii, p. 423b)

However, when Constantino lies down to sleep nearby in the noonday sun, he too has his moment of recognition. A visible tableau of the Wheel of Fortune makes all plain: his fall; Irene's triumph; Carola's vindication; Leoncio's bid for empire. That revelation, delivered in the country, attests to something repeatedly touched upon in the Court scenes: the inexorable linkage between worldly human greatness and falling. Irene evokes it as she renounces the throne (I, ii, p. 384b). Mistrust of unstable worldly fortune is a *leitmotif* of Leoncio's nervous dialogue with his destiny (I, iv, p. 385a; II, vii, p. 401a; III, vii, p. 418a; III, xi, p. 422b; III, xviii, p. 426a). Clodio, marvelling at his own swift advancement, fears – and with good reason – that he may suffer a fall (II, ix, p. 404a). Constantino himself does suffer one, prophetically, at his coronation, dropping his orb and crown, and breaking his sword as he stumbles (I, ii, p. 384a), but it is only now, distanced from Fortune's domain by sleep and the rural setting, that he can read these things aright.

The play's final anagnorisis comes with the recognition (in both senses) of Irene by her army and subjects, and the acknowledgment as heir of Carola's (wholly unhistorical) baby boy. Emblematically, the child is retrieved from a refuge of natural innocence and strength: the hollow of an oak tree (III, xx,

p. 428b). The dispositions which Irene now lays down as Empress bring the play back, too, to its imperial context. Yet the faithful Tarso is co-opted to help her rule. The tensions of justice against mercy go unresolved. Carola's vow to travel to China, rather than live where Constantino is a prisoner, suggests that Tirso's providentialism remained, to the end, anything but glibly prescriptive. Yet the domains laid out imaginatively in the play for Court and country do assist him to a real coherence in its presentation.

The Court here embodies the institutional life of the world. Tirso neither rejects that life nor proposes its radical alteration. He was no proto-revolutionary. But he does seem to be conscious that this aspect of the human world tends not to work very well. As imagined here, Court is the domain of Fortune and the place of the Fall and, because these institutions and hierarchies, and the power that goes with them, are part of a fallen nature, they can, under tyranny, go swiftly and horribly wrong. The countryside, of course, is still part of the fallen world. It includes such unedifying realities as Tarso's quarrel with Italio (and whatever trifling with Melisa preceded it); it includes rustic incompetence and obscenity; even Andronio's corruption happens out there. The venal sailor, too, reminds us that even simple folk can still be corrupt. Yet this is still a place where the room for a greater simplicity allows room also for a sounder understanding. It is a space where more can happen – where, if you go there, you can meet the unexpected; where the long-lost can sometimes be found. It is where Irene learns to know true loyalty, and Carola learns mercy. In a word, it is a redemptive space – the fallen world accessible to grace. That meaning here is delivered through the structures of romance very much as it is in *A Winter's Tale*, and with something of the same sense of release as the play moves from brooding intrigue and fatality into what is still no ideal place, but a landscape of human possibilities.[27]

[27] An earlier version of this paper was presented in November 1996 to the 12th Annual Colloquium of the Department of Hispanic and Italian Studies in the University of Victoria, British Columbia, as part of a session held in honour of Professor Louise Fothergill-Payne, *de buena memoria*. To Louise, as to Victor Dixon, readers and spectators of the *comedia* have cause to be grateful for practising the kind of scholarship which has consciously and consistently enriched enjoyment of the plays.

Syntax and Semantics in the Dramatis Personae of Lorca's *La casa de Bernarda Alba*

JAMES WHISTON

Although other colleagues as well as myself have had the pleasure of teaching *La casa de Bernarda Alba* to our first-year students in Trinity College, Dublin over the past 25 years, it seemed that Victor Dixon had made the play his own, and because of his passion for and knowledge of the stage, he was able to steal a march on the rest of us, and turn this particular drama into live theatre by directing a student production of it. The happy memory of a play directed by Victor Dixon in Trinity – and there were several – the professionalism, the dedication, the attention to detail, the shaping imagination of his direction, have prompted this piece on *La casa de Bernarda Alba* which, out of continuing esteem for, and deference towards, Victor Dixon's incomparably finer knowledge of the play, is restricted mainly to the initial outer confines of the drama, its dramatis personae, the order of the players therein, their ages and likely relationships. It is to be hoped that this piece will not just be a reflection about how things might have been in the Alba household before the fictional time of the play, which begins on the day of Bernarda's second widowhood, but it is difficult for a veteran *galdosista* to discard a lifelong academic relationship with nineteenth-century realism even when confronted with a script as determinedly pared down as *La casa de Bernarda Alba*, and not attempt to add some flesh to Lorca's lean and magnificently hungry text with a supplementary critical narrative.[1] Indeed, because of its brevity the critic of *La casa de Bernarda Alba* is often obliged to read between the lines and supply what may appear to be missing links, but which Lorca, rather in the style of his thread-like drawings, has actually left in interstitial form, thus enabling the reader or viewer – but I should think more likely the reader – to flesh out what is unspoken, or missing, or what

---

[1] Mario Hernández closes the introduction to his edition of *La casa* with an interesting newspaper account of Lorca's esteem for Galdós's writing: '[Lorca] tronaba contra los que se lanzan a escribir comedias sin conocer el castellano; decía su amor a Galdós – "¡Y hay autores drámaticos que no han conocido a Galdós!" '; *Federico García Lorca, La casa de Bernarda Alba* (Madrid: Alianza, 1981). Subsequent references to the play will be from this edition and will be placed in the text.

has been expressed 'llena de segunda intención' (p. 104), as the play's own text puts it. In this regard we may borrow what Francisco Induráin has written (and doubtless many other critics of the play in a similar vein): 'Lo condensado del texto lorquiano hace que al reconsiderar cada frase, cada palabra incluso, broten nuevas referencias posibles y hasta probables.'[2]

In particular, Martirio is a character whose speech and actions allow the critic to subject her words to specially close analysis. In the scene of the stolen portrait of Pepe el Romano, the general air of scandal and shame which centres around Martirio may be explained if we read into Poncia's reply to Bernarda a somewhat more precise placing of where the servant discovered the picture. We firstly see a reference to it from Angustias, who storms on to the stage, explaining that the picture of Pepe that she had 'debajo de mi almohada' (p. 106) has gone missing. When La Poncia finds it she is reluctant to say where. This could mean that she is unwilling to point the finger at one of the sisters, but her hesitation may also suggest that she is scandalized at where she found it. Lorca uses the word 'extrañada' to describe La Poncia at this moment of discovery, which may refer to her expectation that she would find the picture in Adela's bed, but it could also refer to the actual place in Martirio's bed where she found it, 'entre las sábanas', and therefore much closer to Martirio's nightgowned body than under the pillow of Angustias. Bernarda's ferocious response and death wish for her daughter ('¡Mala puñalada te den, mosca muerta!') even allowing for the exaggeration of Spanish curses, suggests, too, that Bernarda may have harboured scandalized thoughts as to why Martirio might have had her sister's suitor's picture under her sheets. With deft touches such as this Lorca can create in the reader's or spectator's critical response a 'theatre of the mind', supplying the links left by the exquisitely light and dexterous text of the dramatist.

I have speculated elsewhere, in the context of a fifty-word poem – 'La vejez en los pueblos' – by Miguel Hernández, that a similar deliberate, anti-rhetorical device is at work on Lorca's title for this play as operates in the repetitive phonics of Hernández's poem.[3] The predominance of the 'a' vowel sound of the title of Lorca's play, its phonic stress on the second, third, fourth and fifth 'a' sound, combine to suggest the pervasive poverty of the lives of the inmates of this *casa*, the repetition of the 'a' sound also creating the phonic equivalent of a prolonged sigh ('ah') throughout the title. (In this connection C. B. Morris's comment is worth noting: that the 'sparse, unclut-

    [2] 'La casa de Bernarda Alba: ensayo de interpretación', in Ricardo Domenech, ed., 'La casa de Bernarda Alba' y el teatro de García Lorca (Madrid: Cátedra, 1987), pp. 123–47, at p. 144.
    [3] 'La inversión de la retórica en "La vejez en los pueblos" de Miguel Hernández', in Miguel Hernández, cincuenta años después (Alicante: Comisión del Homenaje a Miguel Hernández, 1992), pp. 975–82.

tered title is the situation and the theme' of the play.)[4] Did Lorca mean to elide the last 'a' of Bernarda's name into her patronymic? If so, then when used as in the title her name would take on even greater masculine connotations than when on its own.

The preceding paragraphs may serve as a brief prelude to, and justification for, our examination of what strictly speaking may be outside the theatrical experience of the play – the dramatis personae [DP] – but because it was composed by Lorca in the way that he did merits our attention for whatever light it may shed on the piece of theatre itself. (I include the playwright's title, sub-title and *advertencia*, which all appeared on the same page as the DP in the author's manuscript, to be reproduced later.) It has often been noted before that on this page Lorca refers to himself as 'poeta' rather than the more normal 'autor', and it may not be too far-fetched to read this description of himself back into the DP and describe the latter as a 'Poetic Prologue' to the play. Here is the famous DP, and author's comment beneath, as it appears in printed editions of the play (the one given is by Mario Hernández):

PERSONAS

BERNARDA, 60 años
MARÍA JOSEFA (madre de Bernarda), 80 años
ANGUSTIAS (hija de Bernarda), 36 años
MAGDALENA (hija de Bernarda), 30 años
AMELIA (hija de Bernarda), 27 años
MARTIRIO (hija de Bernarda), 24 años
ADELA (hija de Bernarda), 20 años
CRIADA, 50 años
LA PONCIA (criada), 60 años
PRUDENCIA, 50 años
[MENDIGA]
MUJERES DE LUTO
[MUJER 1.a
MUJER 2.a
MUJER 3.a
MUJER 4.a
MUCHACHA]

El poeta advierte que estos tres actos tienen la intención de un documental fotográfico.

The first thing to note about this list is that it is a confection by the first editor of the play (with small amendments by Hernández) and did not appear in this way in Lorca's manuscript. (The names in square brackets represent editors' additions to the original manuscript version of the DP.) In order to

---

4   *García Lorca. La casa de Bernarda Alba* (London: Grant & Cutler, 1990), p. 116.

clarify what has been done to the original text, Lorca's manuscript version of the DP is given in facsimile form on the following page, as reproduced in Mario Hernández's edition. The most striking feature of the printed version of the DP, in relation to Lorca's other plays, is the fact that he added ages to all of the characters who live and work in the house, and also to the character Prudencia. In the context of the absence of characters' ages in his other plays the addition of these in *La casa* therefore seems very deliberate. At first glance, however, the giving of ages to the two serving women and to Prudencia seems like the gratuitous act of a dramatist in something of a hurry, who, having begun adding ages at the top of the list, continued on with those characters who have speaking and acting parts significantly in excess of the other seven (or eight if we count the *niña*) who appear in the play. In the case of Prudencia, the manuscript shows that Lorca inserted her name after he had completed the list (as is also the case with María Josefa), so that assigning ages to these two characters would have been based on a consideration of the ages that he had already assigned to the other characters. Of the ten ages that remain in the printed version, seven appear to be rounded up or down to the particular decade assigned to that character. Again this would suggest that Lorca, as in his treatment of the scene examined in my second paragraph, is concerned only to sketch in the essential details that he wishes to highlight, and leaves any further speculation to ourselves.

The age groupings of the women in both manuscript and printed versions leave María Josefa at eighty years, with Bernarda and La Poncia following on at sixty years each. Morris (op. cit., p. 56: see fn. 4) shrewdly comments that Poncia's 'equality of age with Bernarda does not grant her equality of status'. Criada and Prudencia share a fiftieth birthday; and of the daughters, Magdalena and Adela are assigned the rounded ages of '30' and '20' respectively. Of course, priority on the list of the DP is not given in terms of age because Bernarda comes at the top, although she is not the oldest, and La Poncia comes almost at the end of the listing of principal characters, even though she is jointly second oldest in the play. Does the order of precedence have any special significance? As eponymous protagonist it is probably natural that Bernarda should head the list, but in so doing Lorca breaks the chronological order of age that he could have kept within the family, before moving on to servants and outsiders. As I have indicated, the manuscript version of the DP is particularly interesting in this regard, showing that there was plenty of room between the word 'Personas' and 'Bernarda' in the DP for María Josefa's name, but that Lorca preferred to squeeze her name in with tiny, almost illegible writing beneath Bernarda's name.

Why then does he not similarly break this order when writing down the names of the daughters? From a dramatic perspective, Adela is surely the main focus of the conflict between mother and daughters, although it could be, and has been, argued that Martirio is psychologically a much more interesting character. Of the three generations of the family list, Bernarda is at the

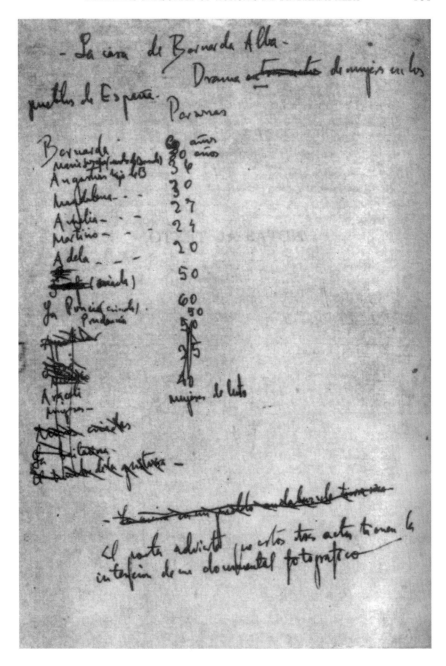

Lorca's manuscript version of the dramatis personae in *La casa de Bernarda Alba*. Reproduced from Mario Hernández, ed. *Federico García Lorca, La casa de Bernarda Alba* (Madrid: Alianza, 1981), p. 154.

top, María Josefa is second and Adela is at the bottom. The implication must
be that while Bernarda can leapfrog chronologically over her mother (¡valga
la figura!) and reach the top, Adela is put firmly at the bottom of the heap,
and must take her place on the lowliest rung of the ladder, immediately above
that of the servants.[5] This positioning is reinforced by the repetition of the
designation of each of the daughters as daughters of Bernarda: by virtue of
their prior birth in relation to the next sister they have their own claim to a
position of respect in the hierarchy of age in the house. (In the manuscript, as
can be seen, Lorca did not actually write the words 'Hija de Bernarda' after
each daughter, but indicated the Spanish equivalent of 'ditto' with three
hyphens after each of the daughters' names. In fact, he did not even write
'hija de Bernarda' after Angustias's name, but 'hija de B'.) Adela's position
at the bottom illustrates how impossibly much there remains for her to do in
order to achieve any position of dominance in the house. In this context we
may note that Adela is included among the seven women's ages rounded-up
to the nearest ten years, which is a small but telling condition that puts her in
with the majority rather than allows her to stand out, as she wishes for and
believes of herself. (C. B. Morris op. cit., p. 26 also mentions 'the round
figures favoured by Lorca' for the ages in the play.) In the manuscript it
appears that Lorca's initial thought was to make Magdalena a twenty-
something, but then changed her age to '30' – the original 'two' has been
changed into a 'three'. Magdalena for her part in Act I rounds up Angustias's
age, referring to her as 'ahora que tiene cuarenta' (p. 75). In the initial order
of speaking in the play Adela is given neither the prominence of first or last
place, but is firmly placed as speaker in the middle of the five sisters.
    One very small deletion in the manuscript beneath Adela's name, which
looks like a capital 'R', may be linked to Lorca's decision to keep Adela at
the bottom of the list of sisters. Could this have been the initial letter of the
name of a sixth sister in an earlier version of the play? The proportionately
greater number of deletions in the DP than in the rest of the manuscript,
noted by Hernández (ed. cit., p. 159: see fn. 3), suggests that the DP belongs
to an earlier draft. In his study Hernández notes a couple of occasions in Act
I when in his view 'Homero [that is, Lorca] dormita' (p. 160) by 'forgetting'
that the number of daughters was five instead of six, 'como si entrara en el
recuento la anciana María Josefa'. It seems unlikely that Lorca would have
mistaken a daughter for a grandmother. A more likely explanation is that

---

5   Herbert Ramsden in his edition of the play uses a similar though somewhat more
elegant figure of speech to describe Adela's position, describing her as 'prepared to over-
leap both mother and convention in the search for satisfaction', *La casa de Bernarda Alba*
(Manchester: Manchester University Press, 1983), xvi. Doubtless the intensely hierarchical ethos portrayed in the play – of age, social class and gender – gives rise to this kind
of descriptive metaphor. Adela shows herself to be very aware of this hierarchy when
talking to Poncia, using a like metaphor: 'No por encima de ti, que eres una criada, por
encima de mi madre saltaría para apagarme este fuego' (p. 96).

Lorca decided originally to have six daughters, and possibly began the name of the sixth under Adela's name, which would make her younger than Adela, given the chronological order followed in the case of the sisters. For the purposes of our analysis, the exclusion of a sixth, youngest daughter is another piece of small, circumstantial evidence of Lorca's decision to keep Adela at the bottom of the DP, where the grouping of the sisters is concerned.

The position of Criada in the DP, and her priority in the list over Poncia, may have been determined by an earlier version of the play, although Poncia is nevertheless clearly a more important character in the play as we know it. Criada was originally assigned the name Josefa, with her status as *criada* indicated in parenthesis, and came before Poncia who was described in the same way. Some editors have reversed the order of the two women in the DP, presumably on the basis of Poncia's importance, even though Criada comes on stage first and is given a speaking part on her own on the stage a little while later, something hardly conceded to any other character in the play. Pepe was also originally called *José*, then *Nicasio*,[6] and if the Josefa/José nomenclature coincided in an earlier draft of the play Lorca may have decided that there was too much confusion in the consonance of the names of these characters (José would have had a physical role on-stage according to this early draft), tried *Nicasio* and finally decided on *Pepe*. What Criada's position in the DP tells us is that while it may not be possible consistently to assign a place in the DP on the basis of age – Bernarda, 60, comes before María Josefa, 80, Criada, 50, comes before Poncia, 60 – Adela does come at the bottom of the list of the sisters on the grounds of age, reinforcing her destiny as one who has found her place, in the words of Poncia herself, in 'un hoyo en la tierra de la verdad' (p. 53).

We should remember that from evidence within the play Lorca invites us to read the play's title as meaning 'The house that belongs to Bernarda Alba', that is as a house that she has inherited from her father: 'esta casa levantada por mi padre' (p. 111), as she says in Act II; hence the play's title refers exclusively to Bernarda and to her possession of the house: Bernarda pulls all, or nearly all, the economic strings in her house.[7] This is perhaps one of the reasons why Lorca places Bernarda's name on its own in the DP, with no indi-

---

6   I rely for this name on the keen eye of Mario Hernández, because from the copy of the manuscript of the DP in his edition it is impossible to decipher the alternative to *José*.

7   Ronald Cueto, in a refreshing article on the play, suggests that the *casa* of the title could refer to 'a *casa*, in the sense of lineage or *linaje*, or of offspring or *descendencia*, which is fated to extinction because of its sterility' (p. 33): 'On the Queerness Rampant in the House of Bernarda Alba', in *Leeds Papers on Lorca and on Civil War Verse*, ed. Margaret A. Rees (Leeds: Trinity and All Saints 1990), pp. 9–43. In his often quoted piece, 'Nuestro teatro' in the September, 1937 issue of *Hora de España* (pp. 29–36) [Glasshütten im Taunus: Verlag Detlev Auvermann KG (Kraus Reprint) 1972] Manuel Altolaguirre calls the play *Las hijas de Bernarda Alba* (p. 36), evidently a follow-on, in terms of its title, from the earlier one *Las hijas de Loth* (Hernández, ed. cit., p. 29). The

cation of any relationship on her part to any of the other characters, until we
come to their own names: they have a dependency on her but she has none on
them. Such self-sufficiency, as we said, may come from her financial independence, for the clear implication in the play is that her second husband –
and possibly her first as well – have come to her house to live and that she has
retained ownership of it. The tragic significance of such self-sufficiency is
that Bernarda, as befits her unrelated name in the DP, is in a position of dominance over others and yet is isolated from all feeling or regard for them. Thus,
the relationship between privilege and responsibility is broken, leading to a
distortion of all the relationships in the house, as is evidenced particularly in
those between the sisters; and it also leads to the unnatural dominance of
Pepe el Romano. From her lowly position in the DP it is little wonder that
Adela's view of the world and of herself is distorted, as when she breaks her
mother's stick and cries out '¡Aquí se acabaron las voces de presidio! [. . .]
¡En mí no manda nadie más que Pepe!' (p. 148). For a liberal-minded audience into the fifth year of the Second Spanish Republic in 1936 the first part
of Adela's spirited cry of freedom would have sat uneasily with the second
part. One other example from the end of Act I – a stage direction not
emphasised by critics in relation to Adela – shows how all the sisters turn on
their grandmother to lock her up as she taunts them about not getting
married. The stage direction – 'Todas [our emphasis] arrastran a la vieja' (p.
83) – means that it includes the sister, Adela, who is often thought of as being
in some way different from the others. She, too, however, plays her part in
refusing to face the reality of her situation, ground down as she is by the
tyranny of Bernarda.

Similarly in the scene with Martirio when Adela exclaims that 'a un
caballo encabritado soy capaz de poner de rodillas con la fuerza de mi dedo
meñique', a dispassionate audience, while admiring the bold stroke of
Adela's imagination, will conclude that Adela's trust in her own strength
owes more to absurd romantic fantasy than to physical reality.[8] It is also clear
to the audience, given the fate of the 'hija de la Librada' at the end of Act II,
that Adela's proclaimed readiness to live openly with Pepe would not have
been tolerated. She fails, too, to take into account her mother's age and lack
of experience in using a rifle (at night), and Pepe's youth. Bernarda does not

change from *hijas* to *casa* was simple yet inspired, opening up many interpretative possibilities, some of them explored by Cueto in the article mentioned.

   8   Ramsden's simple opposition between vitality and repression leads to an uncritical
assessment of the flaws in Adela's character, taking her at her own estimate when he
describes her as 'strong enough to bring a bucking horse to its knees with the strength of
her little finger' (ed. cit., xvi). C. B. Morris also enthuses that Adela 'convinces us that she
is capable . . . of subduing a wild horse with her little finger' (p. 87). Carlos Feal, too,
quoting Adela's sentence, finds in it a 'profound' example of her desire for male power (p.
103), but without characterising it as the outlandish fantasy that it is, be it masculine or
feminine.

even know the whereabouts of what we assume is her late husband's rifle ('¡La escopeta! ¿Dónde está la escopeta?' [p. 149]) and Adela is easily duped by Martirio, whose thoughts she claims to know well, into thinking that Pepe has been killed. It is as if Lorca in this play has determined that there should be no conventionally theatrical heroine, and that the one who thinks she is the strongest turns out to be the weakest. As the Cátedra editors of the play put it: 'Lejos de ser una heroína que se rebela gloriosamente contra el mal, [Adela] es una pobre joven que muere víctima de unas circunstancias muy específicas.'[9] Although supposedly a main character in the play, this reader at least understands why Lorca would not have given Adela the star billing up alongside Bernarda in the DP.

An interesting confusion in the history of the DP is the question of the age of the eldest daughter Angustias. The manuscript puts her age as 36, and some later printed editions have followed this chronology, but others follow Bernarda, who gives a very exact age – '39' – in response to Poncia's speculation that 'Angustias ya debe tener mucho más de los treinta' (p. 68). In passing we may wonder why Poncia, who has been in the employ of the house for thirty years (p. 52), does not know how old Angustias is. We know from the DP that Poncia is sixty and therefore came to the Alba house when Bernarda was thirty, had married for the second time, and had had her first child, Magdalena, in that year by her second marriage. The difference in the ages of Angustias is important in illustrating the corruption of Bernarda's authority. If her daughter is '39' then it is to be assumed that Bernarda has observed the eight-year period of mourning before marrying again that she now requires of her daughters – the nine-year difference in age between Angustias and Magdalena – but if Angustias is thirty-six Bernarda would have married within five years of the death of her first husband. This would then appear to be the reason why Bernarda replies to Poncia in such a precise way that Angustias '[tiene] Treinta y nueve justos' (p. 68). It could well be that Lorca wanted the two different dates, that of the DP and that of Bernarda's reply to Poncia, to stand in contradiction of each other, underlining Bernarda's hypocrisy.[10] Poncia's linking of Angustias's age to her thirties, on the other hand, points towards an age that would be somewhat younger than Bernarda's answer, thereby not conceding the generational validity of her mistress's proclamation of eight years of mourning.

The question of the corruption of authority is certainly a live issue in this

9 Alan Josephs and Juan Caballero, eds, *La casa de Bernarda Alba* (Madrid: Cátedra, 1976), p. 96.

10 Josephs and Caballero suggest that the eight-year period chosen by the dramatist is 'Otra probable exageración numérica de Lorca. No es costumbre general que el luto dure ocho años' (ed. cit., p. 129). C. B. Morris (op. cit., p. 23) has more precise information on this, from 1918, quoting two years of mourning for the widow, and one year for the widower, which makes Bernarda's impositions on her children grotesque in the extreme.

play, and the DP plays its part in the matter by drawing our attention to the probable ages of marriage of Bernarda and her mother and Angustias, the eldest daughter. The gap between the two older women is only 20 years, which gives us a maximum marriage age of 19 for María Josefa, while that between Bernarda and Angustias (if the latter is 39) is 21 years, a maximum marriage age of 20 for Bernarda, and a second marriage – if we believe Bernarda concerning Angustias's age – at the age of 28. Thus, Bernarda may have experienced marriage and motherhood twice before her twenties are over, while denying them to her daughters, two of whom are in their thirties; and as Poncia suggests with regard to Angustias (p. 95), Bernarda may be putting her daughters' lives in danger by delaying their motherhood for so long.

Much has been written of Lorca's choice of names for the women in the play. As emblems of the angst-ridden house, some of the names certainly have an appropriate ring, but it is surprising that Lorca chose some names that in their phonic range are quite similar to each other. In such a brief play that proceeds at times at a fast visual pace, although much may not always be said, it seems unwise, theatrically speaking, to have chosen names such as Magdalena, Amelia and Adela, unless we are prepared, as is this critic, to see in the names a phonic representation of Martirio's chilling line: 'Yo veo que todo es una terrible repetición.' Another revealing name that emerges from the scene in which this sentence is quoted is that of the young girl Adelaida whose *novio* will not allow her to leave her house; here again the similarity of this name *Adelaida*[11] to the ones just mentioned brings us back to the element of sameness and repetitiveness in the young women's lives, and suggests that, as with the plight of Soledad Montoya in the 'Romance de la pena negra', neither the kitchen nor the bedroom will offer an escape route for those 'mujeres en los pueblos de España' about whom Lorca was writing. One notices in general in the DP the phonic poverty of the women's names (except for Bernarda and María Josefa), the sisters' names beginning with either 'A' or 'Ma', the phonic similarity of 'Poncia' and 'Prudencia', and the typification in the play of the other lesser women characters as 'Criada', 'Mendiga', 'Mujer' or 'Muchacha'. C. B. Morris writes of the daughters: 'their identities are submerged in the group, disciplined and depersonalized by their mother' (op. cit., p. 41: see fn. 4). (He does, however, go on to give an account of the differences between the sisters [pp. 43–55].) Two of the minor characters, incidentally, combine to produce a wonderful early example of Lorca's use of close repetition in the play, when the *criada* asks Poncia '¿Por qué no me das para mi niña?', to which Poncia accedes. Mendiga also has a *niña* and asks Criada for some leftovers, but is refused. The mirroring of one scene by another, with its unspoken reminiscence of the hypocrisy of the

---

[11] Cueto, art. cit. [see fn. 7], p. 37 also sees a close link between two of the names, and quotes an authority on nomenclature to the effect that *Adelaida* is a diminutive of *Adela*.

unjust servant of the Gospel story, demonstrates Lorca's uncanny skill in extracting the maximum from scenes that appear at first glance to be mere prologues or preludes to the main action.[12]

It may be relevant to mention here the monochrome atmosphere of the play (in that word's current cinematic/televisual meaning of black and white). The play's mood and mode fit in well with the restricted phonic range of comparison of many of the women's names; and of course there is the sentence at the end of the DP, quoted earlier, referring to photography – black and white, we assume, rather than sepia coloured, if the photographs are to be exhibited in some professional fashion, as is suggested by the word 'documental'; in addition this word 'documental' would carry with it the connotation of the sober, unrelieved, indeed repetitious, depiction of matters of major concern to society.[13] Marie Laffranque has linked an earlier letter of Lorca with this *advertencia preliminar*, quoting the poet's plans for a play in which 'La escena ha de estar impregnada de ese terrible silencio de las fotos de muertos y ese gris difuminado de los fondos'.[14] We might also add the lines from *Poeta en Nueva York*, 'New York Oficina y denuncia', which suggest a similar mood: '¿Qué voy a hacer, ordenar los paisajes?/ ¿Ordenar los amores que luego son fotografías,/ que luego son pedazos de madera y bocanadas de sangre?': another reference, very familiar to Spaniards, to the mental link beween photographs and death.[15] Lorca's sombre mood on writing the play is confirmed by Manuel Altolaguirre's account in *Hora de España* of 1937 (quoted in note 7): 'He suprimido muchas cosas en esta tragedia, muchas canciones fáciles, muchos romancillos y letrillas. Quiero que mi obra tenga severidad y sencillez.'[16] We can see confirmation of this severity in what the playwright crossed out in the manuscript version of the DP, with the removal of 'La bailarina' and 'El hombre de la guitarra', probably replaced by the dramatically relevant – and brief – off-stage song of the reapers, the latter more concerned to engage in amorous pursuits, but forbidden to the Alba women both as migrant workers and *jornaleros,* and

[12] In this context see the excellent commentary by Morris op. cit., pp. 86–87 on the repetition of the reapers' song by Martirio and Adela.

[13] See Cueto, art. cit., pp. 23–25, for a discussion of the 'photographic realism' of the play.

[14] 'Federico García Lorca: teatro abierto, teatro inconcluso', in Domenech, ed. cit., pp. 211–30 (at p. 222).

[15] Gwynne Edwards suggests that the light or lighting for Acts 1 and 2 'will be one, not of brightness, but of dullness, a faded quality like the skin of the characters themselves; perhaps, indeed, like one of those old pre-colour photographs'; *Lorca: The Theatre beneath the Sand* (London, New York: Marion Boyars, 1987), p. 276.

[16] Cf. C. B. Morris's interpretation of the reference to photography as 'presupposing the suppression of the bright colours endemic to Andalusian poetry; it can also be found in the firm control over grand gestures, operatic modes of acting and declamatory speeches in the play' (op. cit., p. 25).

hence lacking any lasting financial or social respectability. As C. B. Morris has thoughtfully observed (op. cit., p. 20): 'the reapers' song serves the demands of the play rather than making [a] social or political statement'.

We may also recall the bizarre stage direction referring to the entrance of 'doscientas mujeres' for the domestic obsequies of the funeral. One could justify this direction by imagining Lorca's uncompromising mood on writing this play, a mood that saw the undifferentiated and indifferent human being (the latter exemplified by Magdalena in the play ['Lo mismo me da', (p. 62)], once her father has died) as always in danger of being easily ground down by corrupt authority because of the lack of an individual spark of rebellion, here represented by María Josefa and Adela, but also too easily snuffed out in their cases by this authority. (We should not forget that any positive assessment of María Josefa's role in the play must also take into account that her rebellion remains at the level of words, and that she too is easily duped by Martirio as she makes her exit, trusting that her devious granddaughter will help her to escape [p. 143].) Since no acting ability would be required to play a non-speaking part as one of this multitude of women mourners, each extra anonymous and similarly clad body being used on-stage would accentuate the monotonous and featureless destiny that awaits them, as well as the female inhabitants of the house.

This small army of women is subsumed into the entry 'mujeres de luto' in the manuscript of the DP, which does not offer any individualization for the four speaking parts of the mourning women, as do the printed versions. Lorca evidently wished directors of the play to take the stage direction concerning the two hundred women seriously, since he underlined the number in the manuscript. The generalized sub-title of the play, too – *Drama de mujeres en los pueblos de España* – together with the proverbial references to the confined lot of women in the play itself, reinforce the sense of anonymity and reduce Adela's own significance as an individual in rebellion against authority.[17] The original sub-title in the DP was *Drama en tres actos de mujeres en los pueblos de España*. The most likely reason for the change is that, when Lorca decided to replace the brief description of the play's setting ('La acción en un pueblo andaluz de tierra seca') with the reference to the photographic character of the play's three acts, part of the sub-title at the top of the page became redundant. (The deletion of the reference to the three-act structure of the play, however, has also had the syntactic effect of changing

---

[17] Josephs and Caballero (ed. cit., p. 89) argue strangely that the sub-title is specific in its reference, and that if Lorca had wanted to write about women in general he would have used the phrase 'drama de *las* mujeres en los pueblos de España'. Whatever about the semantics of the phrase, with or without the feminine definite article, the use of 'pueblos' is enough to give the phrase a general meaning. Induráin also sees the sub-title as 'de . . . radio . . . local o localista' (art. cit., p. 132), which it is, in its reference to village or small-town life, but surely general as regards the women who inhabit these places.

the literal use of the word 'drama' in the sub-title into a figurative one, drawing attention to its intensity: a small but significant addition to the connotative wealth of the DP.)

Lorca's own words as to the kind of reader that he wanted for his works come at the end of one of his lectures on poetry – that is aptly named for our purposes – 'Imaginación, inspiración, evasión': 'La poesía no quiere adeptos, sino amantes. Pone ramas de zarzamora y erizos de vidrio para que se hieran de amor las manos que la buscan'. There is no doubt that the interpretative rewards that Lorca's poetry – whether dramatic, lyrical or narrative – repays are immense, just as the lover in the Lorca image quoted, who risks scaling the wall's severe defences hopes to be rewarded by the beloved. C. B. Morris has seen in the interpretative freedom offered in Lorca's last play the essence of its greatness: 'it possesses the elusive quality inherent in a great work of art: that of suggesting many interpretations' (op. cit., p. 115). We are fortunate to have access in print to Lorca's original disposition of his characters in the dramatis personae in *La casa de Bernarda Alba*, through the manuscript version published by Mario Hernández. Lorca's roughly and perhaps hurriedly written page is itself a gem of suggestive possibilities in the way that the ordering and relationship of the characters are presented to us. As such, one could not think of a more fitting prologue for the play itself, whereby the dramatis personae not only performs its primary function as an information sheet but conveys it to us in a manner that may truly be called poetic.

TABULA GRATULATORIA

Kenneth Adams
Alexandra Anderson
Susana Bayó
Bernard Bentley
Peter Bly
Gwyn E. Campbell
Rodolfo Cardona
Barbara Collins
Ciaran Cosgrove
D. W. Cruickshank
T. J. Dadson
Frederick A. De Armas
J. A. Duggan
Fiona Feely
Dian Fox
Derek H. Gagen
A. M. García
Audrey Gleasure
Nigel Glendinning, Professor of
    Spanish, T.C.D., 1970–1974
Iris Annette Gordon
Martha Halsey
Michaela Heigl
Leo Hickey
Richard Hitchcock
Instituto Cervantes, Dublin
Instituto Cervantes, London
Dennis Kennedy

Robert Lima
C. A. Longhurst
John Lyon
Lucy MacDonnell
Ann L. Mackenzie
Michael McGaha
Melveena McKendrick
Barbara Mujica
Alan K. G. Paterson
Sheena Price
Edward C. Riley, Professor of Spanish,
    T.C.D., 1964–1970
    (*In Memoriam*)
Geoffrey W. Ribbans
Daniel Rogers
Alison Rossi
N. G. Round
Anamaría Crowe Serrano
Clíona Sherwin
Alba Smith
Walter Fitzwilliam Starkie, Professor
    of Spanish, T.C.D., 1926–1947
    (*In Memoriam*)
Bruce Swansey
Taylor Institution Library, Oxford
Jonathan Thacker
Jennifer Price Toner
James Whiston